Marguerite van Geldermalsen is from New Zealand. In 1978 she married Mohammad Abdallah and they had three children. She was widowed in 2002 and now divides her time between Sydney and Petra.

Married to a Bedouin

Marguerite van Geldermalsen

Virago

VIRAGO

First published in Great Britain in 2006 by Virago Press

A CIP catalogue record for this book is available
from the British Library.

ISBN-13: 9 781 84 4 082193
ISBN-10: 1 84408 219 9

Typeset in Sabon by M Rules
Printed and bound in Great Britain by
Clays Ltd, St Ives plc

Virago Press
An imprint of
Time Warner Book Group UK
Brettenham House
Lancaster Place
London WC2E 7EN

www.virago.co.uk

For Salwa, Raami and Maruan

in memory of Mohammad

The map is not drawn to scale, but covers an area that is approximately 1 km from east to west and 1½km from north to south.

Key:

⌒	rock mountains or outcrops
⌢	hills of sandy earth
⌐	cave home or shop
××	tent site
A	our wedding tent site
B	The big tree and paved road
C	Nazzal's Camp, Gasr al-Bint and the Keenya (gum trees)
D	Wadi Siyyagh
E	The clinic in the Monastery valley
F	The Fum-al-Wadi
G	Pharoah's column
H	Turkmaniya Tomb
I	Umm al-Biyara

The Petra I lived in.

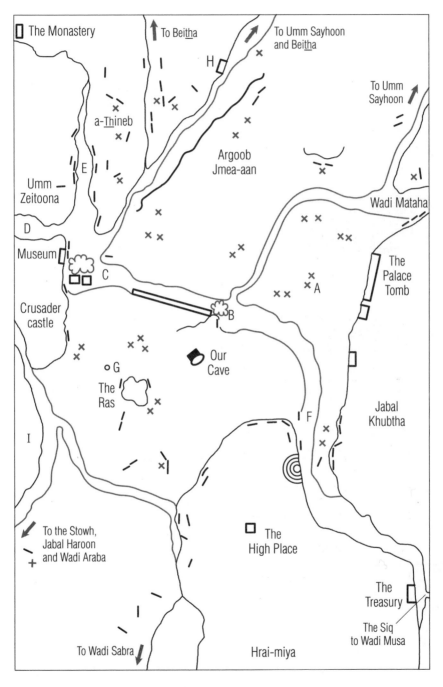

Acknowledgements

There are a few people I want to thank by name. They are Mum, Dad, Ted, John and Anna for being my wonderful family (and also for some of the photos); Lennie Goodings and Elise Dillsworth at Virago Press; Mary S. Lovell who introduced me to them; Jane Taylor (janetaylorphotos.com) for facts and friendship and the photo of the Monastery on the back cover; and Jan Cornall for 'Effortless Memoir Writing'. Also, to those who met me, and said, 'You should write a book,' thank you.

To those who encouraged me while I was writing it – I needed that, thank you, To the Petra Bedouin – even those I haven't named but who shared nonetheless in the 'making of our lives memorable', thank you. And most of all to Mohammad (may he rest in peace). If it weren't for him I wouldn't have a story to tell.

1978: In the Beginning

'Where you staying?' the Bedouin asked. 'Why you not stay with me tonight – in my cave?'

I met Mohammad Abdallah in Petra. My friend Elizabeth and I were sitting on the rock-cut steps of the Treasury with our backs against a gigantic column when the young man sat down on the step below and started to chat. He wore a heavily fringed and tasselled red and white cloth twisted up on his head and a western, synthetic suit: bottle green with flares.

Elizabeth and I had travelled through Greece and Egypt together and had been in Jordan for about a week. We were doing well. In Amman we stayed with a New Zealand couple and went to all the 'places of interest'. We saw the museum, the citadel and the Roman theatre, and we made day trips to Madaba, with its mosaic map, and to the well-preserved Roman town of Jerash in the north. There, some hours after the last local bus had left, we were rescued by a group of Americans with their own air-conditioned bus and local Jordanian guide, who went by the unlikely name of Joe and who spoke English with an exaggerated American accent. They had not only taken us back to Amman, they had taken us to Petra the next day.

The effect of the air-conditioning on the bus was to exaggerate the mid-morning heat when we got out in the dusty car park at the entrance to the ancient city. The group had a tour organised, but before we could even think to make our own plans, Joe introduced us to his friend Rashid, who said very formally, 'Welcome. My name is Rashid. I am from the village of Moses Valley. I show you Petra.'

Moses Valley was the village of stone walls and fruit trees we had just passed through as the bus worked its way down from the mountains, braking heavily. Joe had pointed out the spring where Moses 'struck the rock and water gushed forth' and explained over his microphone that the names of the valley and the village were the same: Wadi Musa or Valley of Moses.

Rashid looked to be in his early twenties, like me. He was thin, dark-haired with pale olive skin, pointy eyes and an uncertain smile. He wore plain trousers and an open-necked shirt. We told him our names and shook his hand.

'Lizabeth,' he recognised. 'Queen Lizabeth.'

Elizabeth was a well-tanned Australian without a line on her face, despite being some years older and wiser than me. She smiled benignly, giving nothing away. She had heard it all before.

There were neither gates nor entry fees and Rashid assured us he wouldn't charge us either, so we just lifted our bags and followed him down the path into Petra.

We had just about reached saturation point as far as ruins go. In recent months we had been to so many antiquity-filled museums and toppled-column archaeological sites that we could barely absorb another historical fact. So I hardly listened when Rashid told us that the Nabataeans were a tribe of people who ruled in the area for hundreds of years. I wasn't interested; I just walked one dusty sandal in front of the other. There was no shade. A horse or two passed, stirring dust, kicking open wet-straw-smelling droppings. For a while the path led between sandstone hills which grew higher and crept closer, then a shady canyon opened in the cliff in front and we entered the Siq. 'This is the only way into Petra,' our guide said. 'That's why it was easy to protect.' And we could see what he meant. It was only a few metres wide and the sheer sides towering in reds and ochres cut out most of the sun, except where shafts of it reached in and caught the leaves of high-up fig trees in splashes of green.

Our bus-load of tourists passed us by on clattering horses, waving and laughing. The men leading them hitched up long robes, and the ends of their head-coverings flicked up as they waved sticks at the horses and shouted to each other. The long robes or *thaubs* were mostly white but occasionally someone wore a grey or tan or dark pinstriped one. The headgear consisted of a square metre of red and white, black and white, or just plain white cotton cloth folded in a triangle, the *mendeel*, with a *mirreer*, a double ring like a thick black rope, on top. They stirred up more dust and the path was stony, our bags became heavier, and despite the shade we were starting to sweat.

Half an hour later the picture I had first seen at the Jordanian embassy in Cairo came to life. Quite suddenly between the brick-red walls of the Siq, above the flowering oleander bushes, a sliver of monument appeared looming and sunlit. The rest of the façade came into view as the Siq ended abruptly and opened into a narrow canyon. We eased our bags to the ground and leaned against the rock in a slice of shade opposite what looked like the front of a towering Grecian temple. A few tourists went up the steps and disappeared through a doorway. The faint and soothing smell of wood smoke reached us from where some men lounged in the shade. A couple of them, in raggedy *thaubs* and suit-coats, came over and tried to show us something but we waved them away, and they went. We were quite obviously travellers, not tourists with money. We looked up at the façade. It was cut right back into the rock. It nearly went to the top of the cliff.

Rashid had his spiel off pat. 'This is al-Khazneh, Arabic for the Treasury. Nabataean people carved it by hand two thousand years ago. We don't know, a temple or a tomb. The Bedouin here think the Pharaoh's treasure is in that urn at the top.'

The urn was part of the living rock but the side we could see was pocked as if it had been hacked at by a pick-axe. 'But not treasure, only rock. You see the holes from Bedouin shooting.'

Bedouin! There was a mysterious, romantic air about that word. Something wide open and free, I thought. Now we were interested.

'Who are they? What's different about them? How can we get to meet some?' We had heard from several travellers, including the New Zealanders we stayed with in Amman, that you could stay with the Bedouin in Petra.

The Bedouin, Rashid told us, were nomads. I could hear the disdain in his voice as he continued, 'They live down here in tents and caves with no education or sanitation.' For us his words conjured up excitement.

Rashid wasn't a Bedouin, he assured us. The Bedouin didn't live in houses like the civilised people of his tribe. In Wadi Musa the families lived in houses with glass windows and running water, some were even made from steel and cement, and a few families shared a generator.

'There is a hotel further down in Petra; there are showers and a generator,' he said. But we were even more curious now and he couldn't put us off. We wanted to stay with the Bedouin. 'I know some of the families,' Rashid eventually admitted, 'and if you are sure, I'll take you to ask.' We were sure.

We picked up our bags and left the shade. Not much further along, the valley opened out. We passed a theatre carved from the rock on our left and a mountainside of monuments up on the hill to our right. There were a few people around: some tourists returning on horses, some more long-robed men lying in the scant shade of oleander bushes and a couple of children driving donkeys clanking with jerry-cans. The hot dust and dry horse-dung smells persisted. Bleached hillsides of dirt and tumble-down walls rose up slowly on both sides of the path. I hadn't realised Petra was so big. I was envious of Elizabeth who, having travelled all over

South America some years earlier, had anticipated the offers of help she would receive and now instead of a backpack she had a kind of kit bag with two handles which she usually slung over one shoulder. Men couldn't help themselves, and now Rashid carried half her load while mine was still squarely on my own back. As we plodded along two black tents came into view. Not much was stirring in the heat. The path turned into a road of stone pavement. It was white and worn and bounced the heat and brightness back up at us. It was June, midday, and I thought of mad dogs and Englishmen. Our sandals slapped. We didn't talk. On both sides of the street what once were shops sprouted dusty scrub and pinkly-flowering oleanders. We didn't want to know about the roofless temple at the end of the pavement and disregarded the impressive stand of gum trees beside it and the shade they promised; we just wanted to get to wherever we were going.

We followed Rashid up a long hot ridge to where a Bedouin family was living in a camp of caves. The strip of swept dirt yard had a rock wall with several dark doorways. The smell of fried tomatoes I recognised was too ordinary for the scene. An assortment of snotty-nosed and smiling-eyed children scrambled about and a heavily dressed woman stood behind a teenage boy muttering with him, eyeing us suspiciously. Elizabeth was very sensitively dressed in trousers and a long-sleeved blouse but I wore shorts and a singlet and had fat legs and it didn't even occur to me that I might offend. Elizabeth felt it was polite to cover up because we were in a Muslim world, but I didn't care. If they wanted to cover themselves, fine. I didn't usually and I didn't see why I should change for anyone.

Another woman came into the yard, just as straight-backed and clear-skinned as the first, but she spoke with a sharper voice. Their husbands weren't home, she told Rashid, and we couldn't stay. Disappointed, we took those glimpses of inhabited caves and Bedouin characters back down the hill and stretched our budget to the hotel with the showers and the generator.

The hotel, called Nazzal's Camp, was secreted behind the tall-walled ruins of the roofless temple, veiled in the shade of the towering gum trees. It had been a tent camp run by Thomas Cook & Sons when Agatha Christie set *Appointment with Death* in it in 1938, but now it was a building of stone and cement with a double staircase leading up to the front door. There was a dining room and a well-stocked bar on the first floor, bedrooms on the second floor, and more bedrooms, one of which we were shown to, set in two-thousand-year-old caves carved into the mountainside behind. Square concrete patches under the trees were the only sign that tents had had to be set up to accommodate the crowds during the hotel's heyday, but it was past that now. In fact, it was to close down later that year; a new hotel already operated outside the site, and we were the only guests at Nazzal's Camp.

In the morning we asked the young men running the hotel what there was to do in Petra. There were no brochures or guidebooks. They told us we could go up to the High Place or the Monastery, but the sun was already beating down and neither name roused enough interest to entice us to climb so we wandered back the way we had come the day before.

Back at the Treasury we were almost alone. I could easily have taken a photo without any other tourists in it but my camera was so basic it wouldn't get half the façade and Elizabeth didn't carry a camera at all. On either side of the main entrance worn horsemen stood beside headless rock horses. Neck-bendingly above us the friezes of flowers looked as fresh as the day they were carved. I discovered later that the Nabataeans had early beginnings as wandering Bedouin. They became important to the incense trade across Arabia from Yemen, initially attacking and later ensuring the safe passage of the camel caravans. From as early as the third century BC they were putting up their tents in Petra, a natural stronghold with many springs and easily guarded approaches. Over the following centuries they built up a thriving kingdom which by the end of the first century AD covered an area from southern Syria to the Negev desert in Palestine and down into Arabia, with Petra as the capital. Traders and craftsmen travelled around the known world and came back with new ideas. Their city spread across the hills, they developed fine pottery, minted their own coins (some with the heads of both the king and the queen), carved great and fantastic monuments in the cliffs that enclosed the basin and harvested every drop of rain the heavens sent them. Petra was a thriving city well into the sixth century but changing trade routes, occasional earthquakes and possibly a drying climate led to its abandonment.

We climbed the steps and looked inside the chambers. The chisel marks made all those years before were still clear and the corners were precise but the floor and the steps were worn. It was as we sat there on the steps, opposite the mouth of the Siq, leaning our backs against the towering column, that Mohammad Abdallah came over and invited us to stay.

Elizabeth's considerate 'What do you reckon?' was wasted because I was already accepting his offer. He seemed enthusiastic – and we were looking for adventure.

To the Cave

We checked out of the hotel later in the afternoon and carried our bags back along the ancient paving to the big tree where our Bedouin host said he would meet us. There didn't appear to be anyone around and we were wondering what we would do if he didn't show up when a calling voice attracted our attention.

'You want Mohammad Abdallah? He ask me show you way.'

We looked up to see a young boy waving his arms on the top of a steep hill of rock walls to the right. We followed his impressive English commands with increasing surprise as they led us left and right around rocks but mostly up until we stood beside him puffing, looking back down at the road we had just been on.

'I know it is you by you bags,' said the little barefooted kid, beaming from ear to ear at his cleverness. A carpet of pottery shards crunched under our feet as we followed him up the hill. We followed him round to where, on a deep, sandy, sun-filled ledge, with the swirly-rock façade of his cave just escaping the envelope of the hill, our Bedouin host stood waiting. He had taken off his *mendeel*, revealing an open face and unruly mop of thick dark hair, but he hadn't changed out of his suit or forgotten his invitation.

'*Ahlan-wa-sahlan* – that means welcome,' Mohammad said, holding out his hand to help us down the deep step onto the ledge. I didn't think it was an excuse to hold our hands – there was a ten-metre drop directly beside the soft dirt step. We stepped one after the other into a kind of corridor that reached into the hillside, where an open door and two wire-mesh-covered windows were set in a rock wall. One window was high, to the left of the door; the other, to the right, was at ground level. Above the stones and cement, the remnants of the living red-rock façade, worn into ellipses and waves, stood against the sky.

Mohammad had moved into this cave only a couple of months before. He had recognised the potential of the spot, even though the sand of centuries had filled the ledge and practically blocked the entrance. Goats had been able to slip into the shade on hot afternoons and on rousing them out he had seen a decent-sized cave, hanging alone on the hillside with a view of half of Petra and no close neighbours. It had taken him some weeks to clear the corridor and build a wall to fill in the worn-away façade.

He was certainly keen to show it off. He ushered us straight in. It was quite different from both the Treasury and our previous night's accommodation – the doorway was just high enough not to have to bend, and when our eyes adjusted we could see we were in an almost square cave about five by six metres, with a low arched roof that was just out of arm's reach and a rough concrete floor. The original floor, with possible tombs and treasures, was a couple of metres deeper, but Mohammad had stopped digging and put in the concrete floor when the roof was high enough. He had also been busy on the paintwork. Chisel marks and fissures in the rock were a rough canvas under his new artwork. He had painted the back wall and the side walls up to shoulder height a very basic and not very nice green. Sprouting from the walls in the same green and stretching across the rocky whitewashed roof above us were six sunflowers with two leaves each, much like I probably made at playcentre with freshly mixed poster paint, but bigger.

'It's beauuutiful.' Elizabeth had a knack for building people's self-esteem. I disagreed, but managed to stop myself from commenting.

On the floor behind the plank door there was a primus, beside it a nickel tea tray with a teapot and glasses, and above it, on a wooden board attached somehow to the rock, were a few plates and a cooking pot. A red suitcase sat on a thin-legged fold-up table of green metal in the far corner. There was a bedstead with a sponge rubber mattress and a blanket thrown on it and a grey and white cotton mat covered half the floor. Pigeons had made a home up in the deep windowsill. We put down our bags and a ginger kitten scrabbled up to play with the straps.

The young boy made himself useful pouring tea. He had deep eyes and big teeth and when Mohammad offered us cigarettes he took one too. We couldn't believe it. He had told us proudly that he was 'eleven years old' but he was still a little kid. Mohammad offered his kerosene-smelling lighter and Elizabeth and I spluttered and coughed, but the boy inhaled so deeply I decided he must have been smoking since birth. He waved goodbye, cigarette in hand, and went off to follow his goats home.

'Let's go to Monastery to see sunset,' Mohammad announced when we had had as much of the tea as we could manage. It was very sweet and very black and there was no milk. 'If we go fast we get there before. *Yallah!* Come on!'

Although it seemed almost too late to catch a sunset, it was cooler now and the Monastery sounded much more exciting than it had this morning, so off we went, rushing back down past the hotel then into a valley and up an amazing rock-cut path, barely stopping while Mohammad picked us caper flowers (soft brushes of pink with white petals and the sweetest of smells), and even on arrival at this most awesome of Petra's monuments, deep gold in the setting sun, we couldn't rest . . . the sunset spot was a few minutes further on, on the edge of the Great Rift Valley. We collapsed laughing on the ledge of rock just before the sun sank behind mountains far to the west.

We were on top of the world. What a view! Caught for ever in my memory – and indeed on film, for we were joined by a Palestinian man who taught and lived at the local school and had caught us up when he spotted the chance to work on his English. Mohammad just as quickly spotted the chance to have a photo taken, of the three of us there in the sunset.

Back at the cave Mohammad lit a lamp, pumped up the primus and cooked dinner. Elizabeth offered to help chop the potatoes but he only had one knife – a fold-up affair which he used to peel and chop directly into the pot, and which he also used to open the tin cans.

While the dinner cooked I sat on the mat on the floor with my back against the rock and wrote a postcard to my sister in New Zealand. The picture was of the theatre, tiers of seats carved from the sandstone, which we had checked out the evening before. The glossy-finish photo made it look sleek and shiny and gave no sense of the dry grittiness that we had sat on. For the date I put June 1978. I had lost track of the days and it didn't matter anyway because it might not get sent for a few more. I described the lamplight I was writing in, the sunset we had just seen, and Mohammad the Bedouin Arab cooking our dinner.

In my cultural ignorance I saw nothing unusual about him living alone, nor did I wonder why he wasn't surrounded by a family of generous proportions. 'I worked in Aqaba before,' he told us about himself. 'At the port and in the Aqaba Hotel. Also I worked at Nazzal's Camp and there, after we did the dishes, we made Bedouin dancing for the guests.' His talk was of the bachelor life he was living and gave no indication of a family.

A tall boy with a teenage shadow on his upper lip came in, put a scarf bundle down by the primus and crouched there looking at us. His sandals were cracked rubber and his belt, tight around his waist, scooped in the folds of old trousers many sizes too big. Mohammad nudged him and told us in way of introduction, 'He doesn't speak English.'

He stood up and came over then and we got up off the floor to shake hands. '*Izayak*,' we said, as we had learned in Egypt.

He looked at Mohammad.

'Here we say "*keef haalak*" or "*masa-al-khair*" or "*marhaba*".' Mohammad lost us. None of the words we had learned in Egypt had been any good here.

We tried '*marahaaba*' and they laughed.

'Say "*shoghilishtayaan*",' Mohammad prompted.

'What does that mean?'

'*Shoghilishtayaan*? It means nothing, just say it.' He laughed. We didn't try; we had already learned enough rude words in Greece to keep us going for a while.

Mohammad served the meal in a flat round dish. It was a thick goulash of potatoes, onions, canned green peas, tomato purée and corned beef. He undid the young man's bundle to produce bread, huge round flaps of it, pancake-thin and still warm, which he called *shraak*. They both tried to teach us how to fold ripped-off bits of it to scoop up the stew. It wasn't easy but the food was delicious. It was obvious our host was perfectly capable of looking after himself, and his visitors.

We went down the hill to pee behind some bushes and before bed we brushed our teeth with a glass of water from the jerry-can outside the door. Although this cave accommodation didn't offer showers, we had a private room because Mohammad took his mattress and blanket and slept outside. We used our towels for pillows and slept in our sleeping bags on the cotton mat. Occasionally the crazy sound of a donkey bray or a dog bark broke the silence and the pigeons cooed in the windowsill for a while. Through the open doorway I could see the dusty yard and, across the valley, stone mountains bathed in the white light of the moon.

I had been right; it had been a good idea to accept Mohammad's invitation. Not only was it cheaper than the night before, it was infinitely more interesting. Taking the chance often was. I usually felt bold and rarely considered the risks other people might have been nervous about. I had hitchhiked in New Zealand since I was about fifteen, to get into town or to the beach, and in the UK I had hitched up and down the motorways time and again. Elizabeth had wanted company on her trip to the Middle East just so she could take up any such offers without putting herself in unsafe situations. It didn't even occur to me to be nervous on this occasion. I suppose we were two and he was small but I don't think even that crossed my mind. We were looking for adventure and we were finding it.

Breakfast was leftover flat bread, a disc of processed-cheese segments and hot sugary tea in little glasses. We agreed that we had been lucky to have had such a 'real Petra experience'. We had met some Bedouin, seen the sunset and slept in a cave. We didn't need to see any more of the ruins pictured in the fuzzy black and white photos of the booklet Mohammad got out of his suitcase. Nothing in the highly descriptive poorly spelled text was inspiring either. We packed our bags ready to move on. He wouldn't take the book back. 'It's for you – keep it to remember me.'

Up at the Treasury Mohammad laid his trinkets out for sale on a table. A pick-up truck came up the gravel track and he waved it to a stop. He cadged us a lift and helped us onto the back with our bags. 'You lucky,' he said. 'This is only car in Petra and going all the way to Aqaba!'

'Goodbye, thank you.' We shook hands and kissed cheeks. 'We will write, we hope to come back some day,' we said blithely, much as we did to every new acquaintance we made, and we settled ourselves in the back.

Through the Siq we bumped. A ribbon of blue sky rippled above us between the towering canyon walls.

Out at the entrance our driver asked us to get off. He obviously didn't share Mohammad's enthusiasm for helping young travellers, but that is travelling for you. We found another ride and before the end of the day Petra was behind us and we were settling into the Samaka hotel and restaurant on the shores of the Red Sea.

A Bit of History

The Samaka was perfect. On the bamboo-roofed terrace we ate garlic-smothered grilled fish with tahina dip which we washed down with brewed-under-licence Amstel beer, and from its crushed-granite beach we swam in the Red Sea. We were just beginning to think we should move on – Syria and Lebanon awaited – when a lanky guy with Peter O'Toole features and

Omar Sharif eyes sauntered in looking for us. He introduced himself as 'the taxi driver: Ali'. Mohammad Abdallah had sent him, he said, to take us back to Petra to see a Bedouin wedding. Ali talked and gestured. One of his thumbs didn't have a bone in it – a strange reconstruction after he had shot it off to get out of the army – and it jiggled around as he talked. We could understand most of what he said but didn't know how much of it to believe.

'I'm Bedwen from Petra; mather . . . father, dead; brathers in Amman, live there; I go at school in Al-Quds – Jerusalem. In '67, war. I come back in Petra. I been England, Virginia Water.' I'd never heard of it but no one would make that up! He held out his slender brown hands and rubbed his forefingers together to emphasise his closeness to Mohammad. 'Mohammad like my brather, I stay with his family, we grow up together. This my taxi, outside.'

The next morning the charming restaurant owner, the balding Abu Majid, loaded a box of fresh fish into the boot of the car along with our packs and we all went back to Petra.

The Bedouin call it 'gismih o naseeb', which means luck and destiny, but if Mohammad hadn't sent that taxi to bring us back I would have gone on wandering aimlessly and Petra would have faded away to a dusty interlude with a spectacular sunset.

And if I hadn't met Elizabeth I probably wouldn't have gone there in the first place. The Middle East had not been my dream destination and I had barely heard of Bedouin, but I had spent the last winter in Britain, damp and grey, in Salt Cottage on the Solway Firth, and despite the Cumberland sausage, the music of Supertramp and the company of Spike and Crowley, I didn't want to experience another. Elizabeth had been looking for someone to travel round the Middle East with and it had sounded warmer to me.

Perhaps I have something of the nomad in me. My parents had emigrated from Holland to New Zealand before I was born. They had said goodbye to their parents and left, Mum on one of the ships, Dad on one of the first commercial flights. The benefits were greater for singles so they didn't marry till they got there. An 'uncle' of Dad's had a penfriend in Auckland he traded stamps with, and that's where Mum and Dad first stayed and where they were married. Mr and Mrs Combes became our New Zealand grandparents, but we didn't see them any more than our overseas ones because Dad got a technician's job at the DSIR (Department of Scientific and Industrial Research) apple orchard at the top of the South Island. I grew up there, on the Moutere Hills halfway between Nelson and Motueka, without a relation in sight.

I had an older and a younger brother, Ted and John, and a younger sister, Anna. My brothers and I biked to Appleby School together and stopped at the pond halfway down Fraser's Hill, on winter days to break the ice and in the spring to collect tadpoles and frogs for 'Show and Tell'. The spelling tests were easy but the maths was hard. The school had vast playing fields and we had fragrant grass fights on the days they were mown. For the annual picnic Mr O'Connor transported all the pupils to Rabbit Island with his horse and cart. The summers were long and hot. Dad took us swimming at the Appleby River or Rabbit Island after work, or we played French cricket after tea and still went to bed before dark. I always had a sunburned nose and we always went camping at Totaranui with its golden sand and native bush. My daily job was feeding the chooks and collecting the eggs, and I took turns with Ted and John drying the dinner dishes, thirty items each, while Dad washed.

I never dried dishes with my sister, who was born eight years after me, because by the time she was old enough we had a dishwasher. I never biked to school with Anna either because by the time she started I was going to high school on the bus, and by the time she got to high school I had left the country.

When I was eleven we had French lessons at school and I brought a real souvenir of the Eiffel tower from home. Until then I'd seen the unusual things we had around our house as different, not special – and I tried not to be different, not to be a Dutchy. My name was Dutch enough though at least I didn't speak any because Mum and Dad had decided to be New Zealanders and spoke only English. We had other interesting things around the house, too, I realised, like the Wayang puppets Dad had brought back from Indonesia where he served in the Dutch army, and the carved wooden chair by the phone with its slippery cushion. When we had dinner parties Mum got out her Dutch Indonesian recipe book and created a 'rijsttafel' with the rice steamed early and kept warm in her bed and the smells of peanut sauce and shrimp crisps.

New Zealand houses usually had uncles and cousins in them, the kitchens smelled of mutton, the bedrooms of lavender, and the sitting rooms had sets of three ceramic ducks flying across their walls.

Mum's way of bringing up children was with a policy of non-interference, a revolt against her own mother, who she felt interfered too much, even in letters from the other side of the world. Dad was the dealer-out of punishment, though I can't remember anything more severe than being sent to my room with my dinner – which only worked, Mum says, until we preferred our rooms.

When I was seventeen I left school, and home, and entered a three-year in-service course at Braemar Hospital, an institution for intellectually handicapped children. I enjoyed it, not because it was what I especially wanted to do, I still didn't know what that was, but it was interesting enough and I was making real money. I wore AMCO jeans, Hang Ten T-shirts and sewed myself fancy jackets. For my hippie days I sewed long skirts with tiny flowers, knitted tank-tops and Inca hats and crocheted knee-high boots.

I met Maureen at work and went flatting with her, and however many others there were bedrooms for in whichever old house we rented at the time. We played our LPs loud: *Tapestry* and *Dark Side of the Moon, Tupelo Honey* and *Goat's Head Soup*; and on weekends we went to the Rutherford or the Metropolitan and danced to the band. There were no bands midweek because there weren't enough young people around. They had gone off to university, or to where the university students were (which meant either Christchurch, a six-hour drive away, or Wellington, separated by the Cook Strait flight or ferry-trip), and of the seventy thousand people left in the district it seemed only a few were looking for a good time. The rest were too young, too old, or paying off the mortgage. As I learned more about cerebral palsy, spinabifida and methods of play therapy, I also grew bored with Nelson. I looked forward to freedom at the end of my three-year course, but I didn't consider dropping out – what a waste of the time that would have been. I liked to finish what I started.

I bought a two-stroke Suzuki and Maureen and I took off in our holidays riding round the country. We saw the calendar-photo scenes and met people looking for adventure from Canada, Switzerland and unremembered but distant and interesting-sounding places.

To come back to Nelson, we joked as we checked out the local pub for talent, was to come back to the 'dead' centre of New Zealand. The actual geographical centre was marked on a hill up the back of Brook Street and I had climbed to it enthusiastically as a child, but now I just wanted to get away. Even the P&O merchant navy ships with their promises of young men with romantic accents were coming into port less and less often since the introduction of container shipping. Nothing exciting was ever going to happen here. New Zealand was too far from the world.

We dreamed but we didn't plan much. As a child I had enjoyed stories of prairies and Halloween and the Wild West and might have gone to America, but Maureen knew people who had been to London and it sounded like a good place to start. As soon as I heard I had passed my final exams, we bought one-way tickets. Mum and Dad gave me pieces of Greenstone jewellery to deliver to my Dutch *oma* and *tantes*, and a list of their addresses, and we flew out of Nelson in June 1976, on a sunny winter's day.

We flitted around. We visited Maureen's relations, the McHughs, in Donegal on the coast of Ireland and my relations the van Geldermalsens and the Camffermans in Amersfoort, the Hook of Holland and s'-Gravenzande. We visited all the people who had ever given us their address and said, 'When you come to the UK give us a call,' and most of them put us up for a night or two. We worked as barmaids, chambermaids and waitresses in Nottingham, Carlisle, Bournemouth and Windermere, and hitchhiked all over the country in between.

Maureen stopped moving when she met the man who became her husband so I was really lucky to meet Elizabeth. She was an experienced traveller with a plan – and a return ticket. She knew about cultural differences and political situations but didn't blink an eyelid at my ignorance. Of course I had heard of the antiquities of Greece and Egypt, but I don't think I could have sworn Jordan was a country before she told me her plans and showed me the map. I know I hadn't heard of Petra. 'Are you sure you want to come with me? That will be gooood.' Joy spilled out around her. So I went along for the ride, to see what I could see and to be able to say I had been there. I knew we were going to have fun.

A Look at the Bride

The evening we returned from Aqaba, Elizabeth went down to the hotel with the driver, Ali, and Mohammad took me to meet the Bedouin bride. The low black-hair tent she lived in was set up on a small cleared area between the fallen-down blocks of ancient buildings. The wrinkly little mother, Fraija, and her daughters Heyaiya and Rakhiya, were the friends I made that evening.

The only light was from a small kerosene lantern hanging from a fork in the wooden tent pole and the smells were strange. Smoky and indescribable. Heyaiya, the elder, married sister, put a cloth mat or *jannabiya* on the ground by the fire-pit and we sat on it cross-legged. Rakhiya, the bride, blew on the embers, perched a teapot over them on a metal tripod and answered Mohammad's comments with a scowl. The language was so incomprehensible I didn't even listen to it but the scowl was clear. I thought it was for me, for coming to look at her, but Mohammad somehow knew what I felt and reassured me it wasn't. 'Her future husband is much older than her, but he is well off and has paid her father a good Bride Price. She hasn't been married before so has not been asked if he is the man she wants . . . and he isn't,' he explained. Maybe she followed his English or maybe she just knew what he was saying; she giggled like a schoolgirl. She can't have been more than thirteen. And, I thought, unlikely to have a more sensible opinion if she had been asked.

Marriage wasn't something I dreamed about. I had never imagined my wedding nor set aside anything for a glory box. The Pill had made marriage if not obsolete, certainly old-fashioned, and I was planning to avoid it. It occurred to me now how lucky I was to have grown up in a society that gave me the freedom to choose.

The girls and their mother all wore dark robes; the light could only detail their faces and hands: Fraija's small and dark, her daughters' lighter and longer. I was glad I had put on my shocking-pink blouse because it was long-sleeved, and I was careful to keep my legs tucked under my skirt. We had arrived in time for the make-up. The wedding party was apparently already celebrating at the groom's tent far away in the mountains and would arrive early in the morning to escort Rakhiya to her husband. Her family had to prepare a breakfast feast for them and even though she was the bride she would have to get up early to help. But she could put her make-up on now.

Heyaiya, crouching by the fire-pit, scraped soot onto a scrap of plastic bag from the inside of a huge wok. 'That soot is from the *mutty* bush, the best kind for kohl,' Mohammad explained. (And the wok was actually a *saj*, used dome-side-up over the fire to make the bread, hence the soot underneath.) The girls had a shard of mirror and applied their home-made kohl with a smooth twig, licked and dipped. They smeared it around their dark eyes.

They transformed me too. Heyaiya went to her tent (set up so close that the tent ropes intertwined) and brought me a black dress to put on over my clothes. The dress was sleeveless but with scraps of material that dangled down the sides like forgotten wings, and it was thick with golden-brown embroidery on the bodice and around the hem. She also put a shocking-pink floral scarf over my hair and tied it behind my neck. I don't know if it was the only spare scarf she had or if she had matched it specially with my blouse. Then Rakhiya sat in front of me and, looking to Mohammad for assurance, put kohl on my eyes. Considering I rarely wore any make-up it was quite a submission, but a small price to pay for such an insight into their world, and I leaned forward so she could apply it inside my eyelashes (with the same twig she had used, licking and dipping and smudging) and her smile was reward enough. When we had finished our tea and were ready to go they put henna on the palms of my hands. The thick paste was like mud and smelled of kerosene – the better to make it dark apparently. Giggling, they smeared it on, then Rakhiya held my hands together while Heyaiya wrapped a rag around them. They helped me up and Rakhiya said, 'See you tomorrow' and 'Goodnight' in clear enough English and I made an attempt, with all of them instructing, to say the equivalent in Arabic. The results even brought a laugh from Fraija.

Mohammad led me in the starlit darkness down to Nazzal's Camp. I needed his hand on my elbow – what with my hands tied and my feet as good as tied in the long dress – but I think I would have reached for his hand anyway. I was glad of the excuse to have him close. 'Careful, *derri-baalki*, now here'; his constant chatter showed he was too. I hadn't expected that. I had come to see a Bedouin wedding and had found a holiday romance.

'Take it off.' I was shy of the scrap of rag, and maybe at the quickness of our closeness, for I made him untie it and I walked on my own as soon as we got into the light of the hotel. I went straight to the bathroom and washed my hands. I couldn't imagine the colour the bride and her sister were hoping for – they were going to apply their own henna before bed and sleep with it on to get deep, long-lasting colour. Although I scrubbed, my palms were already a dark honey colour. And as for my eyes, that kohl was made from the genuine kohl bush and guaranteed to last for days. I gave up and went out to join Mohammad and Elizabeth and Ali and the assorted Bedouin Abu Majid had invited for the fish dinner.

A Bedouin Wedding

By the time we got across to the bride's tent the next morning the groom's party had already arrived and the *mensef* was being served. *Mensef* is the traditional Bedouin feast made from freshly slaughtered and butchered goats or sheep. The meat is boiled in goat's or sheep's yoghurt, *laban*, and served on a bed of *shraak* bread and steamy white rice.

The tent looked small in the daylight, dwarfed by stony hills and perpendicular rock-faces. There were mats outside and Mohammad stayed there with the men but Heyaiya ushered Elizabeth and me into the tent. Women pulled children back to make room as pairs of young men came in with huge trays of steaming food and put them on the ground. A child poured water and we washed our hands again – it was easier than trying to say we had just washed them, and next time we would remember to stand back so it wouldn't splash on our clothes. Six or seven women crouched round each tray; we were pulled down to join them and urged to eat with little scooping motions of their hands. One of the women pushed chunks of meat towards us but we ate as little as we could. The meat was a greyish colour and the smell was rich and strange. This was our first ever *mensef*, and although we couldn't see any eyeballs or tongues, or heads for that matter (they were all on the men's dishes), goat meat cooked in yoghurt, especially as breakfast, took some getting used to.

Heyaiya had made a room by hanging rugs from the roof; Rakhiya sat there looking beautiful. Her dark eyes were exaggerated by the kohl; a pure white chiffon scarf set off her white teeth and the gold-trim of her black *aba* picked out her gold one. Her hands, with palms nearly black, were tucked into her lap.

The food was cleared away; women and girls sang loudly and the piercing trilling sound they made echoed off the cliffs. A woman sprayed perfume on everyone – emptying a couple of bottles. When Rakhiya's father went into her 'room', the women crowded round and peeped over the rug curtains. He gave her some money, I learned later, and they wanted to see how much. There was running around; men and boys sang outside, and women veiled the bride's face with a scarf and covered her completely with the *aba*. Then they escorted her from her home in a procession of colour and noise, of singing and shooting (into the air with real bullets from real pistols and rifles), round the hill and down to the waiting pick-up trucks.

Mohammad squeezed us, along with uncountable Bedouin, onto the back of one truck which had a high cage round it so we couldn't fall out, though we did consider the possibility of getting crushed. The singing and shooting continued. We went up through the Siq – that ribbon of sky again – up through the village of Wadi Musa, then along the mountains and down again on a winding gravel road into the Beitha valley.

There wasn't a black tent or a stone house in sight but suddenly there was an old man standing in the middle of the road waving a pistol wildly in the air. 'My father,' Mohammad said (and why shouldn't it be in the middle of nowhere). 'He wants to invite the *gtaar* to his tent. It's a custom because if we were walking we would need tea.' Apparently this was a history-maker, one of the first *gtaars*, or processions, to go by car. We didn't need tea so Mohammad's father fired a few joyful shots in the air, put his pistol away in its holster and climbed onto one of the bumper bars. There he rode as we continued down to the end of the dwindling dirt track to where the groom's family was camped.

What a scene that was: among the rounded, honey-coloured rock-mountains that bubbled up in sheer cliffs from the flat plain, the tents had been set up with flags fluttering in the precious breeze. The pick-ups released their loads. The almost continuous shooting, singing and hoarse ululating accompanied the bridal procession to one of the tents. The men stayed outside (and we stood with them) but the women swept Rakhiya in and crowded in behind her. As they ducked under the low roof, their headscarves, and the hats of the children they carried, were changed momentarily by the coloured patches decorating the length of the tent front, and then all we could see were their long dresses to which their other children clung, pushing, singing and crying.

There was another tent for the men to sit in. I could see the bright mats along its length slowly filling now that the bride had been delivered. There was a Jordanian flag – green, white and black with a red triangle and a white seven-pointed star – poking out from one front pole and a plain white flag poking up from another. Mohammad said he wasn't allowed to stand around outside the women's tent, but that we should go in and sit. He introduced us to two young girls, Fatima and Wath-ha, and left us with them.

Wath-ha and Fatima practised their English with us; they said they lived and went to school in Petra and were in grade six. We were impressed; every word was more than our Arabic. They were both wearing knee-length dresses with trousers underneath, and their headscarves were puffed up by thick dark hair. Wath-ha insisted on taking Elizabeth off immediately to get properly dressed as she hadn't been to the Rakhiya and Heyaiya Salon the night before. They didn't take long to find a dress and headscarf, and the kohl was abundant; everyone seemed to wear it, especially the women and the babies in swaddling clothes, and even, I decided, most of the young men – their eyes couldn't be that dark naturally. Elizabeth, with her brown skin and black hair, looked almost Arabic. Then they decided we should have Arabic names.

I hadn't yet heard any Arabic names that I could pronounce,

let alone prefer so when Fatima suggested hers, and it seemed to make her happy, I saw no need to argue. It didn't occur to me that it might last longer than that day, or I might have put a bit more thought into the decision. The advantage I discovered was that as Fatima was the name of the Prophet Mohammad's favourite daughter and almost every family has one, a namesake, or two, identified with me on every social occasion.

Elizabeth chose Basma – a name she had heard and felt related to her own (and her sister still writes to her 'Dear Bessma').

As the women sat down, the tent was filled to the edges of its shade. The singing went on. They squeezed up in little cross-legged groups, put their heads together in pairs, and sang backwards and forwards at each other in hard voices. Their babies, concealed in bundles of cloth and sleeping despite the heat, the dust and the noise, lay beside them, and mothers put their arms out to warn us not even to step over them as we tried to move around the tent. Rakhiya had a hot little room of blankets here too, a *khula* she called it, and we sat with her for a while. Women came in to give her money but she seemed a bit lonely. She said she had never been to school but learned English from tourists. We could understand her well enough. 'This man I not like,' was obviously her husband.

Our cigarettes were accepted when offered. Delicious lollies were given out, boiled sweets with soft coconutty centres, factory-made in Amman. 'Nashed Sweets' we read on the wrappings and empty boxes, which were soon scattered about, sticky, but adding to the colour. The women sucked their sweets but the children all seemed to be taking theirs out of their mouths and snatching them from each other with sticky, sandy fingers and crying for more.

Mohammad and Ali came and resupplied us with cigarettes. Mohammad had a camera and took a photo of us with Fatima and Wath-ha, who told them about the names they had given us. The Bedouin gathered, like a crowd to an accident scene, to get their photos taken, and so we have a colourful record: a dusty foreground, a row of crouching children, a collection of brown faces with squinting eyes, and dresses and *thaubs* and shirts and pants, and headscarves, white, green, pink, red, blue and lots of black. Fraija the bride's mother and Heyaiya her sister are there, and Abu Majid and Salaama al-Mokhtar (Salaama the Mayor), who comes into my story later. They were all told our Bedouin names and no one forgot. Mohammad put the camera away and Ali said, '*Yallah*, let's go.'

They transported us out of the noise and dust to a place beyond our imaginations. We followed them into a ravine just a minute from the tents, and there, hidden behind a pink curtain of oleander bushes, was the secret entrance to another world. A passageway, hand-carved through the rock, opened into a soft, golden valley with a sandy floor and towering cliffs. It was like walking through the 'wardrobe'. We could occasionally hear the singing and gunshots from the wedding, but mostly not.

The valley was quite narrow and full of trees and bushes. There were blackened caves and deep cisterns carved into the base of the cliffs on both sides. Our Bedouin guides drew us on, pushing more trees aside to go deeper into the canyon. We followed them up a carved stairway to a cave high in the rock wall, but where they leapt, where the steps had worn away, we stretched across carefully and held their hands tightly. The cave had two carved benches and a plastered alcove with an arched roof at the back. The roof of the alcove was painted with vines and birds and some figures we would have missed if Mohammad hadn't pointed them out. What a treasure. The natural patterns across the roof of the main cave, in yellows, browns and mauves, looked just like a satellite photo – of the Mississippi, I thought, with its delta flowing down to the sea. Mohammad lit us cigarettes, we sat back on the bench enjoying the silence of crickets, lizard rustles and birdsong, and Ali offered us swigs of gin disguised in a bottle of orange.

We returned to the party as the evening meal was in the making. Some guys were showing off their marksmanship, shooting at charcoal marks on a faraway rock with various guns. They offered me a go and I managed to hit a mark. It was chance, and probably a well-kept rifle (I had been hunting only once before – at night up the Wairoa Gorge, shooting possums caught in the spotlight rigged up on the back of the truck), but I didn't let on, I basked in their admiration.

And after dinner there was dancing, like no dancing I had ever seen before. They called it the *samer*. Only men stood there, in a row out in front of the tent, shoulder to shoulder, swaying slightly, side to side and rocking almost imperceptibly from their knees. There was just a little lantern on the middle tent post. I could pick Mohammad out by his suit and his smile. Their feet were still and their *thaubs* swung languidly as they recited; a wonderful, poetic sound different from anything we knew but to which everyone else seemed to be listening intently as if to catch the words. I couldn't imagine how words could be detected in the flow. Two women slipped out of the darkness of the tent to dance in front of the row of men; their black *abas* flowing and dipping, disguised eyes shining, excitement tangible.

Later Mohammad and his friends started a faster dance, still side by side in a row, but more like a snake winding behind the leader who swung his *mendeel* as they all stamped their feet in time. Someone was playing on a pipe flute and another was drumming on a tin jerry-can. It was irresistible music and, although no other women were dancing, as soon as Mohammad asked me I took advantage of being a tourist and danced the night away in that crowd of joyful guys, continuing long after the groom had gone to his bride in the *khula*.

We eventually took our sleeping bags and went to sleep on the rock veranda of the Nabataean façade. Half a moon appeared over the mountains but did little to fade the brilliance of all the stars.

Too soon the morning sun rose, and hot, so we couldn't catch up on lost sleep. Lots of the guests had slept over but Elizabeth and I found ourselves honoured as we were sent in to have breakfast with Rakhiya. Her husband had his breakfast with the men. She gave us bright headscarves from her trousseau, and whispered defiantly that she would be back in Petra in a couple of days. 'You will see.'

It was time to leave. The pick-ups had gone back the night before but Mohammad said, 'It's a nice walk through the hills.' For a Bedouin, we realised when we finally got home several hours later. But it was a short cut: seven kilometres compared to fifteen around the road. Abu Majid and Mohammad's Saudi Arabian friend Mahedy were walking too. Mahedy didn't speak a word of English but that didn't stop him from flirting with Elizabeth, and he looked so elegant in his silky white *thaub* and rich red *mendeel* that she didn't mind. We set out from the tents beside a dry riverbed which turned between high hills of honeycomb rock. Mohammad indicated with a sweep of his arm to a sand-hill. 'That is where the *Ingleeziya*, the English lady, excavated,' he said, but we didn't stop to inspect the Neolithic ruins. They had been excavated by Diana Kirkbride, an English archaeologist, but you had to go up onto the mound to look down into the trenches she had made.

'*Yallah*,' yelled our gallant *mendeeled* guides as they led us down goat paths, along the valley and up onto a plateau of harvested stubble fields. Mohammad and Mahedy sang – it seemed they couldn't hold the music in. A startled bird flew out of a bush in a flash of black and white. Our sandals thudded slightly on the dusty path.

We descended into a valley and the mountains towered above us, rounded on the tops but with natural scoops in the sides where dramatic patterns – whorls and waves of reds and browns, creams and pinks and all the shades between – hung like an outdoor art gallery.

We stopped for refreshments. The Nabataeans had carved a pool into the mountainside and water trickled into it from a crack in the rock. We drank daringly from an old tin can Mohammad found lying there, but were glad to have a corner of his *mendeel* to filter out the bits of grass we could see floating on the surface.

On we went. The valley narrowed and we clambered in and out of the sandy stream bed. We had oleander flowers in our hair and sunburned noses. Here we saw worn stairs disappearing like a dream on the rounded rock face, and now to the left tombs with staircased façades, and on in front a façade with an arch. We could hear children's voices and a donkey bray. Our guides no longer held our hands. (I have since discovered that the Bedouin and Arabic way is about *sutra*: the safeguarding, or preservation, of modesty.) We passed an occupied dark and smoky cave, and then a palatial-looking one with inset windows, a door and a living rock terrace. There was young Fatima. She called to me, reconfirming our connection by name, and to Mohammad to bring us in for tea, but we didn't stop and by midday we were home catching up on lost-in-dancing sleep.

It was as Mohammad guided us singing through rocky, oleander-crowded canyons that I fell in love with him. Why I hadn't noticed his quick, eye-crinkling smile the day we met I don't know, but I noticed it now. I loved his simply confident, fun-filled manner. He lit our cigarettes, and gave us a hand up, and had other gentlemanly habits which I would have scorned as a liberated woman in New Zealand, but which appealed to me now. He fixed his red and white *mendeel*, throwing the knotted ends up over his head into an exotic Bedouin turban, and flashed me a smile. I could no longer see his synthetic suit. I was fascinated.

But I didn't know it was love. Much as I fancied Mohammad and enjoyed the days we spent together, there were other places to see and other people to meet and Elizabeth's ticket home from Beirut expired in a few weeks so we had to get on.

We said goodbye again.

Fate and Destiny

If there had been a Lebanese embassy in Damascus or if we could have gotten Lebanese visas at the border I might never have realised I had more than a fancy for Mohammad, but God works in mysterious ways. The only way we could get into Lebanon was to go back across the border to Jordan to the Lebanese embassy in Amman. As the Jordanian border officials stamped us each another month's visa to enter their country, I had an idea. I didn't *need* to go to Lebanon, only Elizabeth's flight left from there. I had neither a commitment nor a forward plan. I could go back to Petra and stay with Mohammad while I decided where to go next. He was fun and staying with him cost next to nothing I reasoned. Elizabeth could see more than me and sent me off with a goodbye, a good-luck and a promise to keep in touch.

I came into the Treasury forecourt yet again and Mohammad raced over. 'I was just thinking about you,' he said, with such amazement that I could tell he had been, and that he was as happy to see me as I was to see him. We shook hands and kissed on both cheeks but held off with the embrace because his friends were all watching. In the future whenever Mohammad was asked about how we met, he joked, 'I was fishing, and she is what I hooked.' And I think this is when he knew I had taken the bait. He didn't take long to reel me in.

Within days everyone was talking about us getting married. In

Nelson in the 1970s – in a world of women's liberation, mixed flatting and 'living in sin' – marriage had been the trap to avoid. (I had joked that I would consider it in order to get rid of my complicated Dutch surname, but even taking your husband's name was being phased out.)

Here marriage was everybody's goal.

I now know that they just said what they thought – because to them it was clear that I was looking for a husband, Mohammad needed a wife, and we loved being together – but at the time I thought he had retained the services of the whole tribe. I laughed in the late afternoons when the *mendeeled* twinkly-eyed men outside whichever cave or tent we were sitting asked if I was going to marry him, '*Widki ta-khuthee?*' and tried to convince me, 'Mohammad *quayas*' – Mohammad is good. But it sounded more serious when his laughing friends Ali and Awa<u>th</u> caught me alone. They told me what a good man he was, 'Mohammad ferry good, make good husban,' and what a good idea marriage was, 'Husban *quayas*.' I felt pressured and irritated and I told them to mind their own business, not understanding their Bedouin tactics.

The trouble wasn't Mohammad. I had never had such a handsome boyfriend. He was small and strong and as agile as a mountain goat. He had brown skin, a black moustache and a smile that really did light up. His nose was perfect too, too beautiful to go unmentioned. He joked with meaningless words, cooked delicious meals and made me the centre of his attention. He attracted attention himself; old women kissed his hand, young women baked him bread and when his friends came by they joked and sang. I considered myself lucky he wasn't already married. I wasn't put off by his cave or way of life either. I really liked the idea of no mortgage or electricity bills, and only one room to clean. Nor did I think 'marriage to Mohammad' would mean 'stuck in Petra'. He had a passport he was proud of and seemed keen to use.

The trouble was marriage.

I was enjoying things as they were; walking with him up to the Treasury and drinking tea at the vendor's fire, or down between the western cliffs to wash and swim at the spring; or up to Ali's cave where we sat out on the bedstead in the evening light and they talked and I let the words flow over me and enjoyed not having to take part in the conversation; or with another friend, Ali-f, for a bottle of arak and a barbecued chicken dinner around a tiny fire in a valley filled with juniper trees – and back to the cave with them singing, 'Layla, Layla, Layla, Layyyyylaaaa-a ya Layla.'

But people were becoming suspicious. What was I doing here if I didn't want to marry Mohammad? I might be a spy, they warned him. So I started to think seriously about the idea. Mum and Dad had set a good example which I would want to live up to. Marriage was a commitment, meaning us together for ever, and I wasn't sure that Mohammad, who was always so busy joking and laughing (and I loved him for it), appreciated that.

'I'll grow old and wrinkled,' I said, trying to escape. I had goldy-blond hair and clear, tanned skin but I knew that wouldn't last; I couldn't be bothered with cleansers or toners and already had lines across my forehead, and, Elizabeth had observantly predicted, would soon have squinty eye-wrinkles because I never wore sunglasses.

'So will I, but you will be my wife so I'll love you anyway,' he insisted. Although Mohammad appeared to be the ultimate bachelor he really thought that when you were old enough you kept your eyes open for someone to settle down with and when she showed up you married her and made a family.

Later I learned that he had been waiting for a foreigner. His German friend Karl, whose first visit to Petra had been eleven years earlier, told me about the Mohammad he had met then. 'He had not been content to lead the donkey – he wanted English lessons on the way,' Karl told me, and continued, enjoying every moment, 'When I asked what he wanted to learn English for, he had answered, "I want to marry Urrrropean Woman." And it is so nice to meet you at last.'

But fellow foreigners told me to watch out. 'Are you sure he isn't already married?' I was warned. 'The Bedouin have strange traditions,' someone else said. 'If your husband dies, you will have to marry his brother.'

I realised I knew nothing, except that he wasn't married. Mohammad laughed easily when I told him what I had heard. 'I don't know where they get these stories; that would only happen if she wanted it to, because he would have to support her and her children anyway. It might suit.'

And although I didn't want to consider divorce, I needed to know it was there, like checking out the emergency exits on the aeroplane, hoping you will never need them. 'Of course if it doesn't work we will get divorced,' Mohammad answered, not telling me it would be as simple as him saying 'I divorce you', three times.

I made an attempt to think clearly and flew to London. And after just three weeks in the terraced houses and local pubs of friends in Doncaster, Edinburgh and Carlisle, and three weeks in the well-ordered Netherlands with concerned Dutch relations, I knew there was nowhere I would rather be than in Petra with Mohammad. I flew back to get married.

In years to come, when visitors, on finding out I lived in a cave with my Bedouin husband, called me brave, or courageous, or daring, I felt like a bit of a fraud. I had just done the easiest thing. No politics or philosophy; just a wonderful man, who started his day by praying that God would be pleased with him, and that his parents would be pleased with him, and then went off to his work with a flick of his *mendeel* and a joyful step, while I did what I felt like without a care in the world.

I was just lucky. I hadn't been sure I was doing the right thing, but I had been sure there was only one way to find out.

Courting

Mohammad had laughed when I said it wasn't his friends' business to ask me to marry him.

'They don't mean to make you angry,' he said. 'That is the way of the Bedou.' And he told me this story:

Fraij was about thirty-five and he was still unmarried. He was looking for a wife and heard about a divorcée who lived with her parents at their summer tent-site halfway across the plateau to Ma'an. She sounded like a good choice so he asked his friend Sliman to call in on his way to Ma'an for supplies; to put in a good word for him and to make a proposal.

It wasn't until a couple of weeks later that Fraij saw Sliman again and got to ask what answer the divorcée had given.

'Oh, I'm sorry *ya-khuey*' – my brother – Sliman replied. 'I couldn't convince her to marry you . . . but the visit was not altogether wasted because she has agreed to marry me!'

It seemed highly unlikely and not very funny at the time but nowadays I know the 'ways of the Bedou' myself and I wonder if it wasn't true. It was certainly a favourite of Mohammad's; I think he liked how it described the unexpectedness of life.

A Wedding Certificate – What For?

Two and a half months after meeting each other, in the early hours of a Ramadan morning, Mohammad and I headed to Amman to get married.

The normal Bedouin wedding wouldn't do – we needed official papers so I could get a resident's permit. Traditionally in Petra, as in most of the other Bedouin communities, marriages happened without any paperwork. Later, in the mid-1980s, an amnesty was announced to enable couples to get marriage certificates, and my in-laws went to the temporary office and came home with their certificate and a box of chocolates which they distributed among their children, grandchildren and neighbours, but, before that, marriage was witnessed by the community and consecrated by the slaughter of a goat or sheep.

Back then, once private enquiries ascertained that the families of the couple were in agreement and that no other suitor felt he had a superior right to the bride, the engagement was arranged. The man's family and friends came to the girl's home where her family and friends gathered. Women stayed separate from the men. The future couple's fathers read some verses from the Koran, agreed on a Bride Price and decided when to hold the wedding. The man usually gave money to his fiancée's mother and her sisters for helping secure the girl's favour, and hoped the amount would impress. Couples sometimes met in front of the gathered witnesses and offered each other a token mouthful of sugar, but sometimes they were still young children and didn't even attend. Months or years later, when the man was ready and the bride was 'ripe', the wedding took place and the goat or sheep was slaughtered. No rings were exchanged nor papers signed.

Mohammad knew it wouldn't work for us – we needed

papers so we had to go to Amman. It was Ramadan, the Islamic month of fasting, during which pious Muslims don't smoke, eat or drink from dawn (even before sunrise) to sunset – and it was illegal to do any of these things in public places. Petra was way out of the public eye and Mohammad didn't fast anyway so we hadn't been bothered by restrictions, but now that we had decided to get married we wanted to get on and do it. Mohammad hoped we could manage, but I didn't realise how difficult it would be.

I had been amused the night before when Mohammad wound up the alarm clock, surprised that anyone in the valley had one to borrow, but now he was shining a torch in my eyes and I was no longer amused.

'*Gawmi*, get up. I made tea,' he cajoled.

I rolled over.

'The *service* will be full,' he tried again.

I did, in theory, want to get married but at four o'clock in the morning I was tempted to change my mind. It really was the middle of the night. Mohammad tried again. '*Yallah, habebitee.* Come on.'

We left the cave on the ledge and trekked up through the Siq in the dark. Just after the dawn prayers we left Wadi Musa in a packed Mercedes Benz. In New Zealand it had been a treat to *see* a Mercedes; here I was riding in them regularly, although they were far from the latest models. They were *services*, privately owned vehicles licensed to run along set routes like buses, and we paid only the fare for our seats. The driver this morning wasn't fasting either so we smoked along the way. We arrived at the southern bus station, Karaaj-al-Jenoob, and caught a taxi, winding down through the *souq* and up again to the main civil court perched on the side of Jabal Amman. Jabal means mountain or hill and Amman is built on at least seven of them; Petra is in a basin surrounded by them.

Mohammad asked around and plenty of people were keen to be helpful. First we needed a paper from the British embassy, they told him, to prove I wasn't already married.

We caught another taxi further up Jabal Amman. This time I paid. I gave the driver 5 dinars and, following Mohammad's example, told him to keep the change. It was only as he sped away that I realised the 450 on the meter meant 450 fils (less than £1), not 4.50 dinars. My 5 dinars was 5000 fils! Damn! An expensive lesson. Mohammad saw the expression on my face and asked what it was but I was far too embarrassed to tell him. I shook my head and said, 'Nothing.'

The embassy had a wrought-iron fence and a crowd of young Jordanian men hoping for visas. We tried to line up but they let us through – I thought it was the foreign woman's advantage but they were asking Mohammad how he had had such luck and if I had a sister who would be interested in any of them. It didn't take long to get the paper and I was instructed to get it translated into Arabic and to bring it back to be certified. Why they didn't have a translator on the spot I couldn't understand, but they directed me to a licensed translator whose office was downtown in the bottom of the valley. The day was getting hot and we were getting thirsty but not even water was allowed till sunset. Taxi there, taxi back. I was thankful that the embassy crowd ushered me forward again and the official certified my translation quickly. Then we got another taxi to the courthouse. We thought we were getting somewhere.

Outside the courthouse, lining the pavement and, precariously, on the stairs down to the *souq*, scribes sat at makeshift stalls. The fold-up tables of these literate men were arranged side by side under the shade of faded sun umbrellas and were crowded around with the flowing robes and embroidered shawls of people waving papers and wanting applications for birth, death or marriage certificates to be filled out in classical Arabic.

The scribe Mohammad found free at the top of the stairs

wore a tired suit with ironed-to-a-shine lapels. His face, barely showing under his black and white *mendeel*, was well worn too. He nodded and took a new piece of foolscap paper. As Mohammad answered his questions, he wrote down the relevant information painstakingly, making the usually flowing script spiky and disjointed.

The first complication was my name, and not just because it is so long and Dutch. He and Mohammad inspected my passport. 'Which is your father's name? And your grandfather's?' Mohammad asked me, holding it out.

I cried silently at them in disbelief. Oh come on! 'It's my passport so it has my name.' Wasn't that obvious? 'What do you want fathers and grandfathers for?'

Mohammad tried to explain. He showed me his own precious passport and pointed to the English translation: 'Mohammad, me; Abdallah, my father; Othman, my grandfather; al-Manajah, my tribe.' I hadn't even heard his tribe's name before. There was also a place for his mother – Agaela.

Telling them my father's name was Maarten didn't help because there was no record of that on my passport. I let them figure it out. I didn't care how they did it as long as we got it done – and soon.

Ten minutes later this was the result: Marguerite, me; Jane, my father; van, my grandfather; Geldermalsen, my tribe. In Arabic there are no letters equivalent to 'v' or hard 'g' so it was more like this: 'Marghreet Jeen Faan Jeldrrmalsn.' When Mohammad read it out loud it was hard to recognise. I don't know how they would have got round it if I only had a single surname or no second name. Janny, my mother's name, slipped simply into Arabic and was recorded without comment.

Mohammad handed the scribe some coins and he produced revenue stamps from a little metal box, crimson ones with the head of His Majesty King Hussein on them. He stuck them on his masterpiece, signed it with a flourish (the nearest he came to enthusiastic), and then pointed with the paper to the open doors of the court.

Inside, the noise of the crowd pressed back off the dark polished-wood office partitions and low roof. Our turn; Mohammad passed the paper over to a clerk who read it and pointed to the page. Mohammad looked unsure. I followed him back outside where we could hear.

'He says we go where the man, the husband, lives. I am from Petra, we must go to Ma'an.'

'Oh great. Why didn't that scribe tell us that?' I complained. Mohammad lifted his shoulders and shook his head. His tassels swung and he smiled. This was all new to him too.

We needed food and water so we gave up for the day and went to Kevin and Innes's; the New Zealand couple who had made me welcome when I first arrived with Elizabeth and who would continue to make me welcome whenever I came up from Petra with Mohammad.

Innes was from Nelson and we knew each other through our brothers, my older, her younger, who had been great friends. When we were in Egypt, Mum had found out that Innes and her husband were living in Jordan and had sent me their address. When Elizabeth and I arrived in Amman we found a letter waiting for us at the Poste Restante, and not long after calling the number and asking for 'Mr Kevin' he had pulled up dramatically on a motorbike with a sidecar and introduced himself. We had already attracted a few offers of assistance as we stood on the footpath with our bags, and now a small crowd gathered to see where everything would fit. Kevin pushed Elizabeth's bag down in the front of the sidecar and instructed her into the remaining gap in a whirl of enthusiasm and showmanship. I had to strap my bag onto my back to ride pillion, and I held onto Kevin's leather jacket as he whisked us away. We went twisting up Jabal Amman round the roundabouts to their home.

They gave us a warm welcome even though their own lives were really busy. Their baby Jason was just a few months old and Kevin's parents were staying; another New Zealand couple was also passing through.

Now their place was like a home away from home. 'Help yourselves,' Innes said. I loved the informality and made us a pot of tea and some Vegemite on toast (jam for Mohammad) while we told them about our day. They laughed and told us to take it easy – Kevin worked for a local company and knew how frustrating the bureaucracy could be.

The next morning after a good breakfast we took a taxi back to Karaaj-al-Jenoob. Buildings hung over the narrow, crowded street, cutting out the air. The tables and chairs of the closed food stalls were stacked on the hot pavement. Honking buses and taxis squeezed round vendors selling razor blades or a pair of second-hand shoes, and a crew of Egyptians emptying a truckload of second-hand clothes into a storeroom forced us off the footpath. Toothless men called 'Ma'an Ma'an, Albatra Albatra' (Petra). One of them attracted us with a wave of his arm and opened the door of an old Mercedes full of *mendeels* and moustaches but Mohammad led me further along. I followed closely; no holding hands here. I was wearing a long cotton dishdash that was comfortable and modest (until I washed it, it went down to my ankles), but I didn't cover my shiny hair. Dark eyes looked at me, suspicious, inquisitive, speculating.

There was a *service* to Ma'an with room left for the two of us in the front seat. The car was full then so we could leave straight away and the driver put his hand on the horn and kept it there till he had extricated us from the scene. In the thirty-five-degree, nine-in-the-morning heat, we headed back south across the desert with all the windows down. Cigarette smoke blew out; sand and diesel fumes blew in. Heavily loaded trucks rumbled at us, occasionally side by side filling both lanes of the highway. I liked our driver when he took to the shoulder. I didn't like him so much when he overtook long trucks on blind bends. I wished I didn't know how to drive.

Ma'an took three hours to get to. From the depot we walked along the flat, sandy streets towards the administration buildings which were set on a small rise among scattered gum trees. There were only a few men about but they looked at us as if there hadn't been a foreigner here since Lawrence of Arabia. Probably not a fair-haired female one I decided.

The clerk in the courthouse admired the crimson stamps and read the script. People crowded into the room to look. He announced to all and sundry (and Mohammad translated for me), 'It's where the bride-to-be lives that dictates the courthouse. Return to Amman.'

'I don't believe it! I don't even live in Amman, and Amman sent us here!' I said out loud. I imagine what Mohammad was saying in Arabic was the same, but the clerk pointed to the paper and the stamps and dismissed us.

'Let's go back to Petra and try again after Ramadan,' Mohammad suggested optimistically.

Petra sounded good; I didn't want to think about trying again. It seemed too much like hard work.

A Wedding Certificate – Success at Last

On our way back to the bus depot in Ma'an we were stopped by a man who knew Mohammad. The two men shook hands up and down and kissed each other several times on both cheeks. 'This is Abu Ali, the Father of Ali,' Mohammad explained. 'His mother is my father's sister.'

He was quite the opposite of Mohammad, tall and round-faced with a large padded handshake. He led us away from the bus depot along wide, dusty-white avenues between high, roughly plastered walls and occasional date palms. There was no question about it: we were going to be his guests. He opened a wooden door in a wall and we entered an oblong courtyard with three doors on the right and on the left a block wall over which I could see into the neighbour's yard.

He ushered us through the first door into an immaculately whitewashed room. There was light only from the door and a small window beside it. We took off our sandals and stepped into the shade. The concrete floor was cool and silky smooth. I sank onto the thick wool-stuffed mattress, the *farrsha*, tucked my feet under me and leaned on stacked white bolsters, but Umm Ali (the Mother of Ali) came in excitedly and we had to scramble up again. She bent down and kissed Mohammad's hand.

Mohammad introduced me to her. '*Haathi marrati*,' This is my wife, and she held my face between her large soft hands and checked me out with friendly dark eyes. I had to lean down to accept welcoming kisses on both cheeks. A young girl handed her a tea tray as I settled back among the cushions. She crouched in front of me on the concrete floor and poured the tea from a brilliant blue teapot into two little glasses stuffed with green leaves. A minty aroma erupted into the room. She placed the glasses in front of me and Mohammad; she and Abu Ali were fasting. I took a sip and leaned back. I switched off and enjoyed it, the sweetness and the mint. I let the sound of their chatter blend with the occasional clatter from the yard and the further away shouts and traffic noise of the town. I wondered how they could fast, how Abu Ali, hot off the dusty street, could resist the temptation. And even if you weren't thirsty or couldn't smell, it looked so good – the shiny glasses, the clear amber tea, the greenness of the leaves, even the blue brilliance of the pot and polished metal tray called for attention.

Mohammad included me in the conversation. 'All but their smallest children are fasting.' I could hear admiration in his voice, but also embarrassment, because he wasn't, and maybe a question: what did I think about it?

But I couldn't comprehend. Why stop yourself? What was the point? Who would know? None of which I said out loud because I was too relaxed to bother.

They fed us lunch as well. There was puffy fresh pita bread and a small tin dish of fresh lamb's liver fried with onions. It was good.

'*Quayas*,' I said to Abu Ali, who pushed the tray closer and passed me more bread.

'Don't eat too much – the little kids will get what we leave,' Mohammad warned. I worried that he hadn't warned me earlier. There already wasn't much left.

Later we relaxed. We couldn't go back to Petra now anyway because there weren't likely to be any cars after midday. Abu Ali knew someone at the court and he was going to take us in the evening to see if we could get a new paper saying I lived in Petra too. Give it another go. There was nothing to do till then. Mohammad fell asleep. I discovered the girls in the kitchen and watched them prepare their meal. 'My name is Basma. I am twelve years old,' the oldest girl said. 'In school I learn English. This is sister, this is brother.'

'*Ana* Fatima.' I had learned to introduce myself but that was about all the conversation we managed. They crouched me with them on the concrete kitchen floor; I was thankful for the wall. They watched me with shy smiles and encouraged me to try as they stuffed aubergines and courgettes with minced meat and spicy rice.

Late in the evening we went to see Abu Ali's friend from the court. We sat on sponge-rubber *farrshas*, squashed into the front porch of the big square house. There was a breeze-block wall all round with a couple of olive trees planted in bare white earth.

The friend's wife and mother sat with us and served us half-moons of deep-fried pancake stuffed with pistachio nuts; they were delicious. Sugary syrup oozed out as I bit into the first one.

'Ramadan sweets,' she said. '*Gatayif.*'

However, nothing could be done to change our paper. We had been the novelty I had imagined and everyone in the court already *knew* I lived in Amman; besides, it had all those damn stamps.

For some reason returning to Petra ceased being an option – maybe both of us were afraid we would change our minds. Anyway, the next morning after lots of soft kisses from the children, we repeated our journey: the Desert Highway, the open-windowed Mercedes, the city cab to the court in Amman. I followed Mohammad. We were sent pushing with our papers from window to window, although I was getting impatient and thought we should be able to shortcut after having been sent to Ma'an unnecessarily. I wanted to talk to someone with clout.

'No,' he said, looking round to make sure no one noticed my irritation. 'We have to be careful. We don't make trouble. It will be good soon, *inshallah.*'

And soon he was right. Another official took out another form and filled in the gaps as Mohammad answered his questions then translated the ones that were for me. They were: 'Are you a virgin or a divorcee?' and 'Why do you want to get married?' He told me the acceptable answers and translated them back. We signed the form; the man stapled it to the well-travelled one we had and gave them both to us.

Mohammad headed to another door.

'What now?' I needed to know.

'We just have to pay the fees, and then go to the religious sheikh.'

Wow, getting closer, I thought. But no such luck. It was already midday; the accountant had closed so that he would have time to take the money to the bank before it closed – at 1.30. Ramadan hours.

Kevin and Innes went out for the evening so we could babysit Jason and feel useful.

The 26th of August dawned and when the accountant opened at nine we were first in line. We paid the fees and were given directions to a mosque where we could find the sheikh who would finalise our marriage. We needed to take two witnesses with us, so next we went to the Philadelphia Hotel where Mohammad knew he would find someone.

The Philadelphia was the most famous hotel in Amman then but has since been pulled down. It had been built on the forecourt of the ancient Roman theatre and had an air of colonial opulence about it that I felt quite uncomfortable in (though I made the most of the toilets). The owners also owned Nazzal's Camp and many of the staff had also spent time working there so they got to know the Bdoul (unlike Mohammad, most of the Bedouin who lived in Petra were from the Bdoul tribe). So the Bdoul often came and hung out here when they were in Amman.

We found Awa<u>th</u>, who I suspected had been planted here just in case. He had been to the barber and had his hair tamed by a *shishwaar*. Usually he wore a black and white *mendeel*, which was more macho than this blown-dry and curled-under style. His shirt was tight and his trousers were flared, like most of the other young men on the streets. He was, he said, at our service.

The chef, Abu Sliman, had also worked at Nazzal's Camp and agreed to help us as soon as he had served lunch. He also insisted we eat and, because of Ramadan in the streets, we did. In the evenings people could dine among the stone columns and friezes that lay about in the jasmine-bordered garden courtyard, but now only the more discreet high-ceilinged dining room was open.

As soon as we had eaten and the chef was finished, we got a taxi to the mosque. I had imagined a gilded dome, or at least a dome, but this mosque was on the third floor of a plain concrete-block building, downtown next to the post office. We

climbed up to the open prayer hall, which was carpeted with
rugs, but there was no one there – no worshippers and no
sheikh. We waited. We climbed further up the stairwell to sneak
a cigarette on the flat roof. There was a loudspeaker hanging
from the outer wall of the stairwell, the only outward sign there
was a mosque in the building.

Another wasted day, I thought. Maybe it wasn't meant to be.

There was a noise downstairs at the street door. The sheikh
had arrived at last. He stood shaking his head and pointing to
his watch. Meanwhile Abu Sliman had stopped a taxi, and
Mohammad looked desperate.

'*Yallah ya naas*!' Come on, you guys.

It turned out that this was not the sheikh we desperately
needed. Ours was at home, having his day off. He lived on yet
another hill, Jabal al-Lweibdah, and since there were no street
names or numbers in Amman it would be impossible to find his
house without a guide. And this sheikh didn't want to take us
there because he needed to make the call to prayer in twenty
minutes.

All the more reason to hurry! I thought we should kidnap
him. Maybe he saw it in our eyes. He relented and jumped in the
taxi, all flowing robes. We crowded in after him, thanking him,
'*Shukran, shukran*,' as the taxi raced up and round the narrow
stone-walled streets. Here! Mohammad paid the taxi to take
him back – in time to call? I didn't even think about it. I was
about to get married; my mind was elsewhere.

'*Ahlan-wa-sahlan*.' A woman welcomed us and ushered us
into the front room. It was a cross between a lounge and an
office. We sat on stuffed chairs facing each other across a nest of
glass coffee tables. When our sheikh came in, we had to move so
he could get past and squeeze behind his dark polished-wood
desk. The wall behind the desk was lined with bookcases; on the
other walls gilt-framed tapestry verses from the Holy Koran
hung side by side.

The sheikh didn't complain about being woken from his after-noon rest. Understanding that we had made the trip from Petra, he asked his wife to bring tea and coffee – travellers are exempt from fasting. (Now that, I thought, was a good idea.) He was such a comfortably ordinary middle-aged man, despite his head-dress and robe and pale skin (from his indoor life) that he made me feel at ease.

It took him only a moment to realise that he would not be talking to my male representative. I was twenty-two years old, so it was perfectly legal for me to represent myself, and I was also keen to show them all that I was capable – that it was not my father or brother or uncle who decided my future, but me. The letter telling Mum and Dad of my decision hadn't even reached them yet. This was my life; I barely gave them a thought.

The sheikh spoke reasonable English. He said, as he filled out our wedding certificate, 'Because you are a Christian, you don't have to become a Muslim to marry a Muslim man, but if you want to change your religion now I can make those papers too.'

Christain . . . Muslim . . . religion didn't concern me much and I would have converted if it had been a necessary part of the marriage, or if Mohammad had insisted. (Being a Muslim was important to him though he didn't pray or fast.) But now I had a choice. Islam, Mohammedans, Muslim, I thought – I don't know what it all involves.

'If I don't have to change, I won't,' I replied. Marriage was a big enough step for one day. (And I found I was pleased that I wouldn't be a hypocrite in two religions).

He continued. 'You have to name two sums of money to be written into the marriage contract. The first is the *mahr*, which your husband would usually pay to your parents, and by law it may not be less than a quarter of a dinar.' (I've called it a Bride Price but it is more like a male dowry. If the family takes money they usually supply an equal amount of furnishings for the new home, but quite commonly only the token quarter of a dinar is asked for.)

Mohammad refused to suggest an amount. I tried to guess how much he had left in his pocket – probably not much with all the running up and down we had been doing.

'Five dinars,' I suggested carefully.

The small sum didn't seem to surprise the sheikh, who wrote it down and didn't even ask Mohammad to hand it over.

'The second is to be written down in case of divorce,' he said next. I had made sure divorce was possible but I didn't think it would be part of our marriage! He insisted on explaining: 'If Mohammad wants a divorce, he will have to pay you, and if you want a divorce you will have to pay him, but *you* get to stipulate the amount and you have to do it now.'

This was a bit more serious. I had really only known Mohammad a couple of months, so I figured it had to be enough so that if Mohammad threw me out I could get to Amman and keep myself till I got help, but not so much that I wouldn't be able to produce it if something went terribly wrong and I wanted to leave.

I can't believe I thought so calmly.

'Fifty dinars,' I decided, hoping my calculations would never be tested.

The sheikh wrote that sum down and continued. 'Any other stipulations should be made now too. Some people ask for a house . . .'

I was wondering what that meant, and whether I should write down that Mohammad had agreed we would go to New Zealand one day, but Mohammad stopped the sheikh short and said to me, 'Trust me. You don't need to write anything else.'

We signed the marriage certificate. Awath and Abu Sliman witnessed it and the sheikh opened his stamp pad and put the final stamp on it. And I was still a van Geldermalsen.

Out on the street Mohammad grinned and said 'Now I have no money. I'll give you the five dinars later.'

Awa<u>th</u>, our witness, often joked that Mohammad didn't even pay my *mahr*. Although Mohammad never gave me *that* five dinars, our money very soon became *our* money. I never learned to spend as happily as Mohammad could, and grumbled about many of the things he bought, but I usually ended up enjoying his extravagances or benefiting from the profits he made when he resold whatever it was.

In-Laws

When we finally got home around noon the next day, there was a black-hair tent set up below our cave.

We had hired a pick-up to take us down from Wadi Musa. The driver agreed to tackle the narrow track that curled round the hill down in front of the cave. It veered off the main track as the valley opened out and led to places in the south and west, and people and donkeys often used it, but I hadn't seen any vehicles on it before. Mohammad said the track had been used for the excavation of the al-Katuta Nabataean rubbish dump in the south city walls so it was wide enough for a vehicle, but he had to get out a couple of times to move rocks that had since rolled onto it.

As we pulled up, Mohammad's spiky-haired sisters squealed excitedly and ran into the tent. His father came out as we walked up the hill and Mohammad told me, 'You call him Amm, Uncle, and kiss his hand.'

I hadn't thought about in-laws . . . much less about kissing hands. I couldn't do either.

I mumbled '*marrhaba*' as I took his extended hand and shook it as firmly as I dared. I probably looked him in the eye. He was no taller than Mohammad and they looked quite similar, although his face was a bit narrower and his moustache was bigger and thicker. His eyebrows were quite different too – they reached out to embrace his brow-bones whereas Mohammad's sat straight above his soft eyelids and were smudged down his brow-bones as if by an endearing finger. When he smiled at me – despite my lack of respectful kiss – his cheeks popped high and shiny brown just like his son's.

Mohammad lived independently and although I had met his family miles away in Bei<u>th</u>a, I naively hadn't given them a second thought, let alone imagined them in my life. Now here they were – as next door as you could get.

Mohammad's mother had died about twelve years earlier but his father had married again and now his stepmother came out too and welcomed me with a kiss on each cheek. She was taller than her husband, nearly as tall as me. Her brown cheeks were smooth, she had soft blue tattoos of dots and crescents on her forehead and round her lips, and I recognised her bouquet of goats, wood fires and local tobacco. Her name was a collection of unimaginable sounds, which I avoided ever having to say. Her fine young son, who shook my hand seriously, was called Laafi, and although no one called her Umm Laafi until long after her husband Abdallah died in 1987, I will refer to her by that name from now on.

Whenever I am asked what Mohammad's family thought about him marrying a foreigner, I reply brightly, 'I think they were happy he found a wife . . . and they didn't have to pay for her!' because I now know that with the reputation of a playboy, and neither a sheep nor a goat to his name it would have been difficult for him to impress a prospective father-in-law. I didn't know that then though, neither did I realise that a foreign wife was considered a bit of a catch.

Mohammad's sisters (Tuf-leh, Inzela, Neda and Maryam) followed us up to the cave and watched our every move with big eyes. Mohammad said he was just as much a novelty as I was because they didn't see him very often, but I was relieved when my new in-laws shifted their tent away to the Palace Tomb the next day. There, about a week later, they began our wedding celebrations. Luckily it was their obligation – wedding celebrations were not something I had saved for. With or without us, every evening they made tea and coffee and encouraged the men to dance. They didn't send out invitations for this, nor for the feast which was to be on the fourth day of the holiday at the end of Ramadan, the fourth day of the Eid, but everybody must have told everybody else because whenever we went over, there were plenty of people, and the chanting of the traditional *samer* echoed around the mountains long after we left.

It soon became clear that although I couldn't speak Arabic, didn't know how to milk a goat, make bread or start a fire, and certainly wasn't planning on moving in to look after my in-laws, they were still intending to make a party that would be talked about for years to come.

Geography, and Ancient History

On one of those evenings we listened to our wedding celebrations from a mountaintop.

When Mohammad said, 'We go to High Place?' it sounded more like an order than a question. I knew the High Place was another major site like the Monastery, and I knew it wasn't far, but I hadn't been inspired to climb up there because the name was so nondescript. And then he said, '*Yallah habebitee*' – come on, my love – effectively wiping out dithering and contemplation and off we went.

We made up a bedroll, bought some Gold Star cigarettes, processed-cheese segments and a can of sardines with a key opener, called into a black-hair tent to beg some fresh *shraak* and headed up the hill behind the cave.

I guessed this wasn't the tourist route, though it was spectacular. It was more like the straightest line between the cave and the top of the rock. We clambered up and up. We scrambled through and over and round a natural sandstone exhibition of browns and reds, of white and ochre swirls and waves, of carved staircases and caves, and long snaking water channels. Mohammad sang as he pushed me up rocks, led me along carved corridors and at one wall climbed on my shoulders then pulled me up behind him as if I weighed nothing – a boost to the self-esteem. Wormwood, juniper and plants I couldn't then name clung in cracks and carpeted warm, mountain-smelling pockets. Startled lizards rustled through dry grasses and clattered over rocks.

We reached a plateau of iron-red rock and had a short rest with our legs dangling over the drop-edge. Petra stretched below us like an inhabited map. We could see the rock outcrop of our cave and the tent set up for our wedding. We could see girls driving donkeys laden with jerry-cans, goatherds following flocks down rock steps, wood gatherers, horsemen riding lazily and souvenir sellers – we could see the Bedouin heading home. The once nomadic Bedouin of whose tribe I was to become a part.

I hardly knew what Bedouin meant and still find it hard to describe. Although many families had settled in Petra and no longer wandered the desert with their herds of milk-goats looking for water and food, they insisted they were still Bedouin. It was a racial thing, depending on ancestry, not place of abode, and they felt a closer bond with other Bedouin tribes than with the Wadi Musa farmers (who also kept goats and made hair-tents for summer living) or the gypsies (who did wander the deserts plying their trades but were looked down on for having no roots).

To make things more complicated for me, although he was born in a cave in the Monastery valley, Mohammad was not from the Bdoul tribe like everyone else in Petra, but from the al-Manajah tribe, which lived at Ras-a-Nagb, further south. Mohammad's father had moved to Petra because of his wife – she had grown up with the Bdoul because her Bdoul mother had returned to Petra after her al-Manajah father had died.

That difference had little impact on acceptance – eventually all of Abdallah's offspring were considered Bdoul – but it did have an impact on our lives in a more subtle way. Because everyone wasn't related to Mohammad, he wasn't under pressure from uncles telling him what to do, or cousins getting into mischief or committing mistakes that reflected on him or that he had to pay for, and most importantly, though I didn't know it at the time, no one had felt compelled to give him a wife. I was welcomed and accepted by everyone, but it took me a long time to realise that by marrying Mohammad I had really become a part of something larger, and that it was never going to be just him and me.

We made our camp, hanging the food in the branch of a juniper tree and putting the other things on a rock, then scrambled south for a couple of minutes along the honey-coloured sandstone bubbles, the age-worn spine of the mountain, and came onto the sacrificial altar created by the Nabataeans that was the High Place. We didn't meet a soul.

The High Place was not like the Monastery. That was a façade in a mountainside; this was what Mohammad called the Killing Floor, or Math-bah. To make it the Nabataeans had carved away the very top of the rounded sandstone mountain. They left a raised bench round three sides of the large flat square and a single mattress of stone in the middle. To the west, a higher rock platform with a carved bowl, runnels and an altar was created by carving away a waist-deep, hip-wide corridor of living rock. It must have taken meticulous planning not to carve away too much.

Mohammad searched the little gully behind the altar for Pepsi bottles. He had used to stash them there, he said, when selling drinks to tourists had been his job on the side.

That must have been ten years earlier when he had been working as a waiter at Nazzal's Camp. While serving the guests their breakfast, he found out what site they would be visiting – usually it was the High Place in the mornings – and as soon as the plates were cleared away and he was free, he shouldered his sack with enough drinks for all of them and raced up the short-cut. The tourists came up a path of staircases and through a ceremonial corridor carved for a whole throng of worshippers, but it was a steep climb whichever way you came at it, and Mohammad usually sold plenty of drinks. He stashed unopened bottles rather than carry them back down. After lunch the groups usually went to the Monastery and so did he. When he had a crate of empties he borrowed a donkey and went up to the Hajj Nasser's shop in Wadi Musa to swap them for full ones, before racing back down to serve dinner.

I think he kept a good count of his bottles because we didn't find any.

We sat for a while on the altar in the cooling evening. A hawk circled off to the side, swallows or swifts swooped for insects on the rising air. Slowly over the following years the names of the mountains around us seeped into my vocabulary, but now Mohammad introduced them to me for the first time.

A mountain range called the Sh-rah ran all the way across the east from north to south, cutting us off from the world. On its flank, the village of Wadi Musa was an olive-tree smudge, and below that, so close I felt as if I could reach out and touch them, were the pale stone pillows of Jabal Khubtha. The plateau that stretched south in the lee of the Sh-rah he called the Hrai-miya, and the lower whiter plateau that reached westward, the Stowh. Across the west, shadow blended the mountains into a knobbly outline against the sunset. The silhouetted shape of Jabal Haroon was repeated in the shape of the thirteenth-century mosque on its summit. Al-Barra, Umm-al-Biyara, Umm Zeitoona and Umm Saysabana blended northwards to meet Umm Sayhoon, a long dusk-pink ridge that ran back to the east and climbed halfway up the side of the Sh-rah to complete the circle.

At our juniper camp we gathered dry twigs. Mohammad, singing, made tea. Stars appeared as we ate our *shraak* and sardines. The Milky Way moved overhead. Eventually the sprinkling of lights in Wadi Musa went out. 'They turn the generator off,' Mohammad explained.

There wasn't any electricity for hundreds of kilometres . . . the whole sky became a milky way. Wadi al-Haleeb (valley of milk), Mohammad knew, and the Saucepan and the North Star. I thought of The Eagles song, 'Peaceful, Easy Feelin'. 'An' I wanna sleep with you in the de-sert tonight with a million stars all around,' I sang along . . . only Mohammad could hear and he couldn't tell if it was right or not. It sounded perfect to me. Enjoying the wafts of wedding singing and easily ignoring the occasional dog bark that drifted up from below, we slept on the blanket cushioned by juniper needles and the sandy earth.

At daybreak I woke with the sun and basked in the profound silence. For a while we were in a world of our own. A hoopoe strutted about nodding and flew off with a flash of wing. Slowly sounds of the beginning day filtered up: a donkey bray, a herder urging the goats out, the clatter of horse's hooves heading into the Siq, and here on the High Place more birds calling and cackling, waking the world. We had to get up. Mohammad was expected to get things ready for the wedding so after a pot of tea and some bread and cheese, we scrambled back down to the cave.

My Own Bedouin Wedding

Mohammad had a lot of help preparing for our wedding, which made up for the severe lack of time. Suddenly, besides nine-year-old Laafi, he had two other brothers, Salem and Ibraheem, to assist. They were also sons of Agaela and looked a lot like Mohammad, but they looked exactly like each other. For years, unless they sat side by side I couldn't tell them apart. While Mohammad's friends thought they were talking me into marriage, his brothers had been labouring for the Sherika Seeniya. The Chinese company was building a road along Wadi Araba from the bottom of the Dead Sea, where a potash industry was being established, to the port of Aqaba. After the wedding they went off again with their swags and took jobs with different road gangs across the south, but often they didn't have work at all.

Salem, Ibraheem, Laafi and all the other *nishaama* (the 'guys' but with *thaubs* and *mendeels* and kohl) got a lot of fun out of the preparations. In the mornings they headed for the mountains, and in the evenings, as the goat-girls herded the flocks home, they arrived back driving donkeys laden with firewood.

Mohammad's sisters Neda and Maryam were just little, but Tuf-leh and Inzela were kept busy carting water, making trip after trip with the donkey and emptying the jerry-cans into forty-gallon drums.

They borrowed huge cooking pots and aluminium *siddrs* (round serving platters with the circumference of a bicycle tyre) and stacked them outside the tent. They borrowed wool-stuffed quilts and *farrshas* from the caves and tents around the valley. I worried about these: they looked unused, with covers of clean bright satin and snow-white cotton. Umm Laafi folded them lengthways into fat strips and piled them up on her low wooden quilt cupboard, which had a stone in place of the fourth, broken, leg. The slightest bump toppled them onto the dirt floor in a soft mountain which Neda and Maryam and their little playmates gleefully conquered. I didn't know about the supplies of sugar, coffee, tea, sweets, rice and bullets that they bought until later when I helped to pay off the debt.

In the cool late afternoon of a hot day, I went with Mohammad up the Argoob Jmea-aan to collect a tent. A family had offered to loan it for the wedding – they had moved for the time being into a shady rock arch on the top of the ridge which the wind blew pleasantly through. There were the remnants of a round stone tower up there too; a watchtower in the northern Nabataean city walls.

The Argoob Jmea-aan is a ridge, much like a crooked shin. The Bedouin called many geographical features after anatomy: Ras-a-Nagb, the head of the escarpment; Fum-al-Wadi, the mouth of the valley; a-Thineb, the tail (of the mountain); Butn-al-Wadi, the belly of the valley; a-Thi-ra'a, the forearm (long like an *argoob* but flatter); and there were probably others.

The crowd of helpers soon had the tent folded and rolled into a colossal black bundle around the wooden poles, which served as handles to lift it onto the donkey. The poor animal all but disappeared underneath. They loaded hemp ropes, a sack of iron pegs and a smaller bundle – the back wall – with more poles onto another donkey. We headed back home. Mohammad and I strolled but Salem and Ibraheem raced off looking as if they were pushing runaway wheelbarrows, hanging onto the poles and cursing the kids who ran alongside trying to be helpful by waving their arms and yelling at the donkeys, but who only incited more twists and turns from the overloaded animals and looked frightfully in danger of getting squashed under a falling load.

The three wedding tents were set up in a line facing the Palace Tomb, which the Bedouin call Umm Sanadeeg, Mother of Boxes, because of its huge box-like chambers. Umm Sanadeeg, stood five or six storeys high and was just about as wide, but Jabal Khubtha, into which it was carved, still dwarfed it. During the celebrations Tilley lamps would cast shadows of the dancing men onto the ancient façade. Between the tomb and the tents was a flat area that looked like a field but had no grass growing on it. The Bdoul had used to plant crops here, and on many other flat plots around the valley, and had cleared all the rocks off it, but the Department of Antiquities now forbade ploughing inside the city walls.

The three tents were joined together end to end. One was for the women, the food, the bedding and the water drums; it was divided from the other two (which formed the *shig* or men's area), by a stunning woven rug of black and white geometric patterns that hung like a wall from the back of the tent right out to the end of the ropes at the front.

Mohammad also took me to Wadi Musa to get a *mudraga*, like the dress I had borrowed from Heyaiya for Rakhiya's wedding. Mohammad didn't mind me wearing jeans, or a skirt and blouse, but apparently his stepmother, Umm Laafi, was pressuring him. Even though she didn't have the instinctive connection of a mother with her son, she wanted to treat him like her own. If his bride had been a Bedouin they would have had to produce a whole suitcase full of new clothes which she would have proudly shown off to her guests. If I at least wore a new dress she wouldn't lose too much face.

Usually the dresses were made to order and took weeks to decorate so we were lucky to find one the same day. It was good business sense on the part of Yusra, who sold me the one she had just finished for herself, because after that she became my favoured dressmaker. The *mudraga* was made of synthetic material and simply cut, but the colour was dark blue and regal and the goldy-brown treadle-machine embroidery, which covered the bodice in a deep V and circled the hems at ankle and wrist, was flattering. It wasn't quite long enough but in the time it took one girl to serve tea, Yusra took the sleeves out, added material at the shoulders and put the sleeves back in. The *mudragas* were more often sleeveless, but in any case needed to be worn over something because of the deep neckline, and I was lucky that the cheesecloth blouse I had bought as an excited New Zealander on my first foray into London's Carnaby Street went under it beautifully. I was beginning to feel like a bride.

We spent most days at the wedding tents. The days were hot and still. A lot of the time Mohammad got on and did things and I sat Maryam or Neda on my knee and played 'This little piggy went to market' with their grubby toes. Sometimes I just drifted in a world of my own. Sometimes I was part of the entertainment.

The back flap of the tent was hitched up over the poles and we were facing the breeze that wafted up from the *wadi*. The donkey tied to the tent peg had a hard-on which was difficult to ignore. '*Hamar mabsoot*,' my new brother-in-law Ibraheem said cautiously, and, as I realised I recognised his words (the donkey's happy), so our embarrassment dissolved with a giggle.

I still only knew a few words of Arabic. I couldn't really imagine learning the language. Spoken, it sounded just like the written script appeared – musical and flowing but totally incomprehensible, and so I surprised myself when I correctly recognised sounds that bubbled up. *Mabsoot* (happy) was one of my very earliest words because everyone always asked me if I was. I had a bigger problem with the words for brother-in-law and donkey. They sounded the same: *hamar*, I wrote in my memory for both of them. I tried to hear the difference, and I tried again when I learned there were three different 'h' sounds. I talked about my brothers-in-law as 'Mohammad's brothers' or as Salem or Ibraheem, and I tried not to use the word for donkey in case I called it a brother-in-law. This was a real problem later when we had our own donkey and we let it off to graze and I had to walk the hills looking for it, asking if anyone had seen it. It was years before I found out that the difference was nothing to do with the 'h' at all, but in the roll of the final 'r', and brother-in-law didn't have one. He was a *hamaa*.

Every evening a crowd gathered as soon as the sun went down, sitting on *jannabiyas* around the fire and dancing till late, but on the third day of the Eid things picked up a notch. We went over in the morning and I barely saw Mohammad until two days later when our wedding was over.

People started arriving; everyone was wearing kohl. Mothers came with their children – babies in slings on their backs, toddlers perched on top of loads of bedding on the backs of donkeys, and often an older boy leading a goat or a sheep (a donation to the effort rather than a wedding present). Some families unloaded sacks of rice or sugar and one woman who lived near the village brought a box of fresh tomatoes. The pile of sacks spread along the rug wall and was to make a nice seat in the late afternoon. Bedding was unloaded in a pile in the corner.

Teenage volunteers, boys and girls, commandeered donkeys and raced off to the spring loaded with jerry-cans for the increased water demands. There could never be enough water with all the extra people to feed and wash, and as a bonus the spring valley was cool and shady and out of adult supervision most of the time.

I continued to drift round like a tourist but mostly stayed in the women's tent and watched what was happening. No one seemed to mind; I was pretty much ignored.

Mohammad ran around, tassels flying, welcoming male guests: kissing, kissing, '*salaam, salaam*' and settling them in the *shig*, which was bare of everything except mattresses and pillows. In front of it, beside a stone-bordered fire-pit, Mohammad set up a tray of tea glasses, and a water bowl on the metal table brought over from the cave. Ibraheem and Salem worked by the fire for a while serving tea and coffee, but as soon as younger guys took over they escaped to bring water.

The men didn't come into the women's tent but some of them arrived with rifles which they passed over the dividing wall to be hidden between the quilts.

Neda and Maryam and other little children from nearby tents ran about laughing and squealing but the visitors clung shyly to their mothers' dresses. The women set about straight away filling huge bowls with flour to make dough. As they kneaded, the noise of their chattering and singing started filling the tent. With all those bodies there was little room for the air to move. And they all wore so many clothes. There were lots of dark velvet *mudragas* with varying amounts of embroidery and flaps that might once have been extravagant sleeves but were now turned inside out and tied behind their backs, displaying the bright sleeves of floral under-dresses. When they lifted their best-dress hems to tuck them round their waists and keep them out of the dough or away from the fire as they stirred the huge pots of soup, I could see that their floral dresses were baggy and knee-length and that they were wearing trousers too, and moulded plastic shoes and black nylon socks. So many layers. I wore open-toed Greek leather sandals and my underwear was positively skimpy by comparison, but I was still hot.

They all covered their heads too: triangular scraps of old material were tied under young girls' chins; older girls and young women wore chiffon scarves in blue or yellow; and others – later I learned only married women with babies – wore the more distinctive, face-framing *misfah wa asaba*.

The *misfah* is made of a couple of metres of black muslin joined at the ends. It goes over the head, under the chin and back over the head. The folds of it hang down the front and are tucked with plaited hair into the V of the dress. The *asaba* is a folded scarf which covers the forehead and is tied at the back.

Wrinkled faces tended to have soft black *asabas*, but younger ones used gaily coloured scarves folded to stand up like crowns or tiaras, which Mohammad and Awa<u>th</u> called the Sid-al-Aaly after the Aswan High Dam.

No one had colour coordination in the sense that I knew it. They wore dark blue *mudragas* with pink embroidery over purple and orange dresses; white-striped, red stretchy pants under black *mudragas* embroidered in green and orange, and brown and maroon headscarves with pink and green stitched dresses. The tent was an explosion of colour.

Things picked up some more at about midday; the women got up and scrabbled between the folds of the quilts for rifles, which they passed out to their menfolk. They retied their scarves, straightened their dresses then gathered round the poles along the front of the tent and sang at each other from their clusters. As Tuf-leh helped her mother, untangling a rope of gaily coloured material scraps and rigging it up along the front edge of the tents, a singer curtained her mouth with her hand and let out a long trill of ululation. Others followed, vying to do better it seemed. Umm Laafi secured the *raiyah*, a white cloth 'raised in the face of God' to publicly acknowledge His blessings, onto the middle front pole. Mohammad and his friends stood facing the women and shot bullets up into the air. Mothers covered the ears of crying children. Babies started in their swaddling clothes and the tightly wrapped ones went back to sleep. The echoes ricocheted around the cliffs – the smell of gunshot lasted a little longer.

This was the *ghaza*. Our wedding was underway and in God's hands.

Lunch was *fatteh*, served in aluminium bowls the size of car tyres. The *fatteh* consisted of *shraak* mashed in *rishoof* (lentil and yoghurt soup), onto which Umm Laafi carefully poured bright yellow clarified goat's butter. She was careful because she wanted to be generous, but not wasteful; the *samin* was the ultimate produce from the goat and surprisingly expensive.

After lunch although a few older men lay around in the *shig* most of the *nishaama* gathered just to the south of the tents on a raised tumble of carved stone blocks. I could see why when I clambered up it with Mohammad; besides being able to see all over Petra, suggesting the ruins beneath us might have been an important building in the distant past, there was a discreet view back into the women's tent, which both sides were taking advantage of. I was the only woman out on the vantage point but I felt comfortable enough, and when Mohammad left me I stood with his friends Ismayeen and Ali-f, who both spoke a little bit of English. I wouldn't have missed the afternoon entertainment, supplied ad-lib by the horse boys, for anything.

I call them boys, though many of them were men. They were the ones who earned a living bringing tourists into Petra, and while they were waiting to take their tourists back they made the most of the opportunity to show off. They came galloping up from the Fum-al-Wadi and raised the dust. The wheat field of the past became a race track and a show ring in front of the wedding tents. Beautiful Arabian horses, brown, black, golden and white, pranced and flew. Cowry shells decorating the woven halters and chest pieces glinted in the sun, and tassels dangling from saddle blankets swirled in bright colours around the horses' legs. The riders wore flying *mendeels* and *thaubs* of white and blue over cotton breeches. They were chanting or reciting in rhythm but I could hardly hear it above the pounding hooves. Some of them pranced up to the tent in pairs, tassels and bobbles bouncing, to tap the *raiyah* with their sticks.

A group of Sri Lankan tourists, maybe businessmen, came to watch. Mohammad gave them tea and sat them in the *shig*. They did a traditional Sri Lankan dance for us and some of the *nishaama* lined up in the sun and did a standing-in-line s*amer* for them – to everyone's amusement, since dancing was for night-time.

Singing wasn't, though; it didn't stop all day in the women's tent. I sat on the pile of sacks and observed. The dark, kohled women sought me out, touched my dress, admired my watch (a very ordinary one Mum and Dad gave me when I turned fifteen) and pressed one or two hundred fils into my hand, but they remained a part of the flow of exotic, mysterious people. I wasn't seeing them as individuals or imagining them in my future. I was living the moment and I wished my dress had a pocket for the coins.

They sang, drank tea and cooked more soup and *shraak* for dinner. Salem and a friend, both with profusely applied kohl, stood in the middle of the women and kids and played tin pipes to accompany the girls' singing. Mohammad sent them out. The afternoon passed.

Darkness fell within half an hour of sunset. Straight after dinner the women pulled out their quilts and rugs and filled the tent with beds for their crying children. They let the back wall of the tent down to keep out the breeze that was blowing up quite cool.

In front of the tent the men put down their mats and sat watching the young guys who stood out in front in a row and danced. It was monotonous but sensual; they chanted in pairs and swayed back and forth, barely moving their sandalled feet, slipping in a single clap or two now and then. The women were quiet now too, listening to the words. The children slowly settled down and fell asleep despite the continued singing. It seemed to go on for hours and hours. I couldn't drink any more sweet tea though women crouched round the fire in front and made pot after pot. Between dances guys crouched round the fire too, lighting cigarettes and glancing into the dark tent. I watched Mohammad take his turn in the line of dancers. He seemed to be in his own world, laughing with his partner, but then he looked over to me.

It was amazing to feel the air between us tingling – our eyes could touch but we could not. In the future, I enjoyed this sensation especially on occasions when women sat separate and Mohammad came to seek me out – to see if I was OK or needed cigarettes. It was as if having a 'different' wife gave him a free pass into the women's tent. Everyone always seemed thrilled to see him and they all stood up to shake his hand or kiss his *mendeel*, and I watched him coming till he crouched low in front of me, and I had to stop my hand from reaching out to stroke his cheek – to make do with the brushing of our fingers as he lit my cigarette for me. A touch and a promise.

The children slept through it all: the singing, the occasional pistol shot or raising of voices, the barking of dogs and the braying of donkeys – making love and more children in one-roomed caves would be easy if they always slept like that.

All the best bedding was in the *shig* for the men but finally someone remembered me and sent there for a wool-stuffed *farr-sha*, a pillow and a pure white quilt, which they laid on the ground between the sleeping women and children, and ushered me onto. The square mattress was short so my feet were in the sand; the pillow was made for leaning against, stuffed hard as a rock, and I still had my clothes on so I could barely move beneath the heavy wool-filled quilt. I felt as if I had been put to the test like the Princess and the Pea. Then I was joined by an old woman with jingly bracelets . . . I held my breath and pretended to be asleep.

But she was not, it turned out, partaking in any traditional initiation ritual; she was just taking advantage of my good quality bedding.

Goes On . . . and On . . .

The next morning is when the wedding procession, the *gtaar*, would normally have taken place, escorting me from my father's to my husband's tent, so when Mohammad came into the tent the women crowded round him in a well-wishing throng and apparently begged to be able at least to parade me around the dusty field. Mohammad handed out lengths of cloth, as he would have if they had accompanied me to his home, but refused to let them cover me in an *aba* and walk me round in the heat. I still marvel at how he knew what to do for me.

The incongruous sound of a car engine drew women and children out of the tent as a pick-up pulled up in front of it. The standing Bedouin on the back declared congratulations with pistol shots aimed at the sky. Mohammad's father welcomed them the same way.

They were a group of Mohammad's closest relations from the al-Manajah tribe. Ibraheem had been sent to tell them of Mohammad's wedding and they had put on their best clothes, left their women in their tents on the high plateau of Ras-a-Nagb halfway to Aqaba, and come back with him in the rented pick-up.

The only woman was Ataiga, an aunt of Mohammad's father. The men all went to the *shig* and she, all tanned leather and blue tattoos, came into the tent and made me sit with her on a new sponge *farrsha* that had been kept carefully on top of the quilt pile until now. Ataiga gave me a brown scarf, which I tied over my hair, and ten dinars, which I knotted in the corner of it. Some little girls touched my covered head and approved. '*Quayas*,' they said.

Mohammad knew I was getting bored. He was too busy to entertain me and knew I wasn't going to run away (a worry some grooms have when the weddings are arranged), so he sent me off with a young woman called Maryam who didn't speak English. Clear-skinned and straight-backed she led me off down the hill behind the tents. Her Sid-al-Aaly made her as tall as me. Down in a narrow valley, where the air was heavy and no sound from the wedding reached, we used an oleander thicket for a toilet before climbing up another steep gully to her home. It was the cluster of caves on the flat ledge of rock that Elizabeth and I had visited on our first day in Petra. Today, though, Maryam's husband was at home, crouched on plump haunches on the smooth concrete floor of the biggest cave surrounded by small pots of paint. He had pulled the cabinet, the only piece of furniture, into the middle of the room and was working his way round the white-washed walls painting a strip of hand-sized diamonds in glossy blue, yellow, red and green. My first impression of Salaama al-Mokhtar was to be reinforced over the years, as he strived for better things.

The wedding continued unfalteringly without me. When we got back, horse-racing was in full fling, some guys were target-shooting and there was singing and cooking. Goats – the traditional blessing and several others, freshly killed and butchered – were now boiling in yoghurt in three huge pots in a row on the fire. Goats' Head Soup: the real thing. I posed for a photo.

Ursula, a German woman who lived in Amman, turned up with Ismayeen. 'Come and sit with your bride,' she ordered Mohammad.

Like me, she thought he should have pride of place and let everyone else do all the work. But he said, 'Tomorrow, I will sit with you,' and off he went. She did manage to catch him and take the nearest thing we have to a wedding photo. Mohammad is between Ismayeen and myself and the evening sunlight warms up the Sh-rah behind us.

What had I expected? At home we didn't have white-dressed wedding photos of Mum and Dad on the mantelpiece, or albums full of bridesmaids and flower girls to be taken out and pored over when Gran visited. I wondered if the reason I had never dreamed about my own wedding was because all of this was beyond my imagination.

The women ululated in unison as the *nishaama* carried *siddr* after huge round food-filled *siddr* to the guests in the *shig*. Women and crying babies had to wait a little longer. Soon though the same young men bore the trays back to where the cousins from Ras-a-Nagb were crouching by the cooking pots organising the catering. They rearranged the remaining rice and *shraak*, scooped a pile of meat pieces from the pot, ladled hot yoghurt sauce generously over all and it was served to the women and children.

Ursula and I were served by my father-in-law, who brought us a small platter (in comparison to theirs) at the same time as the men. He allowed two women to eat with us and kept everyone well clear so we could eat in peace, and then, immediately after-wards, without allowing us a moment to savour the taste, he ordered a young man to attend to us so we could wash, with generous handfuls of soap powder and a jug of warm water. We were being watched so I washed diligently as I had seen them do, swishing the barely dissolved soap around my mouth and rinsing and spitting onto the ground.

The dancing soon started once more – all right for those who could understand it. Again the mats were put in front of the women's tent and the men sat and danced in the open. Again I watched my husband. Light from the fire and the lamps in front of the tents threw huge dancing shadows of the swaying *thaubs* onto the façade of the Palace Tomb.

Much, much later when they couldn't dance or joke any more, a group of Mohammad's friends escorted us back to our cave. They didn't stop singing all the way; their words reverberated around the basin, echoing from the mountain walls that surrounded us. It had been a long wedding and very suc-cessful from Mohammad's point of view, but for me, I was just happy to have him to myself at last.

What Did Your Mother Say?

For a while we were the *ersan*, the bridal couple, but we spent our honeymoon much as we had spent the days before. I had been living out of a backpack for nearly two years and was happy to settle, and Mohammad was keen to 'open the door of providence' (or get back to work) in order to pay off some of his wedding costs.

I allowed myself to be lured gently into the domesticity of cave life.

At first Mohammad still made the tea in the morning, pumping up the primus while I slept in. Sometimes, when he urged '*Ishrubi shay*,' I woke up enough to have a glass of tea too, but I rolled over to doze a bit longer when he went off to the Treasury. We made our bed outside though, and after a while the sun reached over the top of the cave and I had to get up then – or get cooked. I piled the sponge *farrsha* and blanket on the bedstead in the cave. I washed the dishes, but we didn't have many so that didn't take long, and I put them to dry in the sun. Then I went out, unlike the other women who always had a child or brother to send, and I took my husband some bread and tomatoes or a can of sardines for lunch.

I enjoyed having my little 'plot' and my little routines. I went and sat with Mohammad at the Treasury most days, and when there were no tourists to sell trinkets to we wandered and drank tea wherever we were invited. It wasn't demanding – far from it. It was as lazy a life as could be.

Mohammad was fun. If we were walking silently he would say some nonsense word to make me laugh. The words often meant nothing but I loved the sounds and tried to get them right. He'd laugh back at me and I'd never know if it was my pronunciation or if the word he had taught me was rude or a curse or no longer politically correct. The one I was sorriest to learn the meaning of was the description of the black clouds that came over the western mountains in the winter. '*Jet min gharib zay teez al abd*,' I'd say to announce their arrival poetically until one day, when we might have had visitors, Mohammad told me not to. 'It means "It's coming from the west like a black man or slave's backside" so if you are going to use it you should be careful when.'

Abd can also be translated as 'servant of', as in Abdallah, the servant of Allah.

In early October Mohammad came up from Nazzal's Camp with an aerogramme from Mum and Dad. It contained their response to our marriage.

'We think we have given you a good upbringing with plenty of opportunity to learn to think for yourself,' they wrote, 'so we trust you know well enough what you are doing. And we are here for you anyway, anytime.'

Dad had already found articles about Petra in several of his National Geographic magazines, and Mum had found Ma'an in their atlas.

In the future I was often reminded of this letter because so many women (never men), on hearing that I had married a Bedouin and lived in a cave, immediately exclaimed, 'And what did your mother say?' And I quoted it proudly.

Later Dad thought he had written more about the loneliness of living in an alien culture. He and Mum came from quite different Dutch backgrounds and they both had few experiences in common with the people they had met in New Zealand. But either he never wrote it or I just never remembered it. I didn't keep the actual letter – determined not to gather clutter I periodically burned all that sort of stuff – it didn't matter anyway.

Years later Mum also told me of the dream she had had –

which had been so vivid she had felt compelled to tell Dad and their friends. 'I dreamed of Marguerite,' she had told them. 'It wasn't bad but there is something about her, I'm sure.' And she had realised what it was three weeks later when my letter arrived.

When we eventually got to New Zealand Dad said, 'I can see why you picked him,' but that comes later.

The Daily Grind

Sometimes during the first months Abdallah arrived early with his trowel. If we were breakfasting, he joined us; if we were still sleeping, he stood over us and urged, '*Gawm ya Mohammad. Wahhid Allah*,' until we got up.

Wahhid Allah was just one of the many ways God came into our daily lives. To *wahhid Allah* is to pronounce that there is only One God, which Mohammad did as a ritual as he washed his hands and face. 'There is no God but Allah and Mohammad is his prophet.'

Abdallah was helping Mohammad expand our plot by digging away the mountain of dirt piled up against the rock outcrop to the left of the door. They were hoping to find another cave. During the day Abdallah loosened the sand and sifted through it looking for ancient pottery and coins, and as soon as it was dark Mohammad tipped the day's sand off the ledge. The early-evening breeze that came up the valley carried dust back up over him and the pile of debris in front of the cave below grew flagrantly. We didn't find another cave in the rock, but seven metres from the door Abdallah unearthed a Roman wall of solid blocks with bits of clinging plaster, which ran to the edge of the ledge. As they cleared the sand out from the corner formed by the wall and the rock, they uncovered several metres of flagstones, the floor of an ancient room, and in a crack between the flagstones they found four coins that someone had dropped centuries before. They were bronze, worn smooth and tarnished almost black. They were about the size of Pepsi bottle lids with a cross on one side and a big M on the other.

'They've got our initials on them, look!'

'It's got nothing to do with Marg and Mo though,' Mohammad said, bringing me back to earth. 'The M and the cross and their big size make them typical Byzantine coins. They're only about one thousand five hundred years old' – not as rare or valuable as the smaller two-thousand-year-old Nabataean ones, he implied.

But I was still impressed – antique coins in our yard, with our initials on them.

When the Inspector of Antiquities was unable to ignore the growing pile of dirt any longer, he wandered up to see what was going on. But by then our yard was as big as we needed so Mohammad invited him for dinner and promised to stop digging.

The following year Mohammad made a room there, up against the rock, incorporating the Roman wall and building two thick walls of stone. The tin roof meant it was never suitable as a bedroom, too hot in the summer and too cold in the winter, and it was dusty much of the time too, except when it rained, and then water dripped through the holes his nails had made in the tin roof to collect in muddy pools on the floor. I wanted to use it as a private space but after a couple of years I gave up and we turned it into a kitchen.

In the meantime I worked on the interior decorating. I decided the natural colours of the rock were too special to cover, and the green that Mohammad had used was too crudely green to live with, so I set to scraping all the paint off the walls. He didn't argue, but let me find out for myself. I managed a couple of patches of about half a square metre and gave up. I felt for the Nabataeans. My hand was worn out because I had to chisel under the paint to get it off the rock. Mohammad then easily convinced me to whitewash it all over instead of re-carving the whole cave. It took several layers to bury the green and the blotches I had carved but the brightness of the whitewash made me glad my first idea had been so difficult because the cave felt lighter and bigger.

Over time, especially during the winter months, the natural salts pushed through the rock and dropped occasionally in little spiffs of red and whitewashed sandstone into our dinner or onto our faces while we were sleeping. When it became irritating, by which time the ghosts of Mohammad's painted sunflowers had reappeared as well, I knew it was time to mix another bucket of whitewash.

The 'sleeping in' phase didn't last very long – Mohammad was forward-thinking and soon taught me to work the primus and make the tea. He earned himself curses when the rubber on the plunger turned inside out, or when the jet got blocked (so it needed to be poked with a fine wire – which I learned to extract from the window netting), or when the kerosene in the tank ran out and I had to find the funnel, fill the tank and start pumping all over again – assuming we hadn't run out altogether, which earned him more curses and a trip to the shop.

Making tea looked easy at least. Mohammad just tipped the old leaves over the edge of the bank and rinsed out the pot. He filled it with water, scooped a couple of handfuls of sugar and a small handful of tea leaves into it and popped it on the primus. But I was deceived. It was easy enough to pour in the water and I soon took to measuring the sugar by the glassful so I could get that right, but the correct amount of tea was more difficult and took me ages to perfect. Even then it only went well as long as we got the same brand – Shay al-Fakher, imported from Ceylon by the Palestinian Tea Trading and Importing Company – as otherwise it might be too weak or too bitter or too black.

And the primus, once I finally had it going right, would wait till I glanced away before spewing the sugary water through the tea leaves and sending it streaming down like a volcano erupting to put out the flame, block the jet and billow steam and kerosene fumes into the air.

But Mohammad wasn't very fussy about his tea. Once I knew how to pump the primus, I had to get up early and make it every morning.

There was a reward, though. From then on we had our breakfast together sitting right on the edge of the ledge. It took a while for the sun to get up over Jabal Khubtha and till then it was nice and cool. We had blocks of stone for stools and a round column drum for a table. We drank tea, dipped bread in oil and dissolved pieces of sweet and sesame-seedy *halawa* on our tongues. When we had batteries for the tape recorder, Mohammad put on his tape of the famous Egyptian Abd-el-Basset reciting from the Holy Koran. I didn't need to understand a word – it was made for this world, especially for such mornings as we watched in awesome wonder as the valley awakened and the sunlight slipped down the rock faces in our view.

Shraak, Wobrs and Juniper Wood

In Ma'an a diesel-fired oven produced pita bread but Wadi Musa was still too small to have a bakery and anyway it was an hour and a half's walk away. Within the valley there was nowhere for us to buy bread. We managed pretty well because we needed only a couple of flaps of *shraak* for dinner and break-fast and we got them as we wandered round in the afternoons. Women out in front of their tents making bread for evening meals invariably called, '*Janbu, ta'ashu endina*' – Come, dine with us – and when we didn't they sent kids running after us with a *shraak* or two. And when it got cooler and Umm Laafi set up her *taaboon* oven, she often sent the girls over with a fresh loaf and then we had lunch too.

The *taaboon* bread was amazing. The first time I tried it I couldn't believe it; here in the desert. It was so extravagant! The delicious plate-sized loaf was a few centimetres thick, with chunky crusts of bursting golden brown waves which, when broken open, revealed fluffy insides of yellow wheat. The women baked the loaves in dung-fired ovens made of clay.

But one day, when we hadn't been wandering the evening before and I had to go over to ask Rakhiya to bake us some bread, I decided I would have to learn. Rakhiya had arrived back at her parents' tent a few nights after her wedding and she swore she would not return to the husband of her father's choice, no matter how well he might be able to provide for her. I often visited her family tent and they always welcomed me and made tea and food, but I didn't want to have to ask for bread ever again.

Eventually I would be able to reward myself daily with crepe-thin bread hot off the *saj* – but it took some doing.

Mohammad asked Umm Mahmoud to teach me. Without hesitation but with twinkling eyes she said, '*Budri, budri*' – come early.

Umm Mahmoud and Abu Mahmoud lived up behind us in a cave at the base of the High Place.

I liked to call people by their given names but in this case I couldn't. To distinguish him from other Mohammads people called him Mohammad al-Atrush – the deaf Mohammad – and I didn't like that, and so much of her name, Imhheela, was said from down in the throat that I couldn't pronounce it for years. I had enough difficulty with 'Umm Mahmoud'.

They were a young couple, I could tell because they only had two young boys, but I never thought of them as such. Abu Mahmoud's deafness made him old and because of Umm Mahmoud's joyful competence and the teaching role she undertook I thought of her more like a mother – though she was younger than me.

Bright and early the following morning I arrived at her cave to find I was not bright and early enough and she was throwing the last *shraak* onto the *saj*. She laughed and suggested I start in the afternoon.

I sometimes went to see her in the afternoons anyway. She always made me feel welcome, putting a cloth *jannabiya* in the shade of the rock or, if it was cool enough, on the rise out in front, from where I had a view of the path Mohammad walked home along. She made tea and I watched her young boys Mahmoud and Ahmed playing around.

I watched her too; I liked the confident way she went about her life. She was beautifully dark with luxurious eyelashes and heavy, waist-long plaits, which I admired silently whenever she took her headdress off to retie it. She reframed her oval face with a high, burgundy *asaba*, triangles of black hair at her temples and her net *misfah* under her chin.

When the tea was ready she always cooled it quickly in a bowl for the boys; she didn't keep them waiting, jumping dangerously close to the teapot until it was too late. If a child's shoe fell off she put it back on straight away, and if they wet their pants she had a dry pair ready. And she did it all with undistressed ease.

I watched and admired her and over the weeks, as I learned to make bread, we became friends – able to sit together for hours looking out over the valley without words. When we saw Mohammad on his way home she called him to come up for tea, and then he'd invite them over for dinner. Or she offered to make dinner for us all, or to give me even more than fresh bread to take home. They seemed so poor – the caves they lived in had no alterations, no doors or concrete floors – and her offerings were so generous that I thought of *The Grapes of Wrath*. '*Ma endina ghair batatas, atiki batatas?*' All we've got is potatoes, shall I give you some?

That afternoon she filled a bowl of water from the jerry-can, washed her hands and poured water for me to wash mine under. She put flour with a sprinkling of salt in the kneading pan and told me to say *Bis-millah* (in the Name of God) before I started kneading. I had watched plenty of bread being made so knew what to do. I put my rings and watch in my pocket, folded my *mudraga* back and knelt on the mat in the shade of the cave façade. I started by pouring just a little water, mixing it in, adding a little more and mixing again. Even before I got all the flour into one lump, my forearms were worn out (my knees were OK for a while longer), so Umm Mahmoud relented and crouched opposite me kneading, adding a splash of water and kneading again, till we had a smooth elastic lump of dough so soft it spread out to fill the dish.

Now for the fun.

She got the fire going and balanced the tin *saj* on three stones. She had a piece of material rolled up with some flour in it which she spread out beside the fire. She squeezed off a fist-sized lump of dough, dropped it onto the flour and deftly worked it until she had a flour-covered ball. She splashed a drop of water onto the *saj*, which sizzled expectantly. It was ready. She patted the ball flat, especially the edges, and picked it up, throwing it from one outstretched palm to the other, to create a huge thin circle of dough which she threw over the *saj*. It hissed immediately as it started cooking. In a minute the kids giggled as she commanded me, '*Iglibi!*' Turn it!

I was used to crouching by now so that was not part of the

challenge, but I panicked for a moment. 'Who me?' I had to flick
up the edges from the hot tin till they came free, then, smoke and
flames aside, peel it off in one piece and turn it over. All went
well. The peeling-off sound as I lifted it was very satisfactory and
it settled just perfectly on the other side. The middle was thinner
so Umm Mahmoud lifted it like a tent for the slightly thicker
edges to bake. And there it was again – fresh *shraak*.

'*Doorrki*,' she said. Your turn.

Ever since I first saw *shraak* being made I imagined I would be
able to do it, and I had been dying to have a go. But then, I had
imagined I would be able to knead the dough, too. I did wish no
one was watching this first time. I checked my rolled-up sleeves,
then I flipped up the dough – there was no turning back. And it
was just how I imagined: the dough was so amazingly elastic
that it was easy (after a fashion), and there was my first *shraak*
on the *saj*, with only a couple of holes in the middle.

I went early in the mornings and every afternoon after that.
Slowly my arms hurt less. I loved the mornings as the weather
got colder. The kitchen cave, so small I had to duck my head to
go in, was cosy with the smell of the wood fire, the waking-up
boys were all cuddly, the sweet tea with powdered milk
warmed me to my toes and I would take hot bread home to
wake Mohammad up with. On Fridays I learned to ignore the
crackle on the transistor radio, although I could rarely discern
anything. It's the Koran, it's *quayas*, today is *al-Juma* (the Holy
Day) – Umm Mahmoud said the Arabic words and I guessed
the rest.

The time came when I decided I could throw a *shraak* myself.
Mohammad had already bought a small *saj* and a whole sack of
local flour and that day I collected dry wood on my way back
from the spring. I made the dough and put my *saj* on the fire on
three small rocks. Half an hour later I was in tears; the fire kept
going out and the dough was sticking to the cold tin or getting
too hot and burning. When Mohammad came home and found

the remnants of my fire in the yard with scrapings of burnt and uncooked dough around it, he laughed. He said I would have to go back to get fire-making lessons next, and recognising-wood lessons too, as this was oleander and just about useless for fire-making. Poisonous, too, I discovered later. Salem came and Mohammad suggested he and Awath take me to collect wood.

Salem said, 'Let's go tomorrow.'

In the morning they came with two donkeys, ropes and a shotgun. Salem's shirt was nearly as tight as Awath's; it looked like they had been taken in by the same person, with big uneven stitches along the inside arms and down the side seams. They both wore kohl and their eyes were bright. I climbed behind Salem and we raced off to the base of a rock mountain called al-Barra half an hour away. It was already a hot, bright, sunshiny day. We tied the donkeys and took off their saddles. We worked up a real sweat, soon obvious on the boys' tight shirts, as we climbed up a gully of dark sandstone with clinging shrubs. We must have climbed up over a hundred metres to the top of the mountain, which was a huge bowl filled with the heavy scent and whiteness of the flowering *rattam* bushes. There were juniper trees too, abundant and aromatic, and it was the dry branches of these we broke off and piled up. I didn't do much; it broke easily but splintered to needle-sharp spikes.

We could hear a flute being played on Umm-al-Biyara, the neighbouring mountain, and Salem spotted the musician. She was with a colourful group of goatherds whose flocks grazed the leaning plateau. Salem called out and the music stopped while they exchanged a few excited words. I hoped they were innocent because anyone in the area could hear them – they put an edge on their voices to send the words across on the clear vibrant air.

A year or two later, when Salem set out to ask the musician's father for her hand, with Umm Laafi's father and uncles for moral support, he was rudely rebuffed. The elders consoled him though. 'If her father could ignore all etiquette and not even show respect to us, you want nothing to do with his daughter.'

There was a loud sonic boom. I heard the sound on many days but here it was louder than usual. Israeli fighter jets practised to the west along the Great Rift Valley of Wadi Araba, which was below sea level. Here on Jabal al-Barra we were a thousand metres above, so the jets were just across the way.

When we had a huge pile of dry branches we took a break to unpack our bags in the shade and make tea. It was a magical mountain brew. The teapot was encased in a black crust carrying traces of all the aromatic fires it had been on. We filled it with spring water and brought it to the boil on the incense of a juniper-wood fire.

It was some time then that Salem spied the *wobr* on a ledge basking in the sun. When he shot it the report was swallowed by the sky. It was a furry animal about as long and thin as my forearm and without a tail. I couldn't imagine what it was and I didn't find the English word for it – hyrax – for years. Salem and Awath skinned and gutted it in a few minutes. Salem's *shabriya*, his knife, was as long as the *wobr*, with a black goat-horn handle and a steel blade sharpened on both sides that pierced the skin with its sharp tip. We barbecued the pieces. Awath, like a good boy scout, had a twist of salt in his pocket. It was delicious but without our bread it would have been a meagre lunch.

Then we dragged our branches to the edge of the gully we had climbed up and threw them over. When we clambered down I was relieved to find the donkeys hadn't been hit, and impressed to find all those logs we had barely been able to drag to the edge had smashed and splintered into easily manageable bits. I thought of the North American legend of Paul Bunyan throwing tree trunks down the mountain to arrive much later in the city worn right down and ready to be boxed as toothpicks.

Awa<u>th</u> and Salem set about loading the donkeys – an engineering feat in balance. By hanging two equally heavy bundles
one off each side of the long wooden saddle they made a wide
area across the donkey's back onto which they loaded a third
bundle. I helped control the first donkey while they loaded the
other, and then we were off. The donkeys were raring to go, as
if they needed to keep moving so as not to lose balance. Their
loads were huge and the path was erratic; stony and winding,
narrow and steep, sandy and slow, but those donkeys delivered
their loads of firewood to our ledge and I coordinated my fire
and bread-making abilities to produce perfect *shraak* daily from
then on.

Dear Elizabeth

Petra. 30 Sept.

Dear Elizabeth,
    Well it was certainly great to get your letter today. You
certainly sound more settled and happier. I hope you are.
I nearly didn't get it. One boy took it from the post office
then forgot it when he stayed in a tent by the Rest house.
Then today the people moved into the cave with the
oldest Nabataean inscription. Mohammad's dad saw it
but didn't know it was for me so tonight Mohammad
sent his brother to collect it. So it's been places I
haven't . . .

Complicated it was. Few enough people got letters for everyone
to know they were precious, but they didn't all realise how nice
it was to get them sooner rather than later. After that one nearly

got lost I wondered if there were other letters for me at caves or tents around the valley, and I went up to Wadi Musa to open a post office box of my own.

There was a proper post office now; it was no longer an agency in a shop like when Mohammad had come up to vote. There hadn't been parliamentary elections since the 1967 war so he must have been underage, but he said a representative from Ma'an had come down to Petra and, with the lure of a dinar, enticed as many of them as he could to go up to Wadi Musa to cast their votes for him. Mohammad's eyes lit up whenever he told the story, remembering how proud he had been to be able to sign his name, not just *ubsum* – thumbprint – like most of the older men, and how much the dinar, which was duly paid as he left al-Ghenaimi's shop, had been worth. The post office now had a building of its own, but it looked just like the other shops with its stone façade and roller door in the shade of the weeping pepper trees that lined the street.

Letters addressed to us arrived safely after that. I treasure the one addressed to:

The New Zealand Lady,
Souvenirs, Coffee and Tea Café,
Petra,
Jordan

. . . but that came years later.

Quite a few addressed in English script, but not to us, were put in our box as well.

Elizabeth visited us the following year but her plans were spoiled by the civil war in Lebanon and she settled back in Australia. Slowly we stopped writing to each other and we didn't see each other again till decades later.

Spring Cleaning

Every few days I pulled the wooden cave door closed behind me, secured its tiny padlock, put my backpack of dirty clothes on my back and set out for my washhouse. I followed the path across the hill towards the Crusader castle and clambered down the rock screes at the back of it to the *wadi* floor. Umm-al-Biyara towered, Umm Zeitoona blocked the sky in front and, on my right, way above the tumbled rock-falls, the walls of the castle climbed. The path wound along the dry riverbed in the shade of gigantic oleanders. There were usually others on their way to the spring. A young man playing a tin flute might be going to check his father's olive-tree garden; a goatherd might be leading her goats down for a drink. There were always children on their way to get water, racing their donkeys for the fun of it. Their shouts were music, their bouncing jerry-cans drums, and the whole scene echoing off the mountainsides was intoxicating.

Some of them recognised me and asked, '*Enti marrat Mohammad? Terrkubi?*' Are you Mohammad's wife? Will you ride?

I didn't recognise any of them yet but that wasn't why I refused the offers of rides. The way was over uneven stones, but I had no need to hurry and I loved to hear the echoes as they disappeared.

There was a wide corner around which flash floods swept. Nabataeans had quarried rock here, leaving straight walls several storeys high beneath precipitous cliffs. On the inside was the stony garden of Mohammad's grandfather, more stones than garden really, with just a couple of apricot and olive trees, and grapevines escaping over the wall to climb high and wild in the oleanders and tamarisks of the *wadi*. Just past that, where the high cliffs and flood-hardy trees blocked out the sky completely, was the spring. Water just bubbled up between the stones in the valley floor and poured off down the stream. The children clamoured about making little pools so they could scoop the water up with their battered bowls. Some tethered their donkeys close by and reached up to fill the jerry-cans on their backs, but it was much quicker to stand the jerry-cans in the stream to fill them and then get help to load them.

I watched the haphazard procedure the first couple of times: a brother and sister stand on either side of a donkey they can barely see over. The boy is a little stronger so he swings the first jerry-can high onto its side on the wooden saddle, and that's when it leaks if the lid doesn't have a good seal. His sister balances it there and the donkey tries to take a step to adjust to the weight as the boy lifts the next jerry-can onto his knee, leaning it against the donkey's flank, and threads a loop of rope through the handles. He pokes a stick through the loop and yells '*khallas*' to let her know to pull the jerry-can she's holding off her side of the saddle and lower it – slowly in case the stick doesn't hold – until both jerry-cans sit high on the sides of the donkey's belly. They stuff little leaks with scraps of rag they find caught in the trees, break off new oleander switches for the ride home and launch themselves onto the top of the load from boulders on the side of the path.

And once I figured out how it worked I usually helped, but what with the donkeys moving, the jerry-cans leaking, the sticks breaking or ropes twisting, and the fact that we usually stood in the middle of the slippery stream, I could never get much of the haphazardness out of it.

I scrambled on for a few minutes, in and out of shade, to where there was a natural water-channel worn smooth in the white rock. I sat there with my gear spread around and my feet in the cool running water. The soap powder (*suruf*, Surf, or *tayd*, Tide) came in little cardboard packets which fell apart at the smell of dampness so I always used up the whole packet washing away the sand, the smoke and the remnants of food. My jeans were the hardest to clean even when I hadn't spilled olive oil or other food on them, and when I had it was a real incentive to learn to eat properly – by hand.

I draped the clothes on the overhanging branches and, if the only human sounds I could hear were far away, undressed to my bikini for a wash. Further down was the 'swimming pool', a spa-tub-sized gap in the rocks in which you had to keep your knees up so your feet wouldn't swish the fronds of algae, to which the *nishaama* guided the hot and dusty travellers off the occasional London to Kathmandu bus, but I didn't bother to go that far. Few people came here; I only once shared my spot with a woman who was washing fleeces, so I was usually able to have a refreshing splash without anyone seeing me. They would have considered me naked.

Everyone else carted extra water and washed their clothes at home, which seemed silly at first, but that was because getting water was difficult for us. Now and then Mohammad borrowed a donkey and we carted a load of four jerry-cans – eighty litres – which lasted a few days if we were careful. Once we got our own donkey I had to agree that washing at home was much easier, and cleaner too because I could heat the water. But for now I enjoyed the great outdoors. The cliffs towering above were awesome and the coolness calming; the rocks around me had dropped so long ago that they were rounded and smooth and one of them made a warm mat till I and my clothes were dry. Then, clean and refreshed, pack on my back, I joined the water-carriers on the homeward path – and accepted the first ride offered.

An Adventure for a Cure

Despite accepting the occasional ride home, I had still had very little donkey-riding experience when Mohammad sent me off on an expedition to Wadi Araba. His stepmother Umm Laafi, whom he called 'Auntie', was making a pilgrimage, his brother Salem was escorting her, and they could soon saddle up a donkey for me if I wanted an adventure.

I was excited and didn't give my lack of riding experience a thought. I like to think Mohammad didn't either.

'*Derri-baalki*' were his only instructions as I rode off. Be careful.

I hadn't seen much of Umm Laafi since our wedding. They had moved to a cave twenty minutes away, up the valley behind the Palace Tomb and only the bigger kids occasionally came over. Apparently my mother-in-law had lost her voice. It had been getting worse since the wedding (all that singing) and she had tried herbal drinks and some pills from another woman without success. I thought she should rest her voice, but she had decided an act of appeasement was called for: a visit to the ancestors Ayal Awwad. She was seven months pregnant, but that apparently was no obstacle.

To make a pilgrimage to the graveyard of Ayal Awwad – the Sons of Awwad – was a recent tradition. The grave wasn't that of a biblical or Koranic figure, it was the burial place of Salem-ibn-Awwad, a sheikh of the Amareen tribe who had lived in the early 1900s. All the tribes around now believed he had power and so his tomb had become a shrine. If they made regular pilgrimages to his grave or meals of *mensef* in his name he would be satisfied and bring them good fortune. If they forgot about him he might cause misfortune, sickness or death. The lucky ones were reminded in dreams but retribution could come without warning and Umm Laafi wanted to cover all angles.

We left at first light, each of us on a donkey. Umm Laafi sat side saddle with her brown *aba* wrapped around her. It was cold and I was glad of my jacket until we got into the sun. We followed the dirt path down to the bottom of the western cliffs then along the valley to the south. Red caves looked out haphazardly from the cliffs and to the left was a drop to a dry riverbed.

The donkeys seemed to know the way and walked quickly and steadily. The one I had was just right for me, grey and quiet, not too high off the ground and steady on its high-heeled feet. It was pretty comfortable. I held the halter rope loosely looped around the wooden pommel and my dangling legs were well cushioned from the wooden side-beams by a folded blanket.

After a while the donkeys click-clacked up a winding corridor of white rock and we came out onto a high plain. The land was ploughed, and confined into patches by outcrops of rock and dry, stony creek beds. Plough marks wandered around juniper trees, *rattam* bushes and piles of rocks. Now and then Salem urged the donkeys with a '*hhhrrrwl*' and a wave of the arm but we didn't try to talk. Jabal Haroon came into view – the mosque on its peak white in the morning sun. A couple of bright spots calling to their goats gave themselves away halfway up the side of it. Birds twittered. Startled quails bustled into a short flight. We circled the mountain along dusty white paths and through little *wadis* till we came to a short sandstone canyon which funnelled a cool breeze and framed a glimpse of Wadi Araba between its walls.

We stopped at the edge of the mountains. The sky was pure blue. I took in the view below where white sandy hills lowered to the west and *wadis* between them widened. Beyond that, far off on the other side of the valley in Israel, a blur of a mountain range rose. Salem and Umm Laafi were more practically considering the huge shingle scree that dropped directly below us. It looked impassable to me but obviously wasn't, because they got off the donkeys and prepared to head down.

Umm Laafi hoisted up the hem of her *mudraga* and secured it above her belly. She had another dress on underneath and stretchy trousers. She rolled up her *aba* and balanced it on top of her head. Her shoes were moulded plastic.

I would have preferred to wear just a T-shirt and jeans for donkey riding but since I had become a part of the tribe I tried to consider what the Bedouin thought. This was a pilgrimage; I wanted to be suitably covered. Besides a headscarf I wore my *mudraga* over cotton trousers, and now I tucked it up like her, but I was glad I wore sports shoes.

Salem tucked his trousers carefully into white socks. He was small and good-looking like Mohammad and aptly nicknamed Abu Kohl-eh because he invariably wore kohl smudged delightfully around his eyes. His *mendeel* was pure white against the black twisted cord of his *mirreer*, which he wore at an angle like a big wink. He had a dark suit jacket on over a tight white shirt and a polo-neck jumper. A black leather shoulder holster held a pistol low down on his hip and I reckoned he had polished his shoes before he headed out. Such vanity! I wondered – was he hoping to meet someone? We hadn't yet and I doubted we would from here on – if you could get further from civilisation we seemed to be headed there.

'*Yallah, derru-baalku,*' he said as he led off along a faint dent in the black shingle. I followed and Umm Laafi came behind. We loosened stones onto each other as we slithered, zigzagging, down. Sometimes we dragged the donkeys and sometimes I just held onto the rope and hoped the donkey had a good foothold so I didn't end up at the bottom with it on top of me. We were hot by the time we reached the level ground, and after Salem dusted his shoes we rode back northwards along the flat wide *wadi*.

The mountains to our right towered up in inhospitable black

bluffs of granite; smudges of green plants persisted here and there, brighter where the sun caught them. A gap appeared in the dark rock, crowded with bamboo and oleander standing in clear water. I was amazed. Salem pointed to the water, 'Wadi Siyyagh,' he said, and back up to the east, 'Wadi Musa, Petra.' It had taken us all morning to come round and now we were just below where we started. This was the end for the water, though. It came out of the protection of the narrow rocky valley and seeped away into the sand.

There were a couple of little girls scooping up water with battered tin cans. I couldn't imagine where they came from. They watched us arrive and answered our 'salaam's shyly but were soon getting on with their job, filling the great balloons of black rubber hanging on the sides of their donkeys. We filled our water bottles, our donkeys had a drink and we washed our faces and our feet. The air was warm, the water cool and refreshing.

The *wadi* got flatter and wider as we rode north. There were lots more bushes now – great bunches of branches growing out of the sand and bending back down with the weight of their needle-like greenery; dead and yellow bushes holding their roots up where the flash floods had abandoned them; an occasional acacia promising shade; grasses sprouting wherever their roots found shelter. We passed two black-hair tents, homes presumably of the little girls, but we didn't see a soul. The graveyard finally appeared as a slight rise in the flat bush-studded sand.

Salem unsaddled the donkeys and tied them tightly so they could graze around the bottoms of the bushes but not get loose. I was happy to be out of the saddle but it would be a long walk home if that happened.

The low mounds of the graves were made of soil and stones and were all facing the same way. Not even the shrine of Salem-ibn-Awwad had an engraved headstone, but it was distinguishable by the rough low wall that encircled it and the scraps of disintegrating green cloth wedged among its stones.

Umm Laafi didn't go near it until she had emptied the saddle-bags and filled the teapot and balanced it on the fire. And then she completed the *wathuw*, (ritual washing) before climbing over the wall. I was imagining some seriously time-consuming ceremony but it didn't take long. After reciting a verse from the Koran, and lighting a votive 'candle' (made of a twist of green cloth dipped in *samin*) and wedging it among the stones, she clambered back out and got on with lunch.

Salem and I didn't even go inside the wall. I wished I hadn't bothered with the headscarf and dress.

A warning hiss from the teapot as it came to the boil alerted Salem, who quickly lifted it from the flames with a long stick, then returned it to boil briefly to dissolve the sugar and brew the tea.

I sat against the wall and drank tea as Umm Laafi kneaded soft yellow flour to make lunch; no ready-made sandwiches here. We were to have fresh *fatteh*. Not with *shraak* and *rishoof* but with bread-in-the-fire and *laban*. The wood had burned down so Salem used long sticks to spread the pile of coals out and Umm Laafi set the fat pizza wheel of firm dough straight onto them. Salem carefully scooped coals onto it coaxing them to every bit of the surface, and then, once he was sure he had sealed the crust, he buried the whole loaf right into the hot sand under the fire.

Umm Laafi gave me a smashed-up yoghurt ball soaking in a bowl of water and instructed me, '*Ummrussi.*' This was where I could be useful – the homemaking skill that I understood the word for *and* knew how to do. Besides *samin*, yoghurt balls were the main product and money-earner from the goat and sheep milk. Once the butter was churned and removed, the yoghurt was left to settle. The watery liquid was poured off and the rest was poured into a muslin sugar-bag to drain some more. When it was kneadable, salt was added and fist-sized balls were rolled. They were placed on the roof of the black-hair tent till they hardened like dry clay. They kept for years. Now I rubbed the pieces till the water was all white and only a few lumps persisted in the bottom. Umm Laafi prised the lid off a Nido tin and put it by the fire so the *samin* in it could melt.

When Salem tapped the bread and it sounded nice and hollow, he took it out of what was left of the fire and shook it, then lashed it with the empty flour sack to dislodge persistent grains. We sat down and broke the bread up into the dish – its crust was firm and the inside was yellow and heavy. Umm Laafi poured the yoghurt over and we mixed – right hands only – till we had a lovely creamy and crunchy consistency. They made a hollow in the middle like a bowl and poured the melted *samin* into it – clear and buttercup yellow. We said, '*Bis-millah*,' and ate, scooping and dipping, sitting in the sand beside the graveyard under the vast open sky.

We retraced our steps. My backside and thighs were beginning to get sore but I didn't want to admit it so I copied Umm Laafi and rode side saddle some of the time.

Somewhere along the *wadi* we stopped and Salem called out to the mountainside. As I scanned it, a reply focused me in on a goatherd barely visible way up in the rocks. It wasn't just hello, there was a whole conversation, with echoes. Umm Laafi had left her *aba* on the stone wall and Salem was reporting it to the lost and found. (Some months later I was visiting Umm Laafi when an old man came by their tent on his way up to Wadi Musa and brought it back to her.)

My legs were aching by the time we reached the bottom of shingle scree and I couldn't pretend they weren't. I laboured up. I hadn't thought about the energy I would need when I jumped at the chance to come; I had been thinking about doing something new. Well, being saddle-sore was new. '*Yallah*,' Salem encouraged. Umm Laafi stepped steadily upwards despite her pregnancy. I was thankful that we had a rest at the top but I could barely sit and they laughed when they realised my problem. The sun went down as we started off again.

What a tourist! I walked for a bit and would rather have carried on but soon it was too dark to see the uneven path. I was really holding us up. I didn't know that it never took this long and that Mohammad and his father were getting worried. The donkeys had no trouble walking in the dark, picking their way, and we had to keep going. Salem kept laughing and saying, '*Yallah*,' and I had to resume painful riding.

I was very relieved when I started seeing spots of light pinpointing Bedouin homes. Suddenly there were torches and voices and it was Mohammad on the path with a couple of others in a search party.

'*Lish toweltu?* What took you so long?'

'Only me, sore bottom.' I gave them all the cue to laugh. And they could, relieved that Umm Laafi, miraculously, hadn't miscarried.

The others went on ahead to let everyone know we were safe and Mohammad and I walked slowly, oh so slowly, over to their smoky cave. There his excited little sisters – eyes bright in the firelight – were gathered round the pot where the sacrificial goat was cooking. There was *mensef* for dinner and we stayed the night – I couldn't even walk home to our ledge.

Umm Laafi's voice did not get better that day or the next but she was content knowing she had done all she could, and maybe that knowledge made her calmer and less inclined to talk. In any case by the time the baby was born she was cured.

A Flash Flood

It was cold these days and tonight it had been raining. We had a brazier of coals in the cave and I felt comfortable and warm when Mohammad burst in after a toilet visit saying, 'Come and listen to the flood.' Out in the dark on our ledge we could hear a rumbling sound coming from the *wadi*. 'It sounds strong, let's go and look.'

It was dark and rainy. 'Why don't we wait till the morning?' I asked.

Mohammad laughed and, while I got out my coat, he pumped up the Tilley lamp. A few spits of rain fizzled on the lid of the lamp as we headed down the path in the garish light. It reminded me of my dad, of night-fishing for flounder on the mud flats behind Rabbit Island. I sat in the dinghy as Dad waded. He held the Tilley lamp in one hand and his spear in the other and later we had fresh flounder fried in butter for breakfast.

The rumbling increased and by the time we reached the paved road we couldn't hear ourselves speak. Our light showed a river of mud and stones pounding along the *wadi*. I had only ever seen it as a bed of smoothed boulders and now the water was barely contained by the walls. I could feel the crashing and jarring of the ground as the rocks on the bottom were tumbled along. A wrenched-up tree stuck out a branch like an arm reaching for help. Our neighbour al-Jimedy came down to watch with us, and Mufleh also arrived in our pool of light.

Mufleh pops up here and there in this story, that's his way. He has always been itinerant even by Bedouin standards. He was nobody's brother or (paternal) cousin. His father died before he was born and his mother came back to Petra, leaving Beer-a-Saba'a (Beersheba) and her in-laws, and she never cared or married again. Mufleh grew up in the valley. He was looked after by the tribe (people could gain merit in the eyes of God by feeding or clothing or being kind to an orphan, and if you lost a parent you were an orphan) but he never developed a social conscience or took on any family obligations. He was a bit older than Mohammad, who looked at him with frustration. 'He doesn't have to look after anyone but himself, he should be rich!' But

Mufleh didn't appear to have any such ambitions. He worked occasionally for the Department of Antiquities; set up home in one cave, and then another; was even to dabble in marriage several times in the future – but nothing lasted for long.

The rain had ceased altogether now and the water was already receding. There was a freshness in the darkness, washed free of dust. By the time we got back to our cave and closed the door on the night, the sky was pricked with stars. No wonder Mohammad had laughed; by morning there would only be pools captured here and there.

1979: A Beautiful Bedouin Baby

On a dark February evening Salem arrived to *bish'r* – bring the good tidings – of their brother's birth. We were all excited but Abu Mahmoud, who had called in for a cup of tea, said he had seen Umm Laafi earlier but hadn't noticed anything unusual about her when he had had dinner with them.

He wasn't the only one – no one had known she was in labour while she made the dinner, though she did send young Laafi off to call a neighbour from across the *wadi*. The visitors were drinking tea in the men's area behind the woven wall when the woman quietly came and took Umm Laafi off to an empty cave just down the hill where the baby entered the world without complications. *Al-humdulillah-a-salaama*. Praise God for their deliverance into safety.

Mohammad sent me to see them the next morning – he wouldn't be expected till much later, he explained. They were living in their tent again. The sheltered north-facing clearing where their low-slung tent was set up, crowded around by the ruins of ancient buildings, was only ten minutes away. Umm Laafi was lying in pride of place in the middle of the tent on a thick wool *farrsha*. She lifted a floral scarf beside her to show me her *bebe* in a greatcoat bassinet. His sleeping eyes were half-moons with dark eyelashes on mushroom cheeks and his black hair escaping from the headband tied round his little head was enough to tell me he was the most beautiful baby I had ever seen. His mother seemed justifiably proud and called him Hussein, 'Like the king.'

I was the daughter-in-law so I went over daily to put in an appearance. Women visited; most of them were from around Petra, but Umm Laafi was from the Amareen and so her sisters came between the hills from Beitha. I wasn't competent yet in the ways of the tent and the chaos this one was in made it difficult to imagine where one would start. Tuf-leh disappeared with the goats early every day and came back late. Laafi went to school and had to be cajoled daily to bring a load of water when he got back at midday. Inzela, who was eight by then, and five-year-old Neda ran round helpfully, but housekeeping – as in washing dirty dishes, house-training pets and keeping a tidy wardrobe – was practised by few of the Bedouin.

Things changed with education and running water and later they all learned to keep immaculate homes, but then the girls threw the bedding haphazardly onto the quilt cupboard, picked clothes off the ground and slung them over the tent ropes (to be washed when they next needed to be worn), and poured water for the chickens into a cooking pot that sat, with last night's stew dried on its edges, among the blocks of stone and jerry-cans out in front of the tent. And all the time baby goats, separated from their mothers during the day, bounced bleating in and out, dribbling piddle and sloppy droppings here and there.

The visitors arrived in such clean *mudragas* and tall *asabas* I had to remind myself that their homes were often in similar states. The women brought gifts of eggs and *samin* and small amounts of money. They sat and gossiped and drank tea, but they usually stayed for the day and churned butter, turned goatskins of buttermilk and put balls of creamy yoghurt to dry on top of the tent. Umm Laafi's cataract-blinded aunt Fa<u>th</u>iya kneaded dough for lunch once someone put the flour and water in front of her.

I usually enjoyed it – there was plenty going on and most of the women were friendly, if curious, but they always talked about me and on one occasion I couldn't help getting angry.

'*Haa<u>th</u>i marrat Mohammad?*' A round ball of wrinkled woman looks from under her headscarf and, pointing with her head at me, asks Umm Laafi if I am Mohammad's wife. Then '*Keef haalki?*' she throws at me. How are you?

I mumble a response and more faces turn my way. The wrinkled woman is Imghee<u>th</u>a. She already shook my hand when she arrived and has seen me down at Rakhiya's place often enough to know exactly who I am.

A younger, colourful mother, with a generously kohled baby at her breast, asks, '*Tahki arabi?*' Glancing at me but looking round the tent for an answer. Do you – does she – speak Arabic?

'*Shwaya,*' I venture. A little.

At least that gets a direct question. One that I understand. '*Ummki tayebah?*' Is your mother well/alive?

'*Aywa.*' Yes.

They peer at me, smiling and nodding; assessing.

'*Fi bebe?*' The lady beside me leans over and puts her hand on my tummy. Is there a baby? Her hair-oil smell is in my face but I resign myself to her behaviour because she smiles so excitedly as she catches the arm of her toddler to show him off.

'*Ma fi.*' No, there isn't.

They discuss this answer, and chatter together.

'*Takhu<u>th</u> ma'naa,*' I hear Imghee<u>th</u>a announce with her chin on her chest. She is nodding up and down but carefully not looking my way, and I look down, too, pretending not to realise she's talking about me, pretending I don't understand that she's telling everyone I use contraception.

I fume silently. What would she know about it? Why would she even have an opinion, the sour old hag? What's it got to do with her?

But I also feel as if I want them to know I don't take the Pill. Why do I want to justify myself, I wonder, wishing I had the Arabic words to be blatant.

'No I'm not,' I would like to be able to say. 'We are working on babies every chance we get but we haven't had any luck so far,' and I'm sure they would laugh.

But I can't express myself so I look the other way and ignore her as best I can.

Umm Laafi didn't do anything except tend to her baby. For forty days she shouldn't make food or even a pot of tea. She was unclean. She had her own cup tucked in a plastic bag under her mattress and was served separately from the communal dish, which all seemed a bit drastic to me considering the general uncleanliness. I noticed she didn't show Hussein off to anybody else either. 'To keep him safe from the evil eye,' she made me understand. Later, when my own week-old baby caught the flu, either from my sharing tea glasses with everyone else to prove I was not unclean, or from my letting everyone kiss her to prove there was no such thing as the evil eye, I understood the wisdom in their superstitions.

The gifts were welcome; we fried eggs in *samin* for breakfast and Umm Laafi sent Neda to the shop in the Fum-al-Wadi with coins, to buy cinnamon to make a hot brew and incense to waft around the tent. Ibraheem brought tea and a whole sack of sugar up on the donkey. Hussein himself cost very little to keep. He fed from his mother's breast, slept in his father's coat and an old dress had been ripped up to make swaddling clothes.

Their neighbours and some of their children gathered in the evenings and stayed till late getting through pots of sweet tea. Salaama al-Mokhtar and other men from around the valley wandered in too. They kept the fire burning all night, no need for peace and quiet, no need to save on the sugar.

'The woman and new baby are vulnerable for forty days,' Salaama said, and made Mohammad translate for me, so I would understand their almost nightly presence. 'We come to keep Abdallah company.' I almost felt chastised; Mohammad and I only visited on a couple of evenings and enjoyed our own warm cave on the others.

A Bit of Prestige

'*Marratak narsa, lish ma-btishtaghil?*' Mohammad was asked this so often that I came to understand what it meant – your wife is a nurse, why doesn't she work?

They reasoned that I could run the Petra Clinic better than the present nurse because he had to come all the way down from Wadi Musa. By the time I understood what they were saying, enough months of easy living had passed for me to know I needed something else to do, but I wasn't sure about the clinic job. Apart from the fact that the position wasn't vacant, I wasn't sure of my credentials. I had trained specifically with intellectually handicapped children, much more behavioural and much less first aid. My basic knowledge of that had come from the St John's Ambulance course I did at high school. And I couldn't imagine how I would manage with so little Arabic.

'Look.' Mohammad couldn't understand my apprehension. 'That guy doesn't come half the time anyway, he'll be happy to work in Wadi Musa, and as for the language, the doctor writes his prescriptions in English.'

They were all so keen I decided it was worth a try. If I could keep myself busy doing something useful and earn a bit of money for doing it, it couldn't be bad.

At the hospital in Wadi Musa, the doctors tried to talk me into working there rather than at the clinic. They came from Amman for a year each on a rotating basis and the other employees at the hospital were mostly from the village with little formal training, so a permanent registered nurse would be an asset. I really only wanted to work if I could do it without too much effort and that meant not going out to Wadi Musa daily. The Petra Clinic position was for a nurse aide, so that is what I became.

It hardly seemed like a job. I was given it on my word, even before I had a copy of my registration certificate sent over to be put in my file; the monthly pay was so little compared to what I had earned in New Zealand that it was embarrassing to consider it a wage; and the clinic was in a cave so musty and dusty it hardly seemed real – more like just a continuation of my adventure.

For the first six weeks, to see how things were done, I had to go up to the hospital daily. The hours of work were from eight till two, and the day off was Friday like the schools and banks and other government offices. I had to walk up the Siq but got a ride from there, from the beginning of the asphalt road, in the hospital Land-Rover. The driver did the rounds of the village and picked up three other nurses.

I enjoyed leaving the cave early and walking up through the Siq with the first horsemen. As soon as they got used to me and recognised me as *marrat* Mohammad, they would insist I ride and they would walk. They were going to work and would have to walk later guiding tourists on their horses so I didn't like to deprive them of the chance to ride, but one would always insist harder than I could politely decline. It was win-tertime and wonderful. The air was crisp, the pure sounds of the men singing and the horses' hooves clattering echoed through the canyon in the otherwise silence. It was a magical start to the day.

There were no beds in the hospital; it was more of a health centre that closed after working hours. It was in a rectangular cement block set on the way out of Wadi Musa, way above the village, and it commanded a spectacular view, with the moun-tains of Petra below and to the west offering an ever-changing exhibition. Some mornings with the sun on them the mountains came close and the desert and hills of Wadi Araba became clear in the background. When Wadi Araba was hazy I had to remind myself it was not the blue ocean beyond the mountains. Other mornings Wadi Araba was shrouded in cloud and the mountains became a dam preventing it from spilling into Petra. Once, even the Petra basin was covered in a quilt of cloud and Jabal Haroon appeared like an island, with the shrine of the prophet Haroon (Aaron) whitewashed and gleaming in the spotlight of the sun.

The nearest hospital with beds and a laboratory was in Ma'an, fifty kilometres to the east. That is where all the medical supplies had to be brought from, and where I had to go once a month to get my meagre but welcome pay. Mohammad's family and friends were all very interested in this; to be a civil servant carried quite a bit of prestige so I was steadily becoming a more acceptable daughter-in-law, but I was always disconcerted when asked, '*Gid-ish bit jeebi?*' How much do you get? Straight after '*Twathafti?*' or '*Ishtaghalti?*' Did you get the job?

It didn't bother Mohammad. 'You're earning it, not stealing it, so just tell them.'

But to me it was like asking a woman her age – and they did that too without a qualm.

When we decided to save to go to New Zealand (that prom-ised, but not stipulated trip), I arranged to have my pay put into the bank. That freed me from the hot or cold but always dusty journey in the rattly old bus through all the outlying desert villages.

The health centre wasn't very busy; most of the time we just sat around and I would try to talk with the other working girls, but although they were friendly, they spoke very little English. I usually found my way down to the pharmacy where the accountant, handyman and driver, who spoke more, would gather. One day the director told me that it wasn't acceptable for me to sit in a room with the men. At first I tried to explain that my seeking their company was purely for communication's sake, but I realised that he believed the act of sitting with them was unacceptable in itself. I was not there to change the world, so I went and sat with the girls.

I still couldn't imagine how I would manage with the Bedouin in Petra once I was on my own; my Arabic was still practically non-existent. The girls taught me a few words – *raha* (Turkish delight) and *biscotte* (biscuits), which they bought for morning tea and made into sandwiches: a piece of rose or white icing-sugar-covered delight sandwiched between two classic petit-beurres – and they showed me how to boil a glass syringe and stainless-steel needle in a kidney dish and how to spread lots of bright yellow greasy Furazina ointment onto a bandage to apply to a wound or burn. Only basic bandages and cotton wool were available and even these were in short supply. I didn't see a disposable syringe till a month or two later when I met Nuha, the vaccination lady. Sick people came for cough medicine or antibiotics and the doctors were usually able to supply these basics from the pharmacy. People with more serious problems were sent on to Ma'an.

The first time I saw inside the Petra Clinic was probably a Tuesday. The doctor came into Petra once a week and I was to meet him there. I went early to the Monastery valley and waited by the door at the bottom of the canyon wall, which Mohammad had pointed out and I had passed often on my way to visit Rakhiya. Her family spent the winter months in a cave there and now their new 'crop' of baby goats was bouncing about and bleating on a ledge up above. The opposite wall had several other inhabited caves, I could tell – by the donkeys and water drums, the rare clothes line, the playing children and the *tooks* (the black streaks down the rocks like dried-up waterfalls caused by years of washing water, discarded food scraps and rubbish). Chickens thrived.

Sliman, whose job I was taking, was a suave young man with a really thick, black, perfectly trimmed moustache and clean, pressed European clothes. He arrived soon after me and unlocked the door with a huge metal key on a chain. He had to put a stick through the key to give it leverage and it clacked alarmingly in the lock as he turned it, but it never broke. I took to carrying a metal pipe along with the key so as not to break off a new stick each time.

The door was made of rough-hewn juniper slabs. Sliman gave it a strong push and it creaked open and swung to the left, coming to rest with a wooden thud. I had to duck as I stepped over the threshold and into the cave, onto ancient paving stones set in cement. The smell was dusty and cool. The uneven rock walls had been whitewashed once but didn't appear to have been dusted since.

Directly in front, to benefit from the light from the door, was the doctor's table. On it, Sliman showed me, were the patients register, the drugs register, prescriptions and receipts. Behind it, against the rock wall, there was just room for the doctor's chair. Sliman opened a tall wooden cupboard to the left of the table, revealing sparse shelves of medicines and worn cartons of faded pink files. To the left again, almost behind me now, was the rickety wooden table that had stopped the door from swinging back to the wall. Everything on it looked ancient. I could make out a gas cooker, some kidney dishes, cotton wool and forceps; beneath it a gas-bottle and jerry-can and rubbish tin. To the right of the doctor's table was an examination table covered in grey plastic. Beneath that was a wooden bench, and leaning against it was a screen of wood and worn white curtain. Another wooden table between the screen and the door seemed to hold cardboard boxes of dust.

The doctor arrived in the Land-Rover and once again I wondered how I would manage. Quite a few people gathered; some had seen the door open from the opposite cliff, and some came after hearing the vehicle make its noisy way down through the quiet valley. Sliman proceeded to fill out receipts in Arabic as they paid their admission.

'I won't be able to do this,' I said out loud, but the doctor said, 'Yes you will, because the Bedouin of Petra have been granted free medical care by Royal Decree of His Majesty King Hussein and it comes into effect next week.'

What perfect timing – with one decree he had cut out all the Arabic paperwork. The prescriptions were in English, as Mohammad had told me.

When I had finished my time in Wadi Musa and was ready to take over my responsibilities, I met Sliman at the clinic for an unbelievable exercise. He had to sign over all the pills, furniture, syringes and books, no matter what state they were in. In those cardboard boxes under the dust of years was a rusty set of baby-weighing scales; an old Tilley lamp from the days when the nurse had lived in the tiny cave; lots of syringes, unusable due to having been sterilised by boiling in the hard water; charcoal pills which had become dust and were impossible to count, and a ten-litre brass tin – a half-cylinder with a tap – which could be hung on the wall and filled to provide 'running water'.

We spent long hours, interrupted only for tea and to give injections to a couple of robed women, counting and registering every pill and dusty syringe, but not the files in the cupboard. Sliman said they were unimportant. 'For the *Sitt. Thebayer-a-tat-eemat*. Sometimes she comes.'

I couldn't understand what that meant but decided 'unimportant' was the operative word. Finally he went home; he would work in the health centre from now on. I was left to my new job.

The Petra Clinic

It was wonderful to have this little office and reason to go to it. I would pick my way every morning down the hill through the cut stones of ruined houses, across the cleared, ancient marketplaces, past the huge toppled column-drums lying like dominosnakes across the temple courtyard, and on down the grand but dilapidated steps to the paved street. The occasional poppy or wildflower would peek between the rocks, and a prickle bush, which spread out in lines and balls like a chemical formula, took hold as the spring came on.

I took a *Teach Yourself Arabic* book and my writing paper. The sturdy table was a luxury. I made my first attempts at learning the alphabet and caught up on letters home.

One of my first patients was a little old woman, barely as tall as the donkey she arrived on. The tattoos on her dark and deeply lined face, her bent-over back and the layers of *mudraga* that she wore made me think she was old as the hills. She came to get injected with a vitamin B complex – one of the main deficiencies due to a lack of green vegetables – and on her first visit offered me some coins to pay with. I managed to get across to her that I was receiving a wage and didn't expect payment from her as well. However, the next time she came she brought four eggs, nestled in cloth in a battered tin can, and another time a little *samin*, insisting I accept these as 'gifts', not payments.

Others also offered money, and I learned that the custom had started in the 1960s during an anti-tuberculosis campaign when Gublan, a local Bdoul Bedouin, had been trained to give the streptomycin injections. No one had expected to receive the injections without giving something in return. Gublan was an old guy now but people still pointed him out to me – with his precious, thick-lensed, taped-together glasses sitting crookedly on his bony face – as the 'Toktor'.

The generosity made me feel welcome, but uncomfortable. I found it easy enough to refuse the money but didn't have the heart to refuse the produce of which they were so proud, and for which I had rapidly acquired a taste.

And so I got to know the Bedouin. I had met Mohammad's family and a few families he was friendly with, and the guys he worked with at the Treasury, and some of the young women who lived near us and had wandered onto the ledge to see me for themselves, but through the clinic I got to meet the rest of the Bdoul tribe, the Amareen tribe and even some of the Saydiyeen, and to connect them all together. Some came just to see what I looked like – those who hadn't already come to look at me in the cave – some needed a burn or cut re-bandaged, or an injection injected, and some came hoping for a bottle of cough medicine or a pill – vain hopes unless they had a doctor's prescription. Whenever the doctor came, a crowd gathered. Those I had met introduced me to the others and lots of them told me who they were by introducing themselves.

'*Ana Umm Salem.*' I'm Salem's mother, one woman was proud to tell me, naming one of Mohammad's bachelor friends, and her actions helped me understand the rest of the family info she supplied: 'And these are my twin girls, Nayifa and Najda, named by the nurses who delivered them in Ma'an.'

They didn't give up without getting the message across. And I heard more and more words in the flow of language.

'*Jowzi biyishtaghil ma Mohammad fil Jarra.*' My husband

works with Mohammad at the Treasury, another woman, with a round toddler on her hip, told me. (They all called al-Khazneh the *Jarra*, or Urn, despite the tour guide's spiel.)

There were always two doctors, whose years overlapped each other. For their second six months they would direct the health centre but for their first six they did the clinic rounds, so I met a lot of young doctors over the years. They had studied in Amman, Baghdad, Ukraine, Russia or Yugoslavia. Some really wanted to practise and to help, and were frustrated when the old men wouldn't even open their mouths and say 'aaah'. Others were only doctors because of the prestige it brought for their parents, and were quite happy to prescribe pills, creams and injections for the black shapes silhouetted in the doorway complaining of dizziness, fever and spots.

They filled out the prescriptions with the patient's name in three parts – own name, father's name, grandfather's name – and with the age, although that was often a guess. Most said, 'I don't know my age, I neither read nor write,' but some people had a date scribbled on a scrap of paper or an army ID – invariably making them younger than I had guessed. None had birth certificates, but one or two had Estimation of Age certificates like Mohammad, who got his in 1974 when he had gone before a board of doctors in Ma'an and they had taken into account 'his build and general bodily appearance' in case he could be conscripted into the army. (They had estimated he was born in 1950, which made him old enough to avoid it.)

Without Mohammad there to translate I listened very carefully and then put him to work when we got home.

'*Kul ma min-ni eujaani ya toktor*,' I recited for him and, reaching for my back, shoulders and then my chest, continued, '*thehar-i beujaani, kitoofi beujenni, ou bi-hiss kibdi tala a ras gulbi ya toktor*.'

He laughed, but that might have been my acting, because he also seemed embarrassed, or impatient with ill-health, when he explained, 'They're all sick like that. It just means, "All of me hurts, my back, my shoulders, and I feel as if my liver has risen on top of my heart." But that is ignorant talk, you shouldn't learn it.'

Ignorant or not, that is the language the people spoke and that is the language I learned.

'What's she saying? What is *dish beh*?' the doctor asked me one day. Asked me!

I had no idea what the word meant but the lady sounded like she had a cold so I assumed it meant that, but the doctor was confused. 'No, a cold is *rush ha.*'

The Bedouin speak Arabic with a pure and ancient accent which is quite similar among tribes right across the Sinai, Jordan and into Saudi Arabia, but has many colloquial words and phrases that aren't used in the modern urban language of Jordan. Outside Petra I knew when I had used such a word only by the looks I got. Mohammad would look embarrassed, while other Bedouin would chuckle proudly and quote, 'When you've lived with a tribe for forty days, you become one of them.' Modern young women, rejecting the language and the simple way of life it evoked, would pretend they had never heard of the staple diet of their grandfathers.

It was the total immersion way of learning the language. My basic medical vocabulary grew with both modern and Bedouin words but outside the clinic I learned only Bedouin Arabic, and as it was a generally illiterate society I made very little leeway with my writing. Eventually I could understand all the chatter under the tree and knew that if your liver was on top of your heart, or your uterus (the mother of your children) had drifted out of place, you were better off going to Nora or Fathiya to get it massaged back, than coming to the clinic where 'the doctor doesn't understand these things'.

I learned to explain to the mothers how to reconstitute antibiotic syrup with boiled, but no longer boiling, water. I filled packets with pills and drew three lines on them for three times a day. I did learn how to write the Arabic numbers but it wasn't much use because so many of my patients couldn't read them. I put prescribed injections in paper packets too. Sometimes the patients asked me to keep them at the clinic, to save the fine glass vials from getting broken in their tents, but others took them home to impress their families – to be prescribed injections meant you were sick.

On the days we expected the doctor I made a pot of tea and waited with the gathering patients, sitting in the sand in the shade of the oleander bushes that filled the valley. The sand was clean as it was the valley bottom and had been washed by winter floods, but as the summer wore on it became dirtier and I found a stone seat to sit on in the pink oleander pergola. Sometimes tourists passed along the valley on their way up to the Monastery. Occasional sceptical looks (I could see 'hippie gone native') and prying questions made me defensive. I didn't want to appear, to those I sat with, any more different than I already was, so if I saw tourists coming I sat with my back to the path or hid inside the cave.

I still usually wore my jeans and shirt but had started covering my hair. That was partly because we had to cart our water, so when my hair was clean I wanted to keep it clean, and when, too soon, it became greasy, no one could see if I didn't wash it. My reason wasn't important to the women. 'Mabruk al-mendeel,' they congratulated joyfully, and Fraija, who had feared my shining golden locks were an invitation to disaster, a sort of light-ning rod for the evil eye, was relieved that they were safely concealed.

My scarf was called a *mendeel* because it was flowery. Most of the girls wore *ashaars*, which were chiffon and tied under their chins, but I never wore my scarf like that simply because I didn't like how it looked.

The doctor didn't always come on our allotted day; he had

time off and was in Amman, or, more often, the Land-Rover was broken down or being used to bring supplies from Ma'an, and occasionally he went to another clinic first and surprised us by arriving after midday, but there was no way of knowing for sure so we waited. The women gossiped and joked; their babies slept or cried or suckled at breasts released matter-of-factly from the bodices of loose concealing robes; toddlers played or leaned against their mothers and sometimes one of them still suckled – keeping the next pregnancy successfully at bay. Young men passing by stopped to entertain with jokes or tape recordings of the latest wedding's *samer* chanting, especially if young women were waiting. And quite often a dishevelled mother arrived from out on the Beitha Plains or from down in Wadi Araba with a wilted child in a *muzferr*, or sling, then a pinch of thin skin 'tenting' on the dehydrated baby's tummy suggested urgency and I had to decide when the tired mother should give up waiting for the doctor here and make the trek up the Siq to the health centre to be sure.

Whether the doctor came or not I closed the door with the clanking key at around two o'clock. I didn't necessarily finish work then though because there was often someone waiting with an injection when I got back up the hill to my cave.

Clinic Visitors

Most days between the doctors' visits someone came in for an injection or dressing. None of it required much language. Dressings were basic and obvious and they all knew to bare a buttock for the injection – most of them took it standing up.

Husseina was lying on the examination table for hers, though.

She was thrilled to be pregnant but her iron injection could leave nasty bruising if we didn't get it right.

Mohammad had introduced Husseina and her cousin Abdallah as 'the only other couple to have a marriage certificate', so we had a bond, despite her being only sixteen and on her second marriage. They lived with Abdallah's parents not far up the hill behind our home, which meant she was easy to visit. Husseina was very pretty – all the young women looked pretty to me, but there was something special about her round cheeks and enquiring smile. She wore a yellow scarf tied under her chin. She parted her dark yellowish hair on one side, combed it with lots of olive oil down across her forehead and secured it over her cheek with a wall of bobby pins. Thick plaits hung below the bottom of her scarf. Later she asked me to bring a bottle of peroxide from Ma'an – before that, although I had noticed the colour of her hair, it never occurred to me that anyone would bother with such a vanity out here in the desert.

She was up on the examination table watching me prepare the syringe – lying on her side, *mudraga* and underskirts around her waist, finger ready to slip down the elastic of her nylon under-trousers – when a horrified look came over her face and strange sounds came from her throat. Before I could panic she had gathered her wits and was pointing as she swung off the table. There, as big as my hand, waving black legs and pincers as it crawled along the top of the old wooden door, was my first scorpion. Husseina forgot pregnancy and listlessness, pushed me behind the doctor's table, grabbed the broom, knocked the scorpion to the floor and smashed it to bits.

Heads poked in the door to speculate. '*Ya m-akbara.*' I could understand that much; this was a really big one. '*Al-humdulil-lah-a-salaama,*' they said.

'*Al-humdulillah,*' we agreed.

I hadn't seen what scorpions could do yet so I was more interested than scared. I didn't even realise how especially huge it was, though I now think I never saw such a big one again. They were more commonly half the size and there were yellow ones as well – translucent – with their insides and the poison in the tips of their tails showing through darkly.

Scorpion stings seemed to be like bee stings; some people spat on them and rubbed them and went back to work; some, like me when I got stung on the thumb one summer's night reaching for the water bottle on the wall, had a painful but localised reaction. For the rest of that night I had a freezing numbness in my arm that was only just bearable – as if the whole thing had been over-dosed with Tiger Balm – and which wore off so slowly that the following evening my thumb was still too tender to make bread. And there were some people who had violent reactions with vomiting and chest cramps, and if they were lucky they were raced up to the health centre for antidotes. It was in the 'hands of God' whether they made it or not. Babies, who couldn't tell you what was wrong and cried for twenty minutes before the culprit was discovered wrapped up in their swaddling clothes, didn't stand a chance.

Husseina's brother, then in the seventh grade, was to die the day after he was stung, even though he had received treatment and been discharged the night before. The doctor could only speculate that the vicious spasms of the previous night had been re-stimulated when the boy, arriving home thirsty from goat herding, had gulped down some water. His heart had failed before he got back to the centre.

My clinic wasn't much help. Even if someone got stung during my working hours I couldn't stock the antidote. That had to be kept in a fridge and there was no fridge in Petra, let alone the electricity to run it.

The Old Man and the Rababa

As I entered the Monastery valley on my way to the clinic, I passed a cave where I often saw a frail old man sitting cross-legged in the morning shade, playing on a *rababa* and reciting poetry. His music would follow me along the valley.

I asked Mohammad about him and he said, '*Miskeen, mylih weritha.*' Poor guy, he has no successor. The *weritha* was an old word originating before matches and lighters when the only way a Bedouin could keep his fire going was to bury a hard-wood stump deep into the ashes where it smouldered till morning. That log was his *weritha*, and so were his sons, because as the log would continue the fire, so the sons would continue his name.

Everyone called the old man with the *rababa* Abu Argoob, although he didn't have a son. His nickname, the Father of the Shins, seemed appropriate because his were like thin sticks below his hitched-up once-white *thaub*. When he was young he had been a playboy – wearing his *mirreer* at a rakish angle with lots of kohl round his eyes. He had spent his days meeting the goat-girls in hidden valleys; never doing any work. He had had a fun life and it must have flown by till, too late, he realised the girls were meeting younger men than he. Then the only family who would give him a wife was one from outside the Bdoul who had an older and not very competent daughter left in their care. He married her and eventually she bore him a girl, a simple soul but now able enough to help look after her father as he grew old, bringing water and wood, washing and preparing food.

Abu Argoob's *rababa* was typical of the stringed instruments of the Bedouin. It was a goatskin over a few bits of wood about the size of a violin, which he held like a cello. It had one wire, which he caressed with a bow of oleander and horse-hair. The hauntingly beautiful music echoed along the valley with the poetry of the mountains. Often I was his only audience. I couldn't understand the words but I would get goosebumps. The keening of his *rababa* and desolate sound of his poetry conjured up the wind in the juniper trees, a night-fire under the desert sky and the goatherd he loved, married to another man.

When he died that was the end. Whatever his real name was it was buried with him. His daughter was shunted off to some distant relative as a second wife and his wife went back to live out her days with her brother. Even his cave disappeared, bulldozed in 1980 to make way for the Forum Basin Restaurant, and if his ghost does play the *rababa* in the valley it's no competition for the electric generators they installed.

The Settlement Project

Mohammad bought us a little donkey and I went every few days to fill our 20-litre jerry-cans from the spring. I could fill two and ride on top, or four and walk behind. And we could use the donkey to ride around on too – without the water it could carry us both. That summer, when school was out, Mohammad's family moved north to Beitha to harvest barley. They camped in their black-hair tent by the Siq al-Barid, where Rakhiya's wedding had been the previous summer. One afternoon we went through the Eastern Maiserra valley to visit them. That's the valley we had come back through from the wedding and it wasn't much quicker on the donkey. It still took a couple of hours, what with all the climbing off and on, and coaxing the donkey over the difficult bits.

Baby Hussein was sleeping in a hammock strung between the tent poles when we got there, but Neda and Maryam, thrilled at our arrival, jumped up and down like pogo-ing punk rockers. They had spiky hair many a London hairdresser would have been proud of, and for a moment they sent me back to northern England, to the Blackburn town hall where a year ago I had been part of the jumping-up-and-down crowd there when The Clash played live.

As soon as Mohammad's father saw our placid donkey, he swapped it for the mule he had bought in Wadi Musa. He had been at the market and on a spur-of-the-moment impulse (I recognised the father in the son) had bought the strange, strong animal. He only discovered it was too dangerous to have around once he got it home to his tent and the shrill, squealing excitement of the children set it kicking.

I liked our donkey, but Mohammad was excited about the mule and we were both concerned about the children so there was no argument. The mule was too tall to go home the way we had come so we went back by another track further east, winding in and out of the valleys along the bottom of the Sh-rah. Rounding the end of a long ridge sloping down to the west, Mohammad said, 'This is where they are going to move us to. It's called Umm Sayhoon because the wind always blows.'

I had heard about a settlement project; Ali had cited it when he was working on me to marry Mohammad – I would not have to live in a cave for ever, he had explained with enthusiastic innocence. Mohammad would eventually be a worthy suitor with a house, running water *and* electricity. It certainly hadn't been the deciding factor, and I wonder that it hadn't had the opposite effect. I don't think I had believed him really. The idea had been like a wispy cloud on the horizon, a rumour far away and insubstantial, as likely to disperse as to develop into anything.

Only recently the cloud had filled out a little when some UNESCO or USAID people, who had actual drawings and plans of the future village, visited. The idea of the settlement, to remove the inhabitants from the archaeological site, had been put forward ten years earlier by USAID, who had estimated around two hundred tribal members. They were allowing for a few more people now but I still had doubts about their statistics. I knew the cited infant mortality rate of 50 per cent was no longer true. Since I arrived lots of babies had been born (and injected), and still no one had died. The Bdoul were beginning to take advantage of the free medicines and free hospital stays, but not yet of the free contraceptives.

I looked back at the hillside as Mohammad encouraged our mule, 'Dah . . . dah-wll,' down towards Petra. It didn't look big enough for enough little domed houses – with the stables and yards of the drawings – to be built, let alone for each to have a view over the house in front, as the architect promised. And it was barren and isolated; the cloud was still a long way away.

I had to learn a new sound to drive the mule. I had found it hard enough to drive the donkey with the right sound, hrrwl, and now I had to learn another. I couldn't imagine the mule would know the difference but Mohammad laughed if I said anything other than dah-wl. (When we got a horse, I had to learn hirraa, and when we got a camel it was heet, heet.) But I hardly got near the mule. Even without the squealing children it was a kicker. Mohammad tried working it, he tried rewarding it and he certainly tried punishing it, but it kicked, with both legs straight out the back as soon as anyone approached, until one afternoon a couple of months later it blew up like a balloon and died in a snorting heap on top of the cave. The young nishaama gathered with their donkeys and towed it between them down to the wadi where Mohammad poured kerosene on it, set it alight and left it to rot. The smell of our dead mule lingered near the paved road for the rest of the summer.

The Treasury – My Husband's Workplace

Before I started work I had often gone up to visit Mohammad at the Treasury. Now I only went on Fridays but the action still ran like a well-rehearsed play, changing only a little with the seasons, and the number and nationality of the tourists.

As I emerge from the short canyon below the Treasury, the vendors call, '*Ta'ali ishrubi shay.*' Come, drink tea.

Between the mouth of the Siq and the steps of the monument their tables stand in the midday sun in a straggled row. Precious pieces of weathered board balance on thin wooden legs or are propped up on walls of rocks. There is a tin-lined wooden box filled with water in which triangular cartons of orange drink bob. The box's Arabic name *thilaaja* misleadingly translates as freezer. The ground here in the forecourt, like that of the Siq and most of the *wadis*, is rough with rounded boulders, pebbles and sand, and thick with oleander bushes. There are also lighter green broom bushes with longer branches of needle leaves hanging over like horses' tails.

Behind the tables, in between the bushes, Mohammad and the calling vendors (all from the Bdoul: Mohammad-h, two Musas, two Alis, Sliman and Awath-e) crouch around a tiny teapot perched on a little fire. The three stones the pot is balanced on are so close together there is barely room to insert the twigs and there is only a wisp of a flame, but the aromas of wood fire and syrupy tea are overwhelming. They shuffle up among the bushes and arrange a sack for me to sit on. Musa gives me the first glass, which I set down quickly in the sand before it burns my fingers. It is always sweeter than the tea we make at home, and stronger too, so my lips curl imagining the harshness of it, but I never insult them by refusing.

Mohammad-h's eyes glint. '*Mohammad bidu yit-jowaz.*' Mohammad wants to marry. It is his usual line. He glances at Mohammad and waits for my reaction.

In the beginning I don't understand what he is saying so he doesn't get a reaction. Later, when I do understand him but don't have the Arabic to answer, I have to stifle my reaction, which is the frustrating stage. But eventually the day does come when I am able to say, 'Too bad, I'm standing on his neck' – the very satisfying Arabic equivalent of 'I've got him under my thumb' – teasing them both.

Mohammad plays along with them and never reassures me, but I'm sure we have an understanding. He gave up that option when he asked me to marry him. And he can see that most of the men with more than one wife have twice as many problems. Besides, he discovers all sorts of other things to do with his money.

Noises come from the Siq. Mounted on horseback, American tourists pop out exclaiming, 'Wa-ow, isn't that fan-tas-tic.' While they are still trying to capture their first glimpse of the famous façade on film, the horsemen push their feet out of the stirrups and grab at their arms yelling, 'Down now . . . photo down!' – in their haste to get back to the Rest House in case they get another turn.

The little pot of tea and second wives are forgotten as the merchants straighten their *mendeels*, grab fake coins and nickel necklaces studded with blue scarabs off their tables, and fall on the new arrivals from all sides. 'Hey, Mistrr. You look!' I huddle into the bushes.

When the whole group is dismounted and the guide starts his spiel the salesmen hang back, just a little, but as soon as he finishes they follow, first into the Treasury and then on down the canyon. They come back to the teapot discussing their sales and the ones that got away.

The Americans were the best for business. They never had long in Petra, a couple of hours at the most, but they seemed to love being able to bargain and the trinkets all cost very little. Mohammad remembered flattening Pepsi bottle tops and putting them into the fire to render them unrecognisable before selling them as antique coins for a couple of dollars.

Germans, on the other hand, usually stayed out at the Rest House Hotel for several days. They read about the Nabataeans before coming to Petra and took Bedouin guides to find the coiled rock snake guarding the ancient necropolis on the way to Jabal Haroon, or the camels carved in relief in a narrow valley beyond the Monastery. They tried to buy ancient coins and pottery and wouldn't have been fooled by Mohammad's copies, which I suspected those lovely Americans had recognised but bought anyway, to give the enterprising young lad some income.

There were English and French, fewer Italians and Spaniards, and very occasionally a group of Russians. I was surprised they even came, but they did – insipid and cashless, but Mohammad still managed to swap *shabriyas* for binoculars, *mendeels* for cameras, and once an agate necklace for a ladies' watch because mine had stopped working. He put it excitedly on my wrist and it lasted several years.

Arabs were few and far between. A few remembered seeing the TV interview Mohammad had agreed to, which had been filmed and aired shortly after we married. Mohammad had been proud of the attention and for him I had sat uncomfortably through it – in a hot corner of our yard so their lighting would be right, and unable to understand much. Mohammad loved being in the spotlight and sometimes brought groups of school-children up to our cave. Little crowds of girls called 'Hallo, hallo, HALLO' into my face so insistently that even if I could speak their language I could hardly get a word in. It made me angrier that Mohammad found questions like 'How does she get up the hill?'

funny enough to translate, and I would go into the cave and shut the door, or if we were at the Treasury I'd walk away.

Mohammad couldn't understand my behaviour. 'They are just young girls. They find it interesting that you can leave the world of paved streets, cars and houses to live in a cave in the middle of the desert.'

'I don't care what they find interesting,' I'd say, taking it out on him. 'I live in a cave in the desert to enjoy quiet afternoons with you, not to show a generation of Arab girls that there is more to life than a tile floor.'

When it doesn't look as if any more tourists will come, we wander home, calling into the shop for a can of something to add to our *tabekh* for dinner.

One-pot Dinner

Tabekh (from the Arabic for 'cook') is what we lived on – that and bread. *Tabekh* often reminded me of 'Stone Soup', the traditional fairy tale, because it could be made with as little as an onion, water, tomato purée and macaroni, but depending on what vegetables were in season and what cans of food we had, it was usually made with a great deal more.

Here's how.

Put the pot on the cooker (electric, gas, primus, fire) with a dash of olive or cooking oil, or Al-Ghazal vegetable ghee.

Chop up an onion and brown it in the oil.

Add a couple of chopped-up potatoes. Add other vegetables in season; courgettes, cauliflowers and aubergines were the only ones we ever had.

If you have tomatoes for cooking, chop some up now and fry them a bit too. If not, don't worry.

Cover with water and add salt, and if you didn't put tomatoes in, add two big spoons of tomato purée.

Bring to the boil and cook, stirring occasionally. If you would like it thicker, add a handful of pasta now, or a packet of noodle soup.

When the potatoes are cooked and the liquid is reduced, add the canned ingredients: corned beef, green beans, peas, mixed vegetables and sliced mushrooms were our options.

Or leave out the meat and canned vegetables and add buttermilk to the potatoes and macaroni. The variations are endless.

It's good with rice but we usually scooped it up with our *shraak* or *taaboon* bread.

Nowadays I add pieces of meat or chicken once the onion is browned. And I fry peppers, garlic and celery with the onion, too. And we can get carrots and fresh green beans, but I still cook it in one pot and serve it in the same flat-bottomed dish that we all eat out of.

The Local Store

It was before we were even married that Mohammad sent me to the shop for the first time. We needed tea and sugar and we couldn't see a child to send, even from our vantage point on top of the cave.

'I can't speak Arabic,' I pointed out.

1979. Mohammad and me in a tent.

The Siq – the entrance and exit to Petra.

Our cave – beautiful façade and dusty yard. Portable shower basin (against the wall) and fire-place (not quite ready to be taken inside).

Umm Laafi was careful not to enhance Maryam's beauty, in order to deter jealous thoughts – but it shone through anyway.

On our Wadi Sabra adventure with Ali-f and Raweya.

Rakhiya's father fed his goats extra barley so they raced home at the end of the day. Tents, tumbled ruins and ancient façades make up the landscape.

Agaela, and Husseina with her baby, pose with me at a wedding. I've got socks under my *ship-ships* to prevent cracked heels.

Mohammad enjoys a western custom. The proud father holding his baby girl.

The view from our cave ledge.

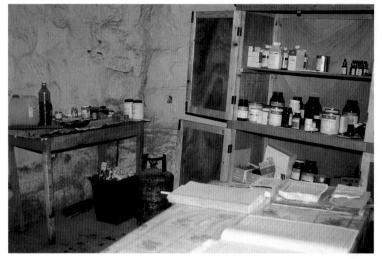

The clinic in a cave. The medications were all produced by Jordanian pharmaceutical companies.

I made bread daily beside the 2000-year-old wall. The best locally grown wheat was wonderfully stretchy.

In the combined kitchen and living room area at my in-laws. The girls have new store-bought dresses to celebrate the Eid.

1982. The *ma-rush* with Mohammad's 'hanging gardens' was where we lived in the summer. Here Mum with Salwa on her lap, Umm Mahmoud with her boys, and Ali, behind Mohammad, enjoy a watermelon with us.

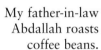

My father-in-law Abdallah roasts coffee beans.

Mum and Dad seemed to fit in alright. Here Dad and Abdallah play *sieja*. Dad considered himself a winner as long as he didn't get the droppings.

Salwa with our donkey. The saddle was Wadi Siyyagh willow-wood.

Raami in the 'high' chair that Mohammad made. A wonderful adaptation of a western innovation.

The view to the east from the top of our cave. Snow covers Petra.

Inside our cave. Unless they were being used, I stacked the blankets and *farrshas* up on the quilt table and covered them with the rug that Fraija brought from Mecca. A leaking jerry-can with its side cut off made a good toy-box.

Helpers (*nishaama*) skinning a goat for a wedding feast.

1984. Salwa was bored and Raami was asleep, but I was thrilled to meet Queen Elizabeth II, and Queen Noor too.

The cave we left had become a real home with glass windows. The climbing *majnoona* and shady *ma-rush* can be seen here from the kitchen door.

Extraordinary tattooed and lined face of Fa<u>th</u>iya, my mother-in-law's aunt.

A wedding procession; lots of *thaubs*, *mendeels* and *mudragas*.

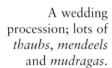

1985. Our cave in the hillside on the ledge: fences and gates to protect children and plants; drum for hot showers; cave for car behind pile of dirt above canvas tent. Royal Tombs beyond, with Palace Tomb far left.

'Never mind, I will tell you what to say.' He was quick! So my Arabic lesson for the day was: '*Nos wagiyat shay wa nos ruttle sukrr.*' Half a *wagiya* of tea and half a *ruttle* of sugar. I loved the idea of having names for 250 grams, and for three kilos, and I loved the words they used.

I said it over and over as I walked along the path to the Fum-al-Wadi. '*Nos wagiyat shay wa nos ruttle sukrr, nos wagiyat . . .*' The slope up to the cave that held the shop was filled with tethered horses. Their stomping had churned the ground up to a powdery dung-smelling dust but that wasn't as bad as the bony flanks, chomping bits and fly-flicking tails I had to walk between, or the eyes of their owners who were sitting about in front of the shop waiting for their tourists to return. I nearly forgot my rhyme. I headed for the dark cave entrance and once I was inside I felt strangely safer, although I couldn't see a thing.

The horsemen came to recognise me over the years and they would call out friendly *salaams* so I got to know them, young and old, but I never felt completely safe when I had to make my way through their crowded, tail-flicking horses.

When my eyes became accustomed to the gloom I recited my order to the man who was standing behind the cluttered counter. His whitish *mendeel* was like an awning over his bearded face, his eyes were in the shadow but he nodded and weighed tea and sugar into paper bags. I would never forget the lesson.

At that time tourists could buy stamps, and have their cards postmarked 'Petra', at the post agency run by Awwad in a cave below the museum. He sold batteries there, too, for the cassette players, so the *nishaama* could weep to Umm Kalthoum singing half-hour-long love songs, and when he went to Aqaba he brought back beer for those same customers. Ali-f's father, the Hajj Mutleg, had a tiny shop in a rescued ruin that sat like a wart on the flat tip of the Argoob Jmea-aan where he weighed *heeshy* (Bedouin tobacco) from sacks, kerosene from jerry-cans and hemp rope from great coils lying by the back wall. Gismih bought the fatal sweet for her son from a musty shop further up the valley, so musty that, tragically, when he started to choke and she cried 'poison', no one thought to turn him over and thump him on the back. Trunks in tents got padlocks and doors in hillsides opened intermittently for as long as it took to sell a carton of cans of Carnation evaporated milk or quality Gold Star cigarettes, exported to Saudi, where there were no taxes, and smuggled back in.

The shop in the Fum-al-Wadi was the closest to our cave. Although it was only about three by four metres with wooden crates turned on their sides stacked up to the roof for shelves, I discovered, as the years went by, that the Hajj Salaama sold practically everything.

Besides sugar and tea he weighed out (irritatingly precisely) long or short rice, brown or orange lentils and sea-green olive oil. Cans – of sardines (with or without pimento), corned beef, tuna fish, humus, *fool* (brown beans), tomato purée, vegetable ghee and evaporated milk – were stacked in pyramids. On the counter he had matches and Ottoman cigarette papers, but the packets of cigarettes were underneath and the sacks of *heeshy* were in the corner behind him. He had little packets of powdered Turkish coffee and pots to cook it in. He had Turkish delight and petit-beurres and delicious shortbread called *ghoraibeh* which was hard to resist. Strangely, for a few months in 1980, the Hajj sold cans of New Zealand 'Fresh-Up' (apple juice and orange) produced in Nelson, with apples from the orchard I grew up on.

Plain black material for *mudragas*, shiny flowery acrylics for under-dresses and satiny stripes for quilt covers were folded into dusty plastic bags. One or two scarves, a *mendeel*, trousers and acrylic socks were there too. There were cardboard boxes on some of the shelves that the Hajj delved into for skeins of black or white sewing yarn and big needles to stitch mattress covers or for huge needles to sew goat-hair tent-strips and even for spools of sewing-machine thread and treadle sewing-machine needles, for which I became a regular customer. Another box contained plain black hair clips which he sold by the dozen to the young girls who used them to batten their long fringes down over their cheeks. There were plastic shoes: black sandals or lace-ups for men, black slip-ons with imprinted bows and squashed toes for women, and *ship-ships* (a kind of plastic flip-flop) for everyone. Mohammad remembered the black plastic dress-shoes his parents had bought for him when they went on a trip to the hospital in Ma'an, and how thrilled he had been to have them and how shiny he had tried to keep them.

The Hajj Salaama had other departments too; if we needed an aluminium frying pan or enamel teapot we could get one. We could choose between good quality 'Arcroc' tea glasses made in France and cheap copies made in Turkey, but the only drinking glasses available were plastic-wrapped sets in polystyrene trays from which the flowers peeled in the first warm wash. He stocked rubber and leather washers for the primuses and Tilley lamps, silky Butterfly mantles for a clear bright light and ingenious *nakashas* for poking clear the jets. There were plastic 20-litre jerry-cans, bulky but light, stuffed in the highest corner. Sacks filled the rest of the space and contained balls of dried yoghurt, rock salt, lentils and sugar. Rope, thick and thin, plastic and hemp, lay coiled on the sacks and sometimes a horse decoration – a woven goat-hair bridle with cowrie shells sewn onto it – hung from a nail.

The other thing each shopkeeper kept was the 'notebook'. If he was illiterate he got the customer himself to enter what he still owed, or he kept the entries in his head till the end of the day when one of his schoolchildren could bring the page up to date. Customers who earned a wage usually settled their debts on pay day, others sold a goat at the Friday market and crossed off their debts then, but there were a few, and they were notorious, who managed to fill, apparently without conscience, a page in every notebook in Petra and some in Wadi Musa too.

But Mohammad had given me the right money to pay for the tea and sugar that day so I handed it over, and carried my paper packets back to enjoy that cup of tea with him, overlooking the world together.

The City and Spirits

Despite the usefulness of the shops in the valley, there were some things we could find only in Amman.

On Mohammad's first trip to Amman after we were married, he came home with a galvanised-iron water drum. It could hold 160 litres and had a lid and a tap. Before that we had used a 40-gallon bitumen drum with the top cut off, and scooped the water out with a bowl. Mohammad built a stone platform for the new drum in the kitchen corner. I put a plastic bowl on the floor below the tap and there was just room above the drum and below the rock roof to lift the lid and empty the jerry-cans. No one ever needed to dip a sandy-bottomed bowl into my clean water again.

On another trip he came home with wedding rings in a little velvet pouch.

'You're crazy!' I couldn't believe his foolishness. 'How could you know my size?'

'I tried it on my little finger. It will fit exactly,' he said determinedly, and it did, I had to admit admiringly. They were beautiful too – plain bands of eighteen-carat gold, just like I think I would have chosen myself but wider (heavier and more expensive) than I probably would have allowed.

A few times a year we went to Amman together. The *services* left the village straight after the dawn prayers at four thirty or five in the morning and they usually filled up for the return trip before noon so we had to leave home early and often stayed over in Amman.

In summer we woke up on the ledge. The white moon slipped behind the Crusader castle as we drank tea and we trekked up through the Siq in the starlight. There were some spots in the Siq where the cliffs leaned right over and no light got down at all. There we held hands. We drove east into the sunrise then onto the Desert Highway with its heavy trucks.

In winter we went up to Wadi Musa the night before and stayed with Abu Ali, the old watchman who, in a photo on the cover of a Lonely Planet Guide to the Middle East, leans against the columns of the Treasury. He lived in a traditional house with the cosy smells of the juniper beams in the roof and the whitewashed stone of the walls. His wife pampered us with woollen quilts. '*Enti dafiyeh?*' she asked every few minutes. Are you warm enough? She got up at four in the morning to light the kerosene heater, make fresh bread and encourage us, '*Kuloo, kuloo,*' to eat olives and creamy yoghurt before setting off.

I didn't like Amman. It seemed to have all the squalor of a city with none of the glamour. We had to go downtown to get souvenirs for Mohammad's stall. The noise of the car horns was constant. In the summer there wasn't a breath of wind, it got up to 40 degrees and smelled. In winter it was freezing and when it rained the passing cars threw up black slop. It was difficult to browse because the vendors practically dragged us into their shops as soon as we slowed down to look. 'Welcome,' they called and, 'You look,' which was enough to make me quicken my step. The prices were seldom marked, never fixed and always higher for a foreigner. I used to send Mohammad back to buy once I'd figured out what I wanted.

I wasn't the only female on the streets. I saw modern young women in trouser suits, with lipstick and long dark hair; round Palestinian matrons in sheer white shawls and dresses heavy with embroidery, and occasionally begging gypsies with thick fair plaits and colourful circular skirts, but I still felt uncomfortable about the looks I attracted. Sometimes I felt someone crowd closer than necessary on the street and I would quicken my pace. Then Mohammad would look around darkly to see who was bothering me.

Slowly though, as I got to know my way round and became a regular sight on the streets, my feelings changed. I didn't fool anyone with my *mudraga* and scarf (once I got pregnant I didn't fit into my jeans) but when I understood a shopkeeper informing his neighbour, 'That's the *ajnebiya* who lives with the Bedouin', I felt a little better . . . still a foreigner, but a recognised and accepted one.

My coup came years later in the narrow Italian Hospital street in Amman, where the balconies are so crowded with second-hand clothes that they seem to touch. I was back in western clothes, once again a foreigner. A young trader with a barrowful of socks was calling out, '*Joozeen jerabat ib dinar.*' When he saw me glance at the barrow, he called out in English, doubling the price, 'Two pairs of socks; *two* dinars.' This attracted more attention so there was quite an audience as I replied, not missing a beat, '*Ya'ani, itha bishtiree bil arabi ahsen li.*' (So if I buy them in Arabic I'm better off). Even the barrow boy laughed and I felt quite at home.

Opposite the central al-Hussein mosque in Amman was the high-ceilinged indoor Souq-al-Bukharia, the market of Bukhara. A narrow corridor ran between the facing rows of booths, each a separate shop with a different specialty, from German Solingen scissors and hair cutters to Chinese plastic dolls with sockets so weak they lost their arms with the first pull. From the first booth, once I rediscovered my ability to sew, I bought embroidery cotton and *marka* – the grid that made embroidering intricate cross-stitch patterns on the plain *mudraga* material possible. From a booth further along I got the 'diamonds' Rakhiya had given me the money to buy for her.

The glittering fake-crystal set of necklace, bracelet and clip-on earrings was mounted on a tacky piece of cardboard and covered in crackly cellophane. I couldn't believe it was really what she wanted but Mohammad assured me it was. 'Frivolous,' he said. 'For the same price she could have bought a ring of 21-carat gold.' But she was young and wanted to be frivolous. Her delightful smile on seeing it was a treasure. She was thrilled, tried the whole set on immediately, and wore it to every wedding for seasons to come.

Halfway along the corridor we had a haven where our friend and souvenir supplier, Badr, greeted us '*Ahlan-wa-sahlan*', put high stools for us in the passageway outside his booth and sent a boy off for drinks. He came back with a tray with hot glasses of black tea stuffed with mint leaves and sugar portions in plastic eggcups. In winter he brought hot yellow camomile or thick white *sah-lab*, a custardy drink with a pile of coconut and pistachio nuts on top and a sprinkle of cinnamon. I warmed my hands on the glass and drank it off the spoon.

Badr was a large man who filled the narrow space behind his glass counter. His beaming smile was nearly hidden behind the fringe of nickel pendants, with bright blue glass beads to ward off the evil eye, that dangled along the front of the booth. The shelves behind him were stacked with beautiful mother-of-pearl-inlaid boxes and backgammon sets, bejewelled *shabriyas* and cheaply carved caravans of olive-wood camels.

Later when I had a baby with me he lifted up a piece of the counter and came out so I could go in and change the nappy privately on the floor.

Now and then we ran into other Bdoul tribesmen. We dragged each other off to the Salaam or Cairo restaurant, for breakfast or lunch depending on the time of the day (the fare was the same, spit-roast chickens, half a one each) and we argued for ages for the honour of paying.

And then there was the trip home. Sometimes we were the last passengers needed to fill the *service* and left immediately. Other times we waited for hours in the back-street bus station for a final passenger. Now and then the only *service* was from Ma'an and we hoped we could get the driver to take us home for an extra fare.

It was 260 kilometres from Amman to Petra and it took over three hours, sometimes well over, even when we got our own car.

'*Twakilna ala-Allah*,' the driver would say as he headed onto the highway. And counting on God we certainly were for the highway was always busy with heavily laden trucks bringing cargo from the port of Aqaba to Amman or on to Iraq.

The trucks looked exciting; the geometric patterns made by the slats that contained the loads were painted in bright colours, and the artists had exercised their creativity on the tailboards by painting 'hands of Fatima' and writing calligraphically '*ma'-sha'allah*' to protect the occupants from the evil eye. But the windscreens were reduced to half; by silken fringes pinned across the top at such exact intervals that the drawing pins were part of the decoration, and by strips of fake long-haired sheepskin pinned to the dashboards in the same fashion. The mirrors served as hangers for prayer beads and fluffy dice, models of the Ka'aba and holograms of eyes that winked as they jiggled. The journey was a game of chance and we would agree out loud with our driver, '*Ala-Allah*.'

Over the years several people I knew were killed in car accidents on that highway and many others had accidents.

Once on the road there were plenty of delays. There was no

weight-restriction control so huge fissures had opened in the bitumen, ten-centimetre steps down to the next level for a metre or two and then bang, the step back up – sometimes our driver avoided them altogether by swerving into the line of oncoming traffic. We stopped at roadside stalls for passengers to buy watermelons or boxes of tomatoes; a radiator boiled or a tyre punctured; once we made an 80-kilometre detour to Karak because our driver recognised the wreckage of his friend's car on the side of the road and wanted to see him in hospital, and another time we met our neighbour al-Jimedy in the Department of Antiquities truck and got a ride with him, only to detour 10 kilometres off our road, within 40 kilometres of home, because he decided he wanted to visit his cousin.

But usually it was straightforward, counting off the landmarks, trucks bearing down on us, trying not to panic as the driver's head nodded sleepily. 'Have a cigarette,' I'd say to keep him awake, 'a date bun.'

Hours later coming through the Sh-rah I'd get my first glimpse of Jabal Haroon over to the west, and even though it disappeared again as we wound down into Wadi Musa, and we still had to find a pick-up driver willing to take us, bumping along, back down the Siq, there was something about that familiar shape that made me already glad to be home.

There were rare occasions when Mohammad and Ali-f needed more souvenirs but I didn't need a new resident's permit or to stock up on tampons, and I took advantage of those times to have an evening all on my own. Mohammad didn't seem to like the idea of leaving me alone and at first I didn't know why he was so hard to convince.

'I'd rather stay by myself.'

'Won't you be afraid?'

'Is there anything to be afraid of?'

'No, but . . .'

'Then I won't be,' I insisted.

Considering our home was possibly the tomb of a whole Nabataean family, I'm surprised I never gave them much thought. By the time I could understand Husseina telling about the strange Bedouin tents she had seen as she escaped from her first husband at night through the mountains – full of people in joyful celebration but of which no sign could be found the next day, or Dakhil-allah telling of the *ghoula* which had over-whelmed him near Jabal Haroon and nearly suffocated him as she forced him to suckle from her breast, I had stayed by myself so often I knew I wouldn't be troubled by any Nabataean or old Bdoul spirits.

'I'll enjoy staying by myself,' I insisted.

'Salem or Ibraheem can come and stay.'

And I'll feel as if I need to stay up to entertain them, I thought.

I wasn't afraid of being on my own. It never occurred to me that everyone would know Mohammad was away and I was a woman alone, way out of shouting distance in my cave on the ledge. And I don't think Mohammad ever doubted me or thought I needed watching. But although I must have had visitors on such evenings, I never felt unsafe (or tempted). I was young and innocent and in love and treated all visitors as Mohammad's friends. If anyone ever had any other intentions, my attitude must have shown them that *I* didn't.

The Plastic Scorpion

Late one afternoon Mohammad was drinking tea out on the ledge when I discovered a flat black scorpion on the floor under the kitchen table. He had just arrived home from Amman and I immediately suspected he had bought it, plastic, from the toy shop in the Souq-al-Bukharia to tease me.

'Ah, I know your tricks! Think you can fool me, do you?' I called out to him.

'What tricks?' His question came back lazily.

'Think I don't know a plastic scorpion when I see one?'

I heard him move even before 'Don't touch it' came through the air and he was beside me with a stick. 'I didn't buy a plastic scorpion, where is it?'

I played cool – it was likely to be part of his act.

'Still right there,' I nodded towards it, 'exactly where you put it.'

He poked it – the scorpion was suddenly a fine natural specimen, venom-filled tail curled over at the ready, moving warily on spidery legs like a boxer in a ring, not sure from which direction the attack would come.

It came from above, and with a disgusting crunch, as Mohammad crushed it firmly with the stick.

Gleefully he looked to me for approval and I read his mind in a flash. The next trip to Amman would bring a bona fide plastic scorpion.

I still wasn't used to scorpions. In New Zealand we didn't have such dangerous things.

I had to remind myself to look whenever I picked anything up off the ground, and I learned to go straight for the kill. And I always wished that there was some way other than the 'yeeuu-uck' that wracked my body and escaped my lips to deaden the disgusting crunch they made.

Tempting Fate

I went alone to Amman when I thought I was pregnant. It was August, the Eid Ramadan again, but ten days short of our first wedding anniversary because the Islamic calendar is lunar and moves forward about ten days every year. Kevin introduced me to their doctor at the Italian Hospital and the test results were positive.

I skipped back down the Siq despite the heat and I remembered to buy a packet of sweets to share with the guys at the Treasury. They asked Mohammad what the occasion was.

'Tempting fate,' they muttered when he told them I was one and a half months pregnant. 'Something is bound to go wrong.'

Their wives didn't mention new babies till they cried. They looked at me sideways and I could see them thinking, 'Irresponsible foreign habits will be the ruin of them,' but they slapped Mohammad on the back, cheered him for his 'good work' and invoked God to give us a boy . . . 'A camel herder, inshallah.'

We didn't discuss such things much but as we walked home Mohammad did say, 'Ili yeji min Allah, hai ya-u-Allah.' That could be translated as 'Whatever God sends we will welcome', but means even more. More like: 'Whatever God sends we will celebrate the arrival of', and I knew we would.

The Makeena

The *makeena*, or sewing machine, was a wedding present from my Dutch relations – they sent the money and we bought it in Wadi Musa. It was a 'Butterfly', made in China. It was just like the old machines I had seen in historic houses in New Zealand, with the same heavy black treadle and wrought-iron metalwork, the shiny veneer woodwork and the curly golden lettering painted across the body. The little wheels faced one way, so I could wheel it sideways but had to drag it backwards and forwards.

The whole community saw the *makeena* arrive – we all noticed if a vehicle moved in the valley and we always watched to see where it went and what it meant, and everyone assumed I was going into business, though I had no such intentions.

Women appeared on my ledge with clutches of children, congratulated me on my new sewing machine and asked if I sewed, '*Bit-khaiti?*', as we drank our tea. They produced heavy lengths of silky polyester and looked hopeful.

I had grown up getting congratulations for things I had attained – a certain age or a place, other than last, in the Waimea Harriers cross-country race on a Saturday afternoon, but now I was learning another use for the word. I was congratulated on our donkey, and then our mule; on the new *mudraga* I'd had made by Yusra; on a silver ring Umm Mahmoud had slipped off and insisted I took when I admired it; on the *farrshas*, blankets and cupboards full of utensils we bought from Mufleh when his Swiss wife went home and he wanted money, quick, to follow her; and I had to get used to noticing my friends' new possessions too, so I could congratulate, and not offend them.

The women had heard that I could sew when we got married;

it had been discussed along with my other merits – my fair skin, golden hair and watch, my being a nurse, and being able to drive and read and write – and besides hoping for a local seam-stress, they also came to support us, which made it even more difficult to evade. I had always sewn for the fun of it and didn't want it to become work. I had never sewn without a pin-on Simplicity pattern, either, so I made excuses.

'I'm pregnant' was the obvious one, accepted without doubt because they all knew how dangerous working the treadle while you were pregnant could be – that, and dancing, were definitely to be avoided. Work was all right, especially lifting – jerry-cans of water to empty into a drum; bundles of firewood onto your head; goat-skins full of yoghurt out of the low back of the tent, where you had to bend over double, to the front where you had set up the tripod to churn the butter; and heavy rocks to secure the tent pegs. So being pregnant was my public excuse. Of course, I knew a bit of sewing would be fine. We scrounged an old chair from Nazzal's Camp and I was able to let my *mudra-gas* out as I got more pregnant, sew pillow covers in the local style (bright satin pockets for the ends with white slip-over sleeves for leaning on), and take up Mohammad's new jeans which were invariably too long.

Salem and Awath found me treadling away and managed to get the better of me. Sewing for them was fun.

'*Thiyegi min hni*,' they insisted. So I made darts down the front of their shirts, against my better judgement. The underarm seams had failed to turn the XLs they had bought into XSs like they were. They didn't care where the seams were or how com-fortable the sleeves were as long as the shirts were tight, and they let me in on who they were hoping to impress.

Rakhiya also had the knack of getting her own way with me. (She still refused to return to her husband but still wasn't divorced. It took another year and many days of anger and frus-tration to convince everyone, father, uncles, husband and brothers-in-law, that she had become a determined young woman and was not going to change her mind.) 'Bring me *kilfeh* from Amman,' she coaxed, and when I found out it was braid and brought it, she got me so caught up in the creation that I was soon sewing it onto the *mudraga*. And I couldn't help putting a facing in the V-neck and tidying up all the other imperfections the seamstress from Wadi Musa had left, by which time I had just about remade the garment. Whenever Rakhiya had a new piece of material I was drawn into the project. From the time we first met she had been giving to me: scarves, chatter, Arabic words, *shraak*, shards of ancient pottery, leftover *fatteh* to take home for Mohammad, drinking yoghurt in season and fresh eggs on occasion, and at last there was something I could give to her. She gave me a chance to perfect my *mudraga*-making techniques with none of the pressure of a commission, and she was a sassy model.

When I realised how simple sewing *madragas* was, I set to to make one for each of Mohammad's sisters for the Eid. But in between times, for the next couple of years at least (even when I was no longer pregnant, then I said I didn't have time), the drive belt hung loose and the *makeena* stayed folded inside its wooden table.

The Pilgrimage to Mecca

The Hajj or pilgrimage to Mecca is the fifth pillar of Islam. All Muslims, male and female, should intend to make the trip at least once if they are financially able. The person who completes the pilgrimage is also called the Hajj (or Hajja).

There were a few people in the valley called the Hajj. I found it confusing but they always seemed to know which one was being talked about. There was the Hajj Nuwaija, a wonderful leathery little man with a teeth-baring grin and carefully trimmed goatee whom I had met at Abdallah's tent; and the Hajj Salaama, who ran the shop in the Fum-al-Wadi and left one of his sons to look after it five times a day while he walked down to the Monastery valley to make the call to prayer. (The big cave next to the clinic was the Petra mosque; it had a door and enough rugs to carpet the concrete floor but seldom any worshippers. The Bedouin who prayed did it wherever they were, and on Fridays even the Hajj Salaama went up to the mosque in Wadi Musa.)

Ali-f's father, the shopkeeper, was also a Hajj. He had wanted desperately to go to Mecca but could not justify it with a wife and eight children to feed, till one night he dreamed he should go out and plough a patch of hillside below his tent. He was a man of faith and followed his vision to unearth enough pottery to pay for his trip and to buy gifts to give everyone on his return.

In 1979, six of the Bdoul prepared to Hajj. Between the Treasury and the clinic and the other social occasions I knew just about every one of the Bdoul now, adults and children too, so I got caught up in the preparations. At last I could do something in return for all the *laban* and *samin* I had been given by the cup and bowl-full.

I made them date loaves in my new gas oven which we bought because, on the day Mohammad saw it in Wadi Musa, a gift cheque arrived in our PO box from my great-aunt for its exact cost. (Despite the PO box, I now and then retrieved my letters from the distant tents of well-intentioned deliverers, but the cheque had been sensibly registered.)

About two weeks before the Eid of the Sacrifice, the pilgrims set off to Mecca in a big old bus with their bedrolls on the roof. The valley bustled as we all went round and loaded them up with food and wishes for God to keep them safe. '*Fi amaan Allah,*' we said in farewell, and off they went. We heard no more till the third night of the Eid when they returned, escorted by the enthusiastic *nishaama* who had gone up to Wadi Musa to meet the bus and bring them home.

If I had thought it confusing as to which Hajj they were talking about before, I could see it was going to get worse.

Dangers

We had another donkey of our own. We tied it to a bush on the side of the hill or, if it was wet, in the big cave almost hidden by the pile of dirt Mohammad had thrown off the ledge. I could go to get water whenever it suited me. My donkey-riding skills had improved and pregnancy didn't stop me either.

We still had a bit of water in the drum one afternoon but I was bored so I saddled up, jumped on and headed for the spring. It was cloudy and cold – I held my jacket round me and was glad of the flowery scarf keeping my ears warm. I passed the Pharaoh's column and as I went round the back of the Crusader castle a head popped out of an illegal excavation hole in the ground lower down the hill and arms waved at me. '*Wheen idki, a duniya sha-tiya.*'

I wasn't sure what he was saying and I couldn't tell who he was – his *mendeel* was folded inside out and wrapped around his head and face and he was the colour of the ground he climbed out of – but he ran up and caught hold of the halter so the donkey stopped. My lack of Arabic was not going to stop him getting his message through. He waved his arms at the dark clouds: '*Shita!*' He pointed emphatically at the valley: 'No!' He turned my donkey round, gave it a sharp slap to get it going and I was sent back home. A few raindrops fell on the way.

A rainbow appeared over Jabal Khubtha and darker clouds filled the sky beyond. It barely rained in Petra but when, within half an hour, the rumble of the flood, wall to wall in the *wadi*, reached my ears, I finally understood.

I was lucky that hillside was so lucrative. I was lucky the digger hadn't been too deep to see me and that he hadn't stayed hidden in case I gave his game away, or I would have been down at the source between the cliffs with no hope of escape.

Why didn't I recognise the dangers?

It was not only the rain that landed on Petra that flowed through the valley, but all the water that fell around the Wadi Musa village. The flank of the Sh-rah range, for a few kilometres north and south of the village, was like half a funnel which for thousands, possibly millions, of years had channelled the rain-water into the valley that ran down through the earthquake-formed canyon of the Siq, through Petra and into the Wadi Siyyagh, to dry up in Wadi Araba.

Usually, if there was actually enough rain to gather and run off, the flood only lasted for a few hours before revealing a fresh layer of land to be searched for coins or pottery shards, but every few decades there was a huge flood. Then it rained longer and harder and for days a river of mud and rocks pounded through the valley. If the flood still travelled through the Siq, it would reach 50 metres up the sides.

That would be why the Nabataeans built the dam. As they settled into Petra they decided to control the havoc-causing blessing. They built a dam across the entrance of the Siq and, by carving a railway-sized tunnel through the shoulder of rock to the north, diverted the flood into the little valley that ran around the back of Jabal Khubtha. They carved cisterns into the base of the mountain and channels to divert the water to them, and what didn't collect there flowed on down the Mataha valley and back into the Wadi Musa at the heart of the city, just below our cave where I had watched my first flood with Mohammad.

But the Nabataean dam hadn't lasted for ever. By the time Johann Ludwig Burckhardt rediscovered Petra in 1812, water had been flowing back through the Siq for hundreds of years. The present dam was built across the entrance after a tragedy in the spring of 1963 when twenty-eight French tourists were caught by a flash flood. The bus driver, who clung onto the water channel, and two girls who clung on to him survived, but the rest were swept away down the Valley of Moses and killed, along with their local guide and donkeys laden with supplies and luggage.

The men of Petra and Wadi Musa went out to help as soon as the flood had passed but they could only help in recovering bodies. Mohammad was twelve or thirteen and remembered most strikingly the oranges strewn with them all the way down the valley, caught in nature's filter of bushes and rocks. That flood of rocks and mud carried some victims all the way down to the Wadi Siyyagh. Some Saydiyeen tribesmen found one body much further down and ten years later they directed a team from the French embassy to recover it from its burial place in Wadi Maruan.

But the Nabataean dam and its modern copy only protected the Siq – the flood still ran through the Siyyagh and now I knew to be careful. There were enough sunny days to get drinking water on and I started using Nabataean cistern water for washing. There was a cistern at the base of the High Place which reaped several metres of water each time it rained. It would have been easy to clean up for drinking, too, but teaching everyone to use clean dippers would have been impossible.

Umm Awwad, who lived just across from it, always got her daughters to make tea and then insisted I stay while they made lunch. Their cave was airy and open enough to have the fire going inside if it rained, and it opened onto a rock terrace where it was lovely to sit if the weather was nice. There was seldom anything I *had* to do at home so it was easy just to sit and watch the children play and the baker curl *shraak* after *shraak* onto the dome of the *saj*.

The donkey grazed happily until it was time to load him up and drive him home.

Whenever I walked past a home with people in it, they invited me in. I found it difficult to get myself away. But I also got very good at sitting comfortably with my thoughts. My hostess might go off to another cave to prepare food. Or she might chat about me with a visiting friend and agree that Mohammad had picked the right woman: how it was good that I wore a *mudraga* and a headscarf and that I was nice and quiet. Knowing quietness was an asset before I could talk too much was a great advantage.

Rattam Stumps

The hillside we lived on was a typical Petra hillside with buried stone walls, pottery shards, sea-squill bulbs and scattered bushes. The Nabataean houses hadn't been excavated then and on cold winter afternoons we took a sack and a pick and went out looking for *rattam* stumps for our fire. Even if the days were sunny, the winter nights were cold, and when the wind brought dark clouds from the west with the promise of rain it was cold in the daytime too. When cruel white clouds scudded across on the wind from the east, the dryness became positively icy.

When Mohammad detected a buried stump he cleared the sandy earth away and planned his attack. Forearm-sized stumps he hammered out with a rock, persistent roots he cut off with the pick. Occasionally we filled our sack from the one big stump, and invariably we got warm digging it up.

Sometimes Rewe'e's daughters, who stayed out with their goats till dusk, came over and scoured the shards of pottery we uncovered for interesting painted patterns to offer the tourists the next day, and Abu Nawas's young boys came down to pass the time and helped us enthusiastically, digging down with their bare, chapped hands, showing off and getting warm.

Back in our yard we tipped out our prize. Mohammad always stacked all of our pickings in a pyramid in the *mangle* ('brazier' sounds altogether too fancy a name for the half jerry-can it was made out of), and ignoring my 'that's far too much, we've got enough here for two nights', doused them in kerosene, flicked his kerosene-filled lighter and set them alight. He loved these bonfires. We stood around the fire out in the yard with the wind fanning the flames until only the embers were left.

Things became desperate if the clouds were dark and released their rain and I had to give in to Mohammad and let him take the fire into the new room. No amount of argument from him got it far inside the door, but the smoke still billowed around the whitewashed walls and into the maroon curtains. We crouched low or sat on sacks on the floor. The flames blazed fiercely, the rain drummed on the tin roof (and dripped through), the smell of kerosene soon gave way to the restoring aroma of the wood and once enough smoke had escaped I got up and balanced a pot of tea on the edge of the fire.

Later, once all the wood had burned, we dragged the *mangle* of red-hot coals into the cave and closed the door. We stuffed sacks into the windows to stop the wind from coming through the netting, put sponge-rubber *farrshas* around the fire, drank mugs of hot milk, played *shish-bish* (backgammon) and, until we had to go to the toilet, forgot the cold and dark outside.

1980: Cards

Later in the winter, Mohammad began disappearing after dinner. He said he went down to the Department of Antiquities cave to play cards with his friends and a bulldozer driver from Amman who was staying there while he worked in Petra.

I made our bed up early but sat in it alone (I refused a fire when it was just for me). I listened to the BBC crackle over the radio, but the reception was pretty poor in the back of the cave so it wasn't a great loss when the radio packed up. I wrote letters – great big long lonely ones that I never sent, and sometimes I knitted, but, even for my own baby, knitting without company or TV wasn't much fun. A book might have helped, but apart from *The Thorn Birds*, which some tourists had left for me with one of the vendors and I had read in four days, I couldn't get one anywhere.

'It's too much. I didn't get married to cry myself to sleep alone in bed.'

'But we don't do anything – just play cards,' argued Mohammad when he came home one night to find me sniffling under the blankets.

'At least you do it with other people,' I accused.

'Come then, but I think it won't be much fun. No other women come.'

'I didn't marry you to be with other women.'

So from then on I went too. The radio they had on crackled with the 'Sowt-al-Filistine min Yerushalim-al-Quds', The Voice of Palestine from Jerusalem, broadcasting stirring songs, understandable even without the language. I'd sit and watch their card games and knit babies' booties in the Tilley-lamp light.

I began to see why Mohammad had stayed away so late – I

was getting addicted just watching the game. They didn't play for money, but they swore often enough: 'By God and my moustache if we were I'd clean you out!' They made great fun of teasing each other the next day and even for weeks after if a play had been particularly embarrassing. One night they only had three players, so I joined in and showed them I had been watching. From then on I had a turn most nights like one of the boys.

After that, Mohammad bought a new set of plastic playing cards early every winter – from Amman, because the shops in Wadi Musa only stocked paper ones. Salaama al-Mokhtar always looked after last year's pack, but after a while we could spot the joker back-on. Mohammad fixed the radio too. Ignoring, or happily unable to read, the 'Caution, electrical hazard, to be opened only by a certified electrician' sticker on the back, he undid the screws and fiddled around until he had the pointer spinning smoothly across the stations once again.

Salaama and his wife Maryam had a young family. He had been a driver in the army and now worked for the Department of Antiquities. He was the *mokhtar*, the mayor, which entailed registering births and deaths, and he was usually the one to represent the tribe on issues like the future settlement, but his effervescent and unselfconscious love of playing cards and *shish-bish*, and almost juvenile desire whenever he went to Amman or Aqaba to catch a Western at the cinema, and to weigh himself for a *shillin*, counteracted the seriousness. (Men, young and old and in-between, sit with old bathroom scales on the footpaths of Amman and Aqaba and I still don't know if they are meeting a need or just providing a means for people to give them alms.)

The bulldozer driver only stayed one year, so from then on Ali, Ali-f and Salaama came to our cave. We started soon after sunset every day, sometimes before, and played till late.

'*Haati a-shish-bish*,' Salaama would say as he settled onto

the *farrsha*. And he'd ask for pillows too – '*Haati m-khudat*' –
he had an arthritic knee and always needed to stretch out.

'You're in a hurry to be beaten,' Mohammad said, opening
the backgammon box. 'Click, click', they stacked up their pieces
to fit in a game before dinner.

Sunset was usually dinnertime but Salaama might have eaten
early or might just get Maryam to heat his meal when he got
home. He thought nothing of calling for the *shish-bish* or pillows, just as at a friend's place in New Zealand we would have
thought nothing of reaching for them ourselves.

'*Tifuthuloo*.' In Arabic I could use expressions that my colloquial English no longer allowed. 'Partake' seems so much more
of an invitation than 'Come and get it'.

They folded the box and I put the dish of *tabekh* down
between them. Salaama always had a taste 'to please our sensi-
bilities', but otherwise rarely ate with us.

By the time we finished one of the others had arrived to make
up the foursome we needed. They all loved to cheat. It frustrated me no end, and I would ignore my partner flashing his
precious 2s or jokers to show me how many he had.
Mohammad would blatantly lick the back of the joker and stick
it to his forehead while he checked out the rest of his hand. For
him the point was to win, and to win by cheating if you could
get away with it was just as clever as winning by the rules; it was
always worth a try. I didn't have a moustache so couldn't swear
to win by it but I was never the favourite partner anyway – neither losing nor being teased about it bothered me.

Mohammad's father lectured him regularly on the amount of
sugar we must be going through because men wandered in
throughout the evening. They knew we were home, and ready to
make another pot of tea, and they knew that our game with its
fiery arguments or derogatory joking was always entertaining.
We thought a few pots of tea were a small price to pay for an
evening's distraction in our own home.

Holy Bread

'You can't do that!' There was a tone in Mohammad's voice I hadn't heard before. Was he aghast (at my stupidity), amazed (at my audacity) or horrified (at my carelessness)? I couldn't tell. He was clearly berating me for something . . . but I hadn't *done* anything.

We were at the Treasury eating the bread and tomatoes I had brought for lunch. To make the most of the warmth of the sun, for the short time it shone into the forecourt at this time of year, we had pushed his trinkets aside and were sitting on the wooden table dangling our legs.

'That's *haraam*!' Mohammad jumped to his feet and picked up the remnants of *taaboon* crust I had discarded. They were too burnt to consider eating. 'You can't just throw them there!'

'Why not? All of you throw your rubbish on the ground. At least the goats will eat my crusts, which is more than I can say for that sardine can or that banana skin.' They were right there in the gravel by the bread crusts but he didn't bother picking them up.

'But this is bread!'

A little silence followed while he waited for it to dawn on me . . . but it didn't so he explained. 'Bread is *ne'ma min Allah*, providence from God, and we don't tread it underfoot.' (So he was aghast at my stupidity.) He put the crusts well under the nearest bush, where only a scavenging goat could get them.

Little food was wasted despite the lack of refrigeration. When Umm Laafi made *fatteh* and there was some left (even after Abdallah had put a dollop on the rock for his mangy dog), she put it in a bowl, covered it with a pot lid or sugar sack 'against the (poisonous) starlight', and sent it with Laafi across the valley to us. I put it in the window and in the morning we fried it in the frying pan and feasted – Bedouin hash browns or refried beans.

The Road to Umm Sayhoon

Work began on the two and a half kilometres of road to the Umm Sayhoon settlement site at the beginning of 1980. It didn't come into Petra but began at the end of the present road, out near the entrance, and ran north along the side of the Sh-rah behind Jabal Khubtha. Apart from the occasional distant day-time rumble of the heavy machinery we might not have even noticed it if Abu Mahmoud hadn't landed the job of night watchman for the project and taken his family to live in a canvas tent on the side of the mountain.

Now I missed sitting with them every day at their cave. I missed Umm Mahmoud's calling from the path below the Ras, donkey loaded with jerry-cans, '*Tirridi mai?*', inviting me to fetch water with her. I missed the cuddles I got from the boys.

I decided to visit them.

It took me all morning to find their camp. Mohammad had pointed out the sand-hill I needed to climb up to get onto the Umm Sayhoon ridge, and that had been the easy part. Then I needed to follow it up to get to where it met the Sh-rah, but rock corridors and goat tracks led me astray and I got hot back-tracking. The ridge was covered in a scattering of crumbly stone that was alarmingly slippery. And it was hot, like a summer's day in Nelson, without a breath of wind, and I was pregnant. I still couldn't see how I could get round the steep side of the Sh-rah. I pulled my *mudraga* over my head and rested for a while in my shirt and trousers. It wasn't until three donkey riders appeared round a spur that I was able to detect the path. A prayer answered, I waved a confident 'salaam,' put my *mudraga* back on and followed the path back till I found the tent.

Ahmed had spotted me and was jumping up and down in front of the canvas tent that clung to the mountainside several metres above the track. '*Hiy ummi Fatima jet, hiy ummi Fatima jet*' – Here comes my mother Fatima, here comes my mother Fatima – he chanted as I scrambled up towards him. He giggled as I scooped him up. My friends were here, their skin was chapped, but these smiles were what I had come for.

The ease with which Umm Mahmoud left the 'comfort' of the cave and camped out here with her two small children amazed me. OK, so firewood uprooted by the heavy machinery was abundant and they could use the water from the tank, but they had a very small spot. If you slipped, you would roll down the mountain. Inside the ridge-pole tent and for a couple of metres in front they had scraped a level floor from the hard earth. The tent flaps at both ends were open now, but it was winter and at night it was cold and a stronger wind blew, which explained the stones holding the sides down. Their beds would fill the floor space.

Umm Mahmoud pulled a *jannabiya* out and made me sit down. She bustled about, apologising for leaving her proper pillows in her cave and rolling up an old quilt for me to recline against. Ahmed sat on my knee and I played 'Round and round the garden goes the teddy bear' on his podgy little hand. Mahmoud, who was always more reserved to start with, held out his hand to play too. They didn't understand the words but there was no confusing the tickles. While Umm Mahmoud built up the fire and made the tea, I played 'Incy wincy spider' and 'This little piggy went to market' with my little friends, ignoring the vastness and the harshness of the landscape – for the mountain peaks and canyons went on as far as the eye could see.

I visited them a few times and sometimes Mohammad came

too. We undoubtedly caused more work, but I couldn't stay away. Ahmed, since my breadmaking days, was claiming me as his mother.

One time I found Umm Mahmoud sifting flour, out of which lots of bran was separating. She said it was *sha'eir* and I, knowing that *sha'eir* was barley, or donkey food, thought I had either misunderstood or she was joking. But she wasn't and I hadn't. She had carefully picked the stones out of a few kilos of barley and Abu Mahmoud had taken it to the miller in Wadi Musa. She kneaded it differently and wouldn't let me help. She baked it deep in the fire under the hot sand. We stayed for dinner, which was *fatteh* of barley bread mushed up in *laban* with a pool of dark green olive oil instead of *samin* in the middle. We made balls and dipped them into the oil. The side dish of crisp raw onion wedges went with the meal like toast with soup. We loved it and went home and cleaned out a few kilos of our own barley for Mohammad to take to the mill, and me to learn to knead.

Work on the road continued slowly but by the middle of 1981 it was finished, bulldozed roughly right through to Beitha, and my friends were back in their cave.

Nabataean Inscriptions

Inscribed into the mauve and red rock on the way down from the High Place is a spot of writing, Nabataean writing in sensuous rectangular swoops like the rows of gold chains in the gold *souq* in Amman. When Mohammad first showed it to me he held back the branches of the juniper tree that protected it, but that has since been used to warm many hands and make many pots of tea so the inscription became vulnerable to attack by wind and rain and kids with sticks.

There are inscriptions and carvings wherever the Nabataeans have been – *salaams* and god-blocks and 'Aretas was here'. In Petra the most famous inscription, the only description in the city of all the gardens, cisterns and feast halls that went together to make up a burial complex, was on the Turkmaniya Tomb. I read about it in a book Ali-d gave me. He had no use for Iain Browing's *Petra*, which some tourists had left in his shop, but I read it from cover to cover. It described hidden treasures in remote cracks in the rocks all over the place and I discovered lots of them on social occasions.

I checked out the Turkmaniya Tomb when we went to visit Umm Laafi's cousin Rakhiya-n, who had just had a baby. I had only encountered her a couple of times and saw her rarely at the clinic so I might not have gone alone, but Umm Laafi suggested that if I wanted to, we could go together. I was a little bit worried about the implications. I knew that whatever gift (money) I gave her would be written on her memory till she could repay me, and as I was seven months pregnant it seemed like a blatant investment. 'That's the idea,' Umm Laafi made me understand. 'People help each other when they need it.' So under my mother-in-law's wing I set out for the Wadi Turkmaniya.

Hussein sat straight-backed on his mother's shoulder, one leg dangling down her back the other down her front, his arms wrapped tightly round her head like her *asaba*. She walked equally straight-backed, in her worn but washed *mudraga* and cracked plastic shoes, a confident guide along a tree-shrouded path. We passed the three-roomed, concrete-block school building, and soon the bamboo and oleander gave way to a garden of grapevines, pomegranate and apricot trees hedged with willow and tamarisk. Then the valley opened out.

I remembered galloping along here when we came back from Beitha on our mule and I knew why I hadn't noticed the tomb.

I had never ridden a galloping animal before and it had suddenly been so smooth and flowing and exhilarating – and I felt so lucky that I had Mohammad to cling to and that the mule had been able to carry us both – that that was all I had noticed.

The inscription, when I saw it, was a disappointment. It was a slab of words; a smoothly finished, unblemished rectangle of a sign, inconsistent with the rest of the melting rock façade. The feast halls and gardens had been erased by thousands of years of winter floods, and the bottom half of the tomb had suffered the same fate, standing soot-blackened and open to the morning sun.

The family – the Hajj Nuwaija of the teeth-baring grin and goatee, his wife Rakhiya-n and their nine children – was just camping here and didn't have a regular settled cave. The floor was sand: deep, loose and black from years of fires and animals sheltering. I was sure the piles of stones in the corners held hibernating snakes. Through the opening in the back wall was a deeper, darker chamber where they had piled sacks of grain and flour and *tanakas* of *samin*. They would move up behind the Shrah mountains in a couple of months when their crops on the high plateau at al-Fujaij had ripened.

I always thought it was called Alf Jeej and remembered the name by imagining *alf* (a thousand) *jeesh* (armies) camped on the vast desert plateau. By the time I realised it was al-Fujaij, nothing to do with armies, the picture had stuck.

The chatter of the visiting women washed around me. I wasn't allowed to do anything. Whether it was because I was an *ajnebiya* visiting Rakhiya-n in her confinement like a real Bedouin, or because I was carrying Mohammad Abdallah's first baby, I don't know, but the family treated me like an honoured guest, and have so ever since with a spirit of hospitality that makes me feel like a precious treasure.

I have drifted away from the Nabataean script. Beautiful as it is it doesn't keep me captivated. Scholars can tell me it has connections with Arabic and Hebrew and that inscriptions have been found in the Sinai, Negev and Arabian deserts, but the best thing the Nabataeans did for me was to introduce me to Mohammad and his tribe.

Jidaya, a Fortune-teller

And despite 'Whatever God sends we will welcome', I wondered how much it really meant to have a boy. The disabled children I had nursed hovered in the back of my mind and I prayed most of all for a healthy baby, whatever sex, but when I congratulated Rakhiya-n on the safe birth of her new baby, she had said, 'Your turn is next . . . a boy, *inshallah*,' and so did Fatima-n and Nora when their turns came before mine. It irritated me that even all the women, just like the vendors at the Treasury, seemed to believe that boys were better.

I *knew* that wasn't true. And was busy proving, every time I got a chance, that I could do as well as them, if not better. Subconsciously I might have wanted a girl so I could prove that I would treat her the same as I would a boy, but it felt like more than that. As if I knew I was carrying a girl. We chose her name easily – Salwa sounded pretty to my English-language ear, and traditional but not very common. We couldn't find a name for a boy.

And one day Jidaya stopped me in the Fum-al-Wadi. Jidaya was the life and soul of many a wedding party, tying a scarf tightly around her hips and belly-dancing to the clapping and singing of the girls and the clinking of the tea glasses she held upside down on her fingertips. She wore her *asaba* tall and bright and applied her kohl thickly around her eyes. Later, when

I took up sewing, she brought bits of material just big enough to sew sleeves from, which she stitched to the armholes of her *mudraga* so it *looked* as though she had a new under-dress, but at this stage I barely knew her. I hadn't even met her at the clinic, so I was surprised when she stopped her donkey under its load of grain sacks and waved at me. 'Fatima.'

'*Keef haalki, shlonki.*' We repeated the various forms of 'how are you?' over and over, kissing each other's cheeks and the backs of each other's hands.

She launched into Arabic . . . '*Halimit*' I could understand (I dreamed) and '*binit*' (girl) and '*rai-it ghenim*' (goatherd), and got the message. Her smile and hand on my arm were commiserating but her eyes as she nodded at my big belly were black dots of fortune-telling certainty.

I couldn't explain that I was excited to have my own instincts reinforced and if it showed on my face she probably thought she misunderstood. We could only wait and see.

Call Him Awwad

Then one day Mohammad-m came wandering over to our cave.

He had visited before and had reminisced with Mohammad. 'Remember when we were working on that dig near Tafila and I had kidney stones and they said beer was good to wash them out. We walked twenty kilometres in the night, we must have been *majaneen*.'

'*Al-humdulillah, ta'agilna.*' Thank God we are more sensible now, they had agreed, sounding pleased with themselves. 'That's what marriage has done for us.'

But today he was hesitant. I put a *farrsha* in the shade and put the tea on to boil. His wife had sent him, he said, and I wondered if the colour of his smooth full cheeks, red under his sun-browned skin, was exaggerated by embarrassment.

'She dreamed that an angel woke her and told her to go to Mohammad Abdallah. "Tell him if his wife gives birth to a boy they should call him Awwad," the angel had said. That was ages ago and she didn't even tell me about it at first but she says she has had the dream again and again. She sent me because it might prove important.'

And, I imagined, if the angel was as persistent as he said, she probably hoped to get a good night's sleep.

From then on I prayed my instincts were right. Our child's name was going to determine our own. I was happy to become Umm Salwa, and for Mohammad to become Abu Salwa but I did not want to become Umm and Abu Awwad; they already lived over by the cistern.

Most of the Bedouin didn't seem to be worried about such things. If someone dreamed a name for their baby, well and good, they considered it a sign or blessing. But it worried me because we had been warned; if we had a boy we could call him Awwad, or spend the rest of our lives fearing retribution. Another chance to choose a name for myself was slipping from me.

An Adventure to Wadi Sabra

Many of the women told stories of arriving home with the goats, a load of wood and a new baby – having given birth in the hills (and having buried the afterbirth in a water course to ensure continued procreation). That was how they did it. They just ripped some material from their scarf or dress to tie the cord and cut it with a stone on a rock.

I, on the other hand, knew of too many things that could go wrong and really hoped, *inshallah*, to be able to get to the hospital when my time came, though our trip to Wadi Sabra might suggest the opposite.

I had been in Petra for nearly two years and had still not visited Wadi Sabra. It sounded lovely. In my book it said there was a small water source there, and a second theatre carved out of the rocks. Mohammad had never been there either. His family had usually lived to the north of Petra, where he knew every mountain path, shade tree and Nabataean signature, while Wadi Sabra was to the south on the ancient caravan route from Petra down to Egypt and Gaza, a southern suburb where few Bdoul lived today.

We talked about going often enough. 'One day,' agreed Ali and Ali-f the card players, but no one moved. Ali had herded his family's goats there when he was little and was unimpressed by ruins but he knew where the water was and was ready to guide us. At the beginning of March as I began my ninth month of pregnancy it dawned on us that I would soon have a small baby to worry about . . . and then it would be summer and too hot, and then some other hurdle would probably be in our way, so we decided to go the next day.

At daybreak I was at our toilet pit with the runs. After a few trips I felt quite weak but when the others arrived with their loaded donkeys I was drinking *baytheraan*, a bitter desert herbal remedy (which tasted so bad it had to be good), determined to be well soon. They were ready to postpone the adventure but I was not. I knew we wouldn't do it again, so while I gathered my strength Mohammad got our donkey saddled and loaded.

In one breath I wanted to have my baby in hospital and in the next I was heading to isolation after a night of stomach cramps! But although it might look like blind stupidity, I think it was different. It was more this blind confidence I had that my life was going to be good and an adventure would be fun. I didn't even formulate the thoughts that I was strong and healthy and not about to have the baby yet, but they were instinctive and true.

Ali-f, with whom I still spoke English and with whom, on boring days at the Treasury, Mohammad still wrestled boisterously, was newly wed. He had brought his wife Raweya from Egypt. (That *gismih o naseeb* again – he had managed to find someone to match him perfectly.) She was a fifteen-year-old matron with sparkling eyes and, having braved the aeroplane flight to her new life with the husband she had just met, she thought she was ready for anything.

Ali, no longer a taxi driver, but still a bachelor, had borrowed a donkey and brought his flute.

Raweya and I rode in the beginning. I didn't feel much like talking so I was glad she knew I couldn't understand her accent. I could read her face well enough though; she didn't know what to make of me. I smiled and found I was starting to feel better already.

The guys sang and joked, anticipating my having to get off and find a place to go to the toilet. They laughed hilariously, and I was able to too – the stomach-ache had gone, I had nothing left to get off for.

The path narrowed through white rocks and we had to get off for the steep climb up to the Stowh. From then on we all rode, Raweya and I with our arms around our men, Ali singing about the woman he wished he had to do the same. We circled the ploughed land of the high plain. Quite suddenly a view opened below us; we were at Ras Sabra. We sat and rested. The yellow photos of the occasion show a strange crew of pioneers: my huge belly and Mohammad's illegal Kalashnikov.

Ras Sabra was the head of a huge U-shaped valley. The sides were ranges of towering sandstone which lessened in height as they veered west in the southern distance. The inside of the 'U' was greener: juniper, wormwood and tamarisk clung to the distant valley sides. The theatre was about halfway along, invisible from here – just a darker shadow. As we picked our way down the zigzag track into Sabra, the heady fragrance of the *rattam* blossom came up to meet us.

We rode along the deeply sandy belly of the *wadi*. I loved it when Ali played his pipe flute and the others shut up so the music could fill the air around my head. Slowly the valley narrowed and the red cliffs rose high above. Around midday we found some stagnant water beneath the huge oleanders and Ali went crashing through the bushes to find the source. We tied the donkeys and followed, pushing the branches back to discover water trickling down the stone-cut steps of the tiny theatre. Plants and even some bushes were thriving on it, badly eroding the benches with their roots. We lay for a bit on the terracotta steps, a motley audience at the base of the sheer sandstone cliff. The blue avenue of sky, the birdsong-enhanced silence and the awesome wonder that surrounded us was a private show. It had been a good idea to come.

Lunch was *shraak*, which I shared, and sardines, which I wasn't ready for yet. The tea was good. Ali and Mohammad went off to see if there was anyone who could sell us a young goat to barbecue for dinner, but before long they were back, saddling up the donkeys, getting ready to move out.

'There's a crazy guy down there. He threatened us with a shotgun! We're not staying.'

I suspected a prank. 'Surely he could see you were Bedou. Are you sure he didn't invite you for tea? Or are you packing up to go there for *mensef*?'

'*Bil aks*' – the opposite. 'He accused us of being *yehood*.' That meant Jews or Israelis.

'Oh, come on.' I still couldn't believe them, although we were soon heading back up the valley. 'It can't be that bad.'

'I wouldn't like to test him,' Mohammad said. 'He must be crazy anyway to make his family live out here.'

'But Israelis?'

'Well, in the late 1960s and early 1970s there was fighting in these hills. That's why the women still run for the caves when they hear a helicopter. Israelis sometimes crossed the border by foot and tried to get to Petra through the mountains; there were skirmishes and some Bedouin even lost their lives. There isn't any trouble these days but this guy's *majnoon* and he's got a gun so there is no point arguing with him.'

We retraced our steps back up to Ras Sabra and as evening approached made our camp in a narrow north-facing gully below a Nabataean dam brimming with fresh water.

We were drinking tea and our potatoes and wheel of bread were baking in the fire when Ali-f, coming in from the dark, said worryingly, 'It looks like rain.' We followed him out of the fire-light and round the rock. Mohammad and Ali agreed the ominous, intermittent flicker to the west implied just that, and they also agreed that it was a long way across ploughed land to the nearest shelter, near the Snake Monument.

'*Yallah*, let's go,' they cheered. As if we hadn't had enough excitement for one day.

By the light of the fire we collected our scattered belongings. The bread was ready, luckily, so Raweya wrapped it in a sugar sack and put in the saddle bag; I counted five glasses and a teapot; the guys saddled the donkeys; we loaded up our beds, flashed a cigarette lighter round to check we hadn't forgotten anything, and headed into the night.

Ali sang as he urged us out of the shelter of the valley onto the plateau – into the wind. The ploughed land was impossible to walk on but the donkeys were likely to stumble so we couldn't ride either. It was very dark. Mohammad was leading our donkey and I was holding tightly to the side of the wooden saddle so it could guide me and take the strain. I stumbled blindly on the primitively ploughed surface, my feet were like boats on a wild ocean, smashing into the tops of the waves and jolting down into the troughs between. I was practically being dragged along, but I got the giggles imagining Mohammad's grin when he yelled back at me, 'You asked for adventure!'

The storm was coming fast. The thunder was louder now and it encouraged the donkeys on.

The flashes of lightning floodlit the land – Jabal Haroon, Jabal al-Barra, Jabal Inmeer, and the Sh-rah mountains. We were in the middle, halfway across the plateau, and seconds later it all plunged into darkness, leaving us blinded as the accompanying thunder boomed. On we blundered, encouraging each other: '*Yallah mish ba'eed.*' It's not far.

The damp wind preceding the storm kept us cool. The lightning, flashing above and all around us now, was a brilliant, celestial fireworks display, applauded fervently by the thunder.

Then we were walking on solid rock. I could smell dung and smoke – civilisation! There were spits of rain on the wind when the lightning showed us the wide-open cave. We all cheered and Raweya ululated in true Egyptian style as we headed straight in, donkeys and all.

There was plenty of room and the cave was protected from the wind because it faced south. There was even a pile of dry firewood. We helped ourselves, making a blaze so we could see. The rainstorm broke, pounding the earth as we ate our dinner. Our sigh of relief was mutual and I said private prayers of thanks too: to Hammooda for bringing the *baytheraan*; to the Nabataeans for carving the cave; to Ghei-<u>tha</u>, who lived nearby, for storing her firewood in it; to the donkeys for getting us safely across the fields without broken limbs before the rains came; even to the crazy Bedouin for frightening us out of Wadi Sabra where there was no shelter at all; and to God for getting the whole show together.

We made our beds on the rock floor. With the soothing sound

of the rain and the satisfying smell of freshly wet earth infusing my senses, I lay with Mohammad beside me, our baby inside me, and slept knowing there was nowhere I would rather be.

Salwa – Our Pride and Joy

I wasn't absolutely sure of my dates – I kept no calendar or diary, but I had now made three visits to the Italian Hospital doctor and he had said I should be due at the beginning of April. My bag was packed and every night I practised my breathing and relaxing. Nothing had happened yet. One afternoon Mohammad invited a rare Jordanian tourist home for a pot of tea, and on seeing my belly he admitted he was an obstetrician. He could understand my uncertainty about the date but said it was unsafe to leave things too long.

'If you don't go into labour in the next week, come to see me at al-Basheer hospital. You understand that, don't you?' he asked Mohammad. 'It's important.'

The next week was uneventful – I didn't even get any of the 'advance' contractions other pregnant ladies gossiped about when their time came near.

Mohammad didn't spend long at the Treasury those days. 'Are you OK? Do you think we should go to Amman?' We were no longer blissfully ignorant. 'Is it still moving?' Everything seemed fine and just the same to me but we finally made the starlit early-morning walk up the Siq to make sure. We caught the *service* for one of my more uncomfortable trips, with my baby nudging my bladder.

The obstetrician worked at al-Basheer hospital, which was the main public hospital on the south side of Amman in a predominantly Palestinian area just minutes from Karaaj-al-Jenoob. He was as good as his word; he had me X-rayed to make sure all was ready, took me to a delivery room and put me on an infusion to induce the birth. Nothing much happened, just a faint example of things to come but slower than expected, so he took me back off the drip and admitted me to the ward before he went off duty. The twinges continued overnight, becoming strong regular contractions by morning, and when my waters broke a nurse took me off to the delivery room and reconnected the infusion. Several nurses gathered round and they called the doctor on duty, a Dr Basaam. I don't know if I was getting extra attention because this was my first baby or because I was an *ajnebiya*, but I didn't mind – I had seen a small darkly tanned Bedouin woman come into the ward this morning and only her baby's first cry had alerted the woman in the next bed to call a nurse. All her traditions had taught her to stay quiet.

I didn't have any such traditions; I cried loudly, our baby was delivered and she too cried loudly (after a quick 'kkhhhhh' of the suction), and there she was, the girl I had expected.

We were taken to a room for new mothers. Salwa was given a separate cot right beside my bed. The other mothers had their babies in bed with them. My baby lay still and sleeping: no screwed-up crying (that came later), no blotchy red face; she was perfect. Mohammad was there with flowers and *al-humdulillah-a-salaamas*. That he had thought to go looking for a real bouquet, in a city of few flower shops, charmed me more than the bouquet itself. Arabs usually gave money. He was pampering his *ajnebiya*, and showed no signs of being disappointed with a girl.

In the afternoon I had visitors. Lynne, an American who had come to work on an excavation in Petra and had married the Inspector of Antiquities, lived just round the corner and came with her sister-in-law and a thermos of cinnamon tea. Kevin and Innes came from across the city. I loved their enthusiastic Kiwi way but was suddenly uncomfortable when Kevin asked, 'Can I pick her up?'

It occurred to me that Mohammad hadn't held his daughter yet. It probably hadn't occurred to him because where he grew up the fathers didn't *see* the babies let alone hold them for forty days – but I don't know why it hadn't occurred to me. It was a good idea – they all took turns and Mohammad's smile captured on the photos was proof that this was another gift from my culture he thoroughly approved of.

I slept wonderfully that night, so was all the more surprised in the morning when every bed except mine had two mothers and nearly as many babies in it, top and tail! There were no complaints. In fact, they were busy swapping labour stories: congratulating the teenage mother with her first boy, commiserating with the older mother who had five daughters at home but had just miscarried her third boy. Their visitors were already arriving; the room was soon bursting with cries of '*Mabruk*' and '*Al-humdulillah-a-salaama*', and an array of Palestinian grandmothers, mothers and mothers-in-law in colourfully embroidered overdresses and fine white head shawls with scatterings of hand-stitched flowers shared aromatic home-cooked food and camomile and cinnamon tea from thermos flasks. They gave out sweets and chocolates in joyful celebration.

Postnatal Support

We took the *service* home the next day and hired a pick-up to take us into Petra. As we drew up below the cave, Bedouin started converging on it. Inside I reached for a *farrsha* but the young mother who now lived in a canvas tent just below us took over. She put *farrshas* side by side. 'Haven't you got a wool *farrsha*? This sponge rubber will open your back. Put the baby on the wall side to protect her. Don't lie that way – you have to have your head facing the west, not the east.' This was going to be hard work.

Soon Abdallah arrived beaming; a boy was best but a girl was wonderful. Salwa was the next generation; his first grandchild, my mum and dad's first grandchild, and my only surviving grandmother's first great-grandchild. (Mohammad had sent telegrams from Amman.)

My mother-in-law arrived with a woollen *farrsha* but I didn't give in. I was used to sleeping on the one I was on; the wool ones were hard and never long enough.

'Why didn't you take someone with you when you went to Amman? What if she came on the way?' I didn't want to try to explain induction so I just ignored her scolding.

'She didn't, everything went well.'

As soon as the guys got a fire going, she produced incense from a knot in the corner of her *asaba* and burned it, crumbling the resin onto coals on a flat stone saucer and wafting the smoke into every corner of the cave.

Umm Mahmoud arrived and busied herself making tea. Mahmoud and Ahmed wanted to see the baby.

'Where's the flour?' Tuf-leh started on dinner.

Ali-f and Raweya arrived with their bedding. Ali-f stood with the men around the fire outside and Raweya cleaned some lentils to make *rishoof*.

Salwa cried and we battled with full breasts. I had to slit my *mudraga* to the waist to get at them. Umm Laafi took Tuf-leh's scarf off her head and draped it over my breasts and infant to protect them from dangerous eyes.

The young mother put her baby to sleep on the bottom of my mattress and he promptly wet it. I cringed. The rest of the day blurred. A long time after dinner most of the visitors left but Tuf-leh had come to stay and so had Raweya and Ali-f. They stayed for the next two weeks.

It was probably just as well because during that time all of the women, lots of the men and most of the children of Petra came to visit us. Men mostly came in the afternoons. Our cave didn't allow much for segregation and they usually just popped in to shake my hand and give me more money before going back out-side to stand around the fire. But the women arrived in the mornings dressed in their best clothes, scrubbed and olive-oiled, and mostly they stayed for the day. The beauty of the children with them was camouflaged for protection against the evil eye by unkempt hair and ragged clothes. The women and girls took over the kitchen corner and the kids took over the rest. I gritted my teeth and stayed on my mattress.

With all the people inside, the cave got hot, and with most of them smoking it slowly filled up with smoke. Mohammad and I and a lot of the younger guys smoked packet cigarettes and we were used to a bit of smoke in the cave, but the women mostly smoked much stronger *heeshy* (which comes from a plant related to henbane). They rolled it in papers which didn't have glue but had to be nipped and wetted along the edge in order to stick. The tobacco was crumbled leaves so plenty spilled in the rolling process, and as the holes in the laps of their *mudragas* proved, plenty more spilled while they were smoking. Our floor was rough concrete, with cracks and waves like invitations to squash butts out in. So it wasn't only the smoke that was irritating.

Everyone brought something: *samin*, *laban*, money or eggs – it was springtime and there was an abundance of everything. Rakhiya-n brought much more *samin* than I could have bought with the money I had given her. Tuf-leh emptied their precious plastic bottles and aluminium bowls and remembered which was whose. By the fifth day we had a hundred and twenty eggs despite frying huge panfuls of them in *samin* for breakfast.

When Salwa's little cries started up the visitors would nod and urge me, 'Feed her, feed her,' and then look at each other surprised when I put her to my breast. I was like them after all! They thought all modern or urban women used the bottle, and I had seen bottle-fed babies here. They were usually fat because the mothers put too much sugar in, or sickly because it was too difficult to sterilise the bottles. We didn't have a fridge, or electricity, for milk cooling and bottle warming, so I was very lucky to have breast milk, always clean, warm and ready, and totally portable.

I didn't wrap Salwa like their babies, though. They wrapped their babies in swaddling clothes, some of them so fastidiously in such straight, tight bundles that they reminded me of the old wooden clothes-peg dolls we made as children; only their heads rolled loose. I declined to follow their example. I pinned Salwa's towelling nappy, snapped shut her plastic pants and stretchy overall, turned her onto her tummy, and shut my ears to the comments *that* produced.

Umm Laafi worried about empty eyes. 'You should cover her at all times,' she insisted. Their babies wore hand-sewn polyester caps with pleated ruffles and little scraps of black veil which they could lower to protect their babies' beauty, or lift up to show it off, depending on the 'eyes' in the room. But I wasn't going to. I didn't believe their superstitions.

'Has she got a *kebass*?' the women all asked Umm Laafi. They considered it my mother-in-law's job to make sure I knew what I was doing. Most of them wore at least a gold or silver ring and their babies all had *kebasses* (square green agate beads with flattened corners and amazing powers) pinned onto the peaks of their cloth caps or threaded onto fabric necklaces. All of these elements could be dangerous, they insisted, if Salwa wasn't protected, and I decided it was much easier to say, 'Yes, she has,' than to try to explain, in my still limited but rapidly expanding Arabic, that I didn't believe in such powers. And it couldn't hurt, so I threaded my gold wedding ring, my silver puzzle ring and Umm Laafi's precious *kebass* onto a safety pin and pinned it to Salwa's blanket. Also to keep the peace, I put a *shabriya* under my pillow; for my own – purely symbolic – protection.

Umm Laafi had already arrived on the morning I found the dried-up umbilicus in the nappy and she wouldn't let me throw it in the rubbish. 'You don't want her to be a scavenger do you? I'll get Laafi to put it on the school. That's the best place, so she will grow up and go to school.'

Years later, a young friend, Haroon, who had still been a schoolboy when Salwa was born, confided to me that he had on occasion climbed with his school friends onto the flat school roof and thrown the little twists of material with shrivelled skin as far as they could into the oleander bushes. But that didn't stop Salwa from going to school.

Nora came and put kohl on Salwa's eyelashes and eyebrows, so they would grow thick and beautifully shaped. I wanted to stop her but she was so quick and self-assured I didn't dare.

She was like that with everything. Although Nora had grown up in a tent in Beitha, she had lived in the city while her husband was in the army and she had picked up all sorts of arts. Her home was always immaculate, her yoghurt was white without a speck of chaff or a goat hair in it, her *shraak* was tissue-thin, and she cooked *shashbara* (pastry pockets containing sheep-tail fat cooked in yoghurt) and *bazeena* (Bedouin pasta that tasted like macaroni cheese); she came and used my machine to make dresses for her daughters to wear to school; and she was a good friend to call if you were having a baby and needed an escort to the hospital or someone to tie the umbilical cord.

Now she smoothed a matchstick with her teeth, poked it into an onion to soften it and applied the powdered kohl generously. Salwa didn't go blind but the huge black smudges took a couple of weeks to wash away and I never could wash it out of the precious white singlets I had bought at great expense from a dingy shop in an Amman back street.

A couple of months passed and it became apparent to the Bdoul women that Salwa was not thriving – they called it *makboos* – despite their precautions. 'What's the matter with her – your daughter?' they asked. 'She's too little. You must have had an unclean visitor.' (Someone who was menstruating or, worse still, someone who hadn't bathed after having sex.) 'Have you tried lentils?'

I wasn't worried; she had been only 2.7 kilos to start with, and though I didn't weigh her I could see she was developing. She looked bigger to me and was already lifting her shoulders off the mat and rolling onto her back. She did cry quite a lot but then I let her suckle, or if I couldn't stand it any longer I gave her to one of her uncles to take her for a walk.

The women told me the remedies for a *makboos* baby anyway and as usual it was easier to listen: I should soak whole brown lentils in water overnight and then use the water to bathe her in; Heyaiya-m had wrapped her baby successfully in the fresh skin of a one-year-old goat – but Salwa probably wasn't that bad a case they agreed. Jidaya brought me her necklace, fifteen pure gold pieces on a black cord (worth more than all our possessions).

'Put it in a bowl of water and put it out under the stars overnight. In the morning use the star-water to bathe your baby in,' were the instructions that went with it.

'*Shukran*,' I said, touched, but I was glad I had a cupboard to lock the necklace in for enough days to be polite. I worried enough about it being in my cave – I wouldn't have slept with it in a bowl under the stars!

I decided Salwa was hungry and started to feed her. At the pharmacy in Ma'an I found a Milupa cereal suitable for babies ten weeks old and soon she was also sharing real food – lapping creamy slurps of *fatteh* or rice porridge off my fingers. If dinner was *mensef*, I mushed *shraak* for her in a glass of sweet tea and fed her that. She didn't look back.

Some months later, when we visited Mohammad's Ras-a-Nagb relations, Ataiga told him about her dream. 'Your wife had a pair of knitting needles, which means she will have two boys', knitting needles being masculine nouns.

When he told me about it, I said, 'I hope they're next. A girl and two boys sounds good.'

What relief when he said, 'Yeah, sounds good.' I had feared he would want many more.

Flexi-hours

I was due to get forty days' maternity leave when Salwa was born, but we had been home only a few days when the hospital Land-Rover pulled up below our cave. The doctor had picked Mohammad up at the Treasury to plead his case. Because I was responsible for every pill in the clinic I either had to go with them to open the cave or deprive the people for forty days. They waited while I got myself and my new baby together and they gave us a ride down.

That was the end of my clinic routine. From that day on people came to our home when they needed me, and on Tuesdays I opened the clinic and waited in the valley for the doctor's visit. It suited us all. I didn't waste hours waiting pointlessly so I didn't mind patients coming to my home, and they got the care they needed when they needed it: two injections a day if prescribed; bandages on Fridays if necessary; and medications, even at night when the hospital pharmacy was closed, as long as they came with a prescription and a vehicle ready to take me down and bring me back.

A few months later there was a measles epidemic. Many patients were prescribed twice-daily penicillin injections and most of them were too sick to move, so I took up home visits as well.

I wished I could have written all that on a note on the clinic door, but I had given up learning to write because so few people could read that it seemed pointless. Word of mouth worked well though, and as I traipsed round the valley or bandaged patients on my ledge I worked on the spoken word instead.

Caves and Tents

I really enjoyed the home visits. The people were all so different and it was interesting to see how differently they set up their spaces, be they caves or tents.

Abu Sha-her, the father of Fatima (who had given me my name) and several other house-proud daughters, had a cave I was particularly envious of – with big glass-paned windows on both sides of the door, a living rock forecourt and a silky cement floor. Mohammad remembered living in it as a young child when his young parents had shared it with three other families, each in a corner. But now Abu Sha-her had a large family and they had it to themselves.

The quilts and pillows were always immaculate and there were doilies hanging from the shelves of a glass-doored whatnot. There were gilt-framed photos hanging from rock loops: Abu Sha-her as a young man in studio pose and Arab Army uniform; his young family, when he had only four children, also taken at the studio when they lived in Amman; and a bigger photo of His Majesty King Hussein. Suitcases on a bedstead against the wall were always closed, scorpion-proof. Next door was a small kitchen cave with a fire-pit in the middle of the swept rock floor, and wooden boxes, black from years in the smoke, as shelves for bright aluminium dishes and enamel plates. In the back was another bedstead for sacks of flour, sugar and rice. They used another cave too; it was bigger, with room in it for water drums, a two-goat and a three-goat cooking pot, sacks of grain and the tethered donkey.

And in summer they set up a well-maintained tent of woven goat-hair strips on the flat ledge of rock in front of the cave and spread out into it.

In summer the hair tents were perfect for the ridges of Petra. With the back flap or *r-waag* up and the breeze blowing through, they provided cool shade. In the late afternoons and evenings, they dwindled to mere reference points from which to bring another *farrsha*, or water. We sat way out in front, in the twilight and the moonlight. Families that didn't have a nearby cave to store their water in or shut their goats up in used their tents traditionally. One end was the *shig*, where visitors were welcomed, where men sat during the day, and where older boys and men might take their *farrshas* to sleep. The middle was the *hareem*, where the women and children lived and slept. The other end was left for the goats, and once they started birthing, for the kids to shade in and for the goatskins of yoghurt and *tanakas* of *samin* to be kept in. In Petra, unless there were guests from outside, the boundaries were pretty fluid – women sat with their men, children sat on their fathers' laps, and goats settled everywhere.

In autumn when the first Shergiya blew in from the deserts of Arabia and we moved our bed inside so as not to be buried on the ledge, I got up in the morning to see downed tents on the opposite ridges. The wind whipped great clouds of sand up and whisked them around the valley, and had lifted the heavy tents up off their poles and let them down again onto belongings and inhabitants.

As the Shergiya died down the heat intensified but I took Salwa across the valley to see how my in-laws were faring. 'Al-humdulillah,' Umm Laafi declared. No one had been hit by the falling poles and she had had the foresight to put out the fire and cover its pit with the *saj*.

Once or twice I heard of tents being burned to the ground. Although the Shergiya got icy cold later in the year, it was always devastatingly dry. There were no fire hoses, and if there was no water in the jerry-cans there was little anyone could do. I was impressed by the speed with which blankets, flour, firewood and utensils were loaded on donkeys from all over the valley, so that by the end of the day the families had been set up again.

The Shergiya, we all knew, lasted for three days, abating around midday only to pick up at dawn the next, so Umm Laafi planned an evacuation. She left the tent as it was, on the ground holding everything in place, and sent Inzela and Laafi scrambling under it to bring out the bare necessities, which we carried with an air of adventure down to the Wadi Mataha to one of their winter caves. I helped cook up rice-in-*laban* porridge, enough for the family from the next fallen-down tent too, and we ate it with a generous scoop of *samin* melting in the middle to dip our handfuls into.

The life of Mohammad's relations in Ras-a-Nagb was much harder. They had no caves to seek refuge in or to shelter their goats in, and although they sometimes moved to the bottom of the escarpment, which was a little warmer, their tents were better prepared for bad weather. A *r-waag* of sacks across the front closed the tent so the wind was forced up and over, and extra ropes held the tents down. Ras-a-Nagb was over a thousand metres above sea level, and most winters snow fell. The damp-ness caused the goat-hair to swell, creating a tighter weave and waterproofing the fabric. They put tins and jerry-cans under the centre row of poles to make the tents A-shaped so the snow slid straight off. That was the only time I could actually stand upright inside a tent – but I never did so for long because the weave was so tight that the smoke from the wormwood fires sat close to the roof.

Tents and caves, summer and winter, one thing was the same. '*Ahlan-wa-sahlan*,' and, '*Au'gaoodi, au'gaoodi, Umm Salwa.*' Welcome, Umm Salwa, sit, sit – I was told wherever I went. Tea always (and a meal often) followed. At Ras-a-Nagb, no matter how late we arrived, we could never leave without a *mensef*, and around Petra I always worried, as I made my way across to give an evening injection of twice-daily penicillin, that I hadn't refused forcefully enough that morning, and that I would find a goat made into *mensef* specially for me.

Nuha, the Vaccination Lady

The clinic job I came to enjoy most was helping with the vaccinations. At first when women asked me about *as-Sitt* Umm The-hayr, I couldn't answer them because I had no idea what they were talking about. But then I learned that *sitt* was a kind of respectful title for a woman (even I was sometimes called *as-Sitt* Fatima), and that *as-Sitt* Umm The-hayr was the one who did the vaccinations. Then one day when I was inside the clinic giving an injection I heard the Land-Rover pull up. I wasn't expecting the doctor, although there were a few people waiting hopefully.

'*As-Sitt jet, as-Sitt jet*,' the lady's come, the lady's come, a kid's voice shrieked excitedly from outside. I stepped out to see a humpbacked woman getting down from the passenger seat. She greeted the women with wide smiles and shook their hands. Her face was round, her complexion fair and her dark hair, which was done up in a thin topknot, was uncovered. She wore trousers, a white medical coat and a cross on a chain around her neck.

She said to me in shy English, 'Hello, I am Nuha.'

Out of the back of the vehicle the driver helped another *sitt*, a younger woman in a full-length white coat and scarf, and together they took chilly-bins of ice-protected vaccinations into the cave, got out the 'unimportant' carton of pink files and set up their mobile clinic on my table. *The̲bayer-a-tat-eemat* . . . so that's what they were – vaccination records.

Umm The̲-hayr was a Christian woman not much older than me whose family, I think, was from Bulgaria. She didn't even come up to my shoulders but she held her large head erect with an air of competence. She was in charge of the infant vaccination programme, the nearest thing to postnatal care there was in the whole Ma'an province (which encompassed thousands of kilometres of desert), and she did monthly rounds of all the outlying villages and many Bedouin tents. I found her son's name The̲-hayr very difficult to pronounce and anyway preferred to call her Nuha. Months later I learned she wasn't married and asked Mohammad how, then, could she be Umm The̲-hayr.

He laughed. 'I hope you didn't call her that. It means "Mother of the Back", because of her humped back. Like Sliman, the humpback who works with me up at the Treasury – we call him Abu The̲-hayr. It's just a joke.' So my language developed.

Women gathered quickly when news of the *sitt*'s arrival spread across the hills, but some mothers stayed away for fear of the scales. They didn't want their babies weighed and it was nothing to do with the cold corroded tray they had to lie on. They feared that someone, jealous of their plump babies, might strike them with the evil eye.

Nuha met this everywhere and rarely insisted on the scales. Instead she encouraged, '*Khuleeni a-shoof-ha*,' and got each mother to undo the layers, invariably wet or filled with sweet-smelling, milk-fed poo, privately behind the screen to make her own visual estimation of the baby's weight. The babies were wrapped in layers of swaddling clothes even in the warm weather. But if you lifted them up they were usually naked from the waist down, and if they peed when anyone picked them up everyone else just laughed and said, 'It's only water.' They invariably smelled of urine and I had to make an effort to dandle them. I did though, that and kiss the snotty wee faces and say, '*Ya thakerallah a-thaafeen*' (a very colloquial equivalent of may the children be in God's care – the accepted compliment), even if I thought they were ugly.

If Nuha suspected poor nourishment she resorted to the scales and compensated with a bag of milk powder. And she always scolded mothers for applying kohl. 'It won't make any difference to how thick or long his eyelashes grow and it could lead to infection.' They didn't take much notice.

She checked the given name, father's name, grandfather's name and family name of each child. There were so many Fatimas and Maryams, Salems and Mohammads it was often necessary to go back to the generation of grandfather to differentiate. She pinpointed the birthdates of newborns with a game of Ten Questions: was it the week after Ali's wedding; after the strong wind; before the snow; the day of the Eid or before Ataima had her baby? Any mother could assist with a clue. The older the child, the harder it got.

Nuha had a register of her own, a back-up to the pink files and while I injected into tight, brown, dimpled bottoms and dropped pink drops into unsuspecting wet red mouths, or older clench-toothed frightened ones, the nurse filled out the information. If the baby was over ten months on the first visit, we would give him the measles vaccine first, otherwise he got polio drops and triple vaccines. These had to be boosted twice with no gaps of more than three months or the poor child would have to start again. Gaps could easily happen because Nuha relied on the hospital vehicle to get down into Petra and if she missed her expected day we didn't know what would happen. Sometimes she came the following Monday, sometimes she didn't. Women might gather for the next three Mondays, only to go harvesting when she came on the fourth, which was enough to put them off for a few months. A telephone would have helped but there were no phones in the valley.

With her erratic programme and the seasonal wandering of some families, it wasn't surprising to get visits like that of Gheitha, who arrived and filled the clinic one day with her beautiful brood of ragged, coffee-cup-eyed children. Their ages ranged from three months to about eight years.

'We have come for vaccinations. It's ages since any of the children had any,' she announced, and proceeded to introduce them with a bright, gold-toothed smile, putting her hand on their heads one by one. 'This is Gasaam, this is Geseem, this one is Geseema, this, Baasema, and this' – holding up the baby – 'is Basaama but we call her "Babeya".' She beamed so proudly and seriously I had to control the giggle that was threatening to escape. Nuha had the job of figuring out who had had which vaccinations and which vaccinations they would now have to repeat because so much time had passed since the last one.

And I tried to remember, from then on, to write down the date whenever a new baby was born.

Winter at Abdallah's

Wintertime: I opened the wooden door of the cave and was in a swirling mist. I threw the greatcoat around my shoulders, pulled the door shut and ran along the path to our toilet pit, which was under an overhanging rock. Some bushes gave a semblance of privacy and on a clear day I could see through them down to the Keenya, but today I could hardly see the path. The mist stilled the world and deadened the sounds of the valley.

In the cave, with the door shut against the cold and damp, it was dim. I made bread in the oven in the winter. I kneaded the dough in the evening and left it to rise and I had put round pebbles in the tray to give the loaves impressions like the *taaboon* bread other women made, but although my bread was good, it was never as light and crunchy as theirs. Mohammad and Salwa woke up as the fresh bread smell filled the cave.

Cold air blew in as Mohammad went out and when he came back in he pulled the blankets round himself. I added a few sage leaves to the teapot for a cosy brew and breakfast was ready. With crusts of hot bread we scooped mouthfuls of fresh white goat's butter and *halawa* mashed in *samin*; we dipped chunks into green olive oil and *zatr*, a tangy mixture of dried thyme and sesame seeds. Mohammad entertained Salwa by nipping the end off a tin-foil cheese segment and squeezing the cheese out so it curled in a quick spaghetti which she licked off his finger.

Mohammad put on warm clothes and secured his *mendeel* around his face. I loved the way he folded it across his nose and wrapped it round his head tucking the tassels into his *mirreer* so that only the sparkle in his eyes and the smile-lines at their edges showed. He went off to see if there were any tourists about and I only stayed in the cave long enough to stack the blankets and *farrshas* on the quilt table and to wash the dishes from last night. Salwa got restless and instead of trying to entertain her in the dark I took her off to visit the grandparents. She lay happily, anticipating an outing, when I put her on the *muzferr* and wrapped her in her blanket.

The women had all laughed embarrassedly when I made the *muzferr* for Salwa.

'*Enti midiniyah*,' they said. You're a city girl. I could feel the implication: a city girl wouldn't be seen dead with a baby in a *muzferr*. They also said, deridingly, '*Al-muzferr lil Bedou*.' The *muzferr* is for the ignorant archaic Bedouin.

Why couldn't they give themselves credit? The *muzferr* was so simply clever – perfect for Petra. They all carried their babies in them for years.

There was certainly no way I would carry my precious baby around in my arms. She would block my view of the path so if I tripped she would fly out and if I fell she would be underneath me. Besides, our walks in Petra weren't short; to get to the clinic took quarter of an hour and to my in-laws half an hour; my arms got tired thinking about it.

So I had made a *muzferr* and now I laid Salwa on the square of material-covered sack that it was. When I pulled up the plaited woollen rope that was looped through the corners, a sling formed, pulled together over her feet but open over her face. I bore her weight across my forehead and she lay across the small of my back. I silently praised this ancient method of transportation again as I threw a greatcoat like a cloak over us both and left the cave.

Down in the Fum-al-Wadi I saw a few horses standing about so some tourists had ventured in. They will have wished they had come on a clear and sunny day, but for me the misty drizzle was magic. Although it had lifted a bit, the damp quietness lingered.

In the Wadi Mataha, on the north-facing wall of Jabal Khubtha, Abdallah's family was living this winter in a big black Nabataean tomb with a floor of compacted sand, ashes, dung and dry grass that was centuries thick and a little springy like a carpet with a rubber underlay. The well-preserved doorway and cleanly carved window in the original façade gave evidence that it was sheltered, but it was big, with several grave-niches like walk-in wardrobes carved into the back wall, so it was hard to heat. The kids were all huddled barefoot and scruffy-haired round a small fire. Hussein on Inzela's little lap, Maryam, Neda and Laafi nudging each other to move over, '*Zehi ghaad*,' trying to get warm and poking twigs under the teapot Tuf-leh was trying to balance there, nearly knocking it off.

When we got there Abdallah went out into the valley with his *shabriya* and cut down a green *rattam* bush as tall as he was. Laafi helped him drag it back and although it barely fit through the doorway he threw the whole thing onto the fire. It soon caught and I lay low on the mattress as it became a huge cracking blaze. Smoke billowed into the corners and the squealing children chased sparks, pouncing to stop them igniting mattresses or clothes. But we were warm and, once the green needles had burned off and some of the smoke had escaped out of the door, we could breathe too.

Later in the afternoon it rained heavily and Mohammad arrived wet. He'd given up for the day – the few people he had met had been too cold to think about Bedouin daggers or the twenty-four coloured slides of Petra he had produced from his pocket.

He pulled little Maryam into his lap. 'Are you my sister?'

'Yes.' She kissed his nose.

Umm Laafi teased, 'Then you are not my girl.'

'Are you Mummy's girl?' he asked.

She looked to her mum. 'Ye-es?'

'Then you are not my sister!' He put her off his lap. They teased her, laughing as she ran from one to the other, beating them with her little fists.

We stayed for dinner and by that time the rain had cleared. When the moon rose we wrapped Salwa up again and made our way home to our ledge.

Eid a-Thehiya

It was nearly Eid a-Thehiya again (the Eid of the Sacrifice) and we were getting ourselves ready to leave for New Zealand soon after.

I dreamed one night that Mohammad was up on the rocky top of our cave preparing to slit Salwa's throat and I was cleaning the big pot when our neighbour al-Jimedy came up the hill with a young black and white goat on a tether calling out to Mohammad, 'This kid will do.'

I wasn't yet a dream teller nor a dweller on dreams and didn't even mention it to Mohammad, but that afternoon he raised the idea of having our own sacrificial goat for the Eid (to celebrate the lamb God sent to Abraham so he wouldn't have to kill his son, who in the Islamic tradition was Ishmael, Isaac's older brother). Abdallah had pointed out that we were a family in our own right now, and his own family goat, although it would be plenty food-wise, might not be enough in the eyes of God.

There was my dream; I understood it now and agreed, so Mohammad went off to look for a suitable animal.

Although many Bedouin fattened their young lambs and kids specially for this high season, it was now only a couple of days away and I was afraid he might not find one. I needn't have worried – he was back within fifteen minutes with the black and white goat of my dream – which he had bought from al-Jimedy!

Before dawn on the day of the Eid we took our goat over to Abdallah's and slaughtered it there as the sun came up. (I discovered that the strange looks I had received, when I congratulated the people we met on the way, were because they didn't consider the Eid started until after sunrise.)

But after sunrise (and *shraak*-making, tea-drinking and meat-chopping), we got into the swing of things.

'*Mabruk a-Eidak.*'

'*Mabruk a-Eidki.*'

'*Kul aam wa enti bikhair.*'

'*Allah-y-barak fi-ki.*'

Congratulations and good-will wishes filled the air.

It always seemed strange to me because for the last hour we had been working together, and the amount of hand-shaking and head-kissing that we were now undertaking seemed more appropriate to a long-awaited reunion.

Everyone had new clothes. Last year I hadn't had a baby to look after or a New Zealand trip to prepare for and had surprised Mohammad's sisters by sewing them *mudragas*, in silky polyester with glittery braid round the necklines and hems. The lights in their eyes when they put them on had made all the fretting over the sizes worthwhile. And little Maryam had continued to show how much she loved hers by wearing it till it fell off, several months later, in shreds. This year they were all colourful in orange and pink flounces, which they wore over their blouses and trousers.

There was an abundance of meat; we put the kidneys, liver and heart straight onto the coals and barbecued them. Salem put a couple of haunches into the *taaboon* (and the aroma of Sunday lunch, reminding me of church with Dad, filled the air when he took them out). Mohammad and Laafi helped the girls turn the fatty large intestine inside out on sticks and grill it – goat crackling – and we put all the rest into the *mensef* pot and cooked it up for lunch. Laafi was promised he could have the head – he would prise or smash it open and scoop out the brains – but first it had to go in the middle of the *siddr* for the men, who only ever ate the tongue and cheeks, knowing there was bound to be a child waiting to get at the sweet meats inside.

Abdallah sent Laafi and Inzela off to invite the neighbours, who all came despite having their own animals to slaughter and eat. We went home after that and in the evening went to Abu Mahmoud's cave to share their sacrifice for dinner. I was quite happy not to see another *mensef* for the next nine months.

Homeward Bound

We flew from Damascus at a time when the Jordanian and Syrian forces were massed against each other along the border. The entry form Mohammad got as we came over the border into Syria disappeared suspiciously from inside his passport at the airport. I thought it must have been dropped and innocently lost, but Mohammad thought differently.

'They want me to offer them a bribe, which I could do, or lose my temper, which I'm afraid I will do, so then they would have something against me.'

We spent ages at emigration. Luckily we weren't in a hurry because we had caught the last bus from the city at midnight and our flight wasn't till three in the morning. Mohammad impressed me by sticking firmly, but oh so politely, to his guns and eventually we were allowed to pass.

On the plane, as the Qantas flight crew fussed over Salwa, I realised I might have been wrong about her name. 'Salawa' they tried, and 'Sow-wa'.

'Sal-wa,' Mohammad and I corrected.

Mum and Dad were at the airport with my sister Anna and a welcoming party of Nelson friends. I had warned Mohammad that it was the opposite of Jordan (here you could kiss the women but not the men), but I didn't watch to see how he

went. I couldn't see for the tears. I had started to become emotional as we neared New Zealand shores, then halfway over the
Cook Strait the tears had started falling. Mohammad was
appalled. He only knew about tears for grief and even those
should never be shed in public, but I couldn't stop.

'It's all a bit much, is it?' Mum took me in her arms. It all was.

But we were safely here now. This was my husband, my
daughter. These were my parents and friends, the skies I grew up
under. We had made it.

I ignored any culture shock I might have caused Mohammad
and relaxed.

Sometimes home had seemed a long way away.

'*Keef Zelanda?*' How's New Zealand?

'*Fi Bedou zayna ghaad?*' Are there Bedouins like us there?

'*Ba'eeda Newzlanda? Zay Masr?*' Is New Zealand far? Like
Egypt?

I found it as difficult to describe as they found it to imagine.
I said, 'It takes an hour to fly to Egypt and twenty-four hours to
fly to New Zealand.'

They answered, '*Sub-haan Allah, al-gismih keef!*' God's amazing, see the destiny!

My father-in-law didn't want Mohammad out of his sight
and he wasn't the only one. Women asked me where I was
taking him. '*Wheen idki fiih?*' They warned us not to stay there.
'*La-t-<u>th</u>uloo ghaad.*'

Mohammad told me to ignore them; he was ready to go and
excited that we might want to stay. He knew my explanations
wouldn't penetrate their ignorance and that they would believe
whatever they wanted to.

Mohammad didn't take long to fit in to New Zealand. He got
a job picking apples and taught himself to ride one of our old
pushbikes. Considering he had only ever ridden animals, which

didn't fall over when you stopped moving, he did really well. Soon he was riding down to the Travellers' Rest, where he taught himself to play pool.

He charmed everyone simply by doing what he had grown up doing. At work he could never start his Vegemite and lettuce sandwiches until he had offered them to the rest of the picking crew, and he wondered that they could enjoy their lunches without doing the same. In Petra I had seen him smash a lollipop into shards so that every child who saw it could satisfy his 'self' with a taste (and ward off the piles that would afflict him if he couldn't). Mohammad's English improved. When the apple and boysenberry seasons finished we borrowed Mum and Dad's car and did a tour of the South Island. Salwa hated the car seat from day one so it was always nice to find a campsite, and after two weeks Mohammad had seen enough 'forest areas' to know he didn't want to see any more. We didn't meet another Arab or another Muslim on our tour.

Mohammad wrote aerogrammes to his father and to Ali and Ali-f. Now and then they wrote too, mostly *salaams* but scattered with news: Ali-f and Raweya's first baby died when it was just four days old; Mohammad's grandfather died; Ali, whose Bedouin dream-woman had been married for some years now, resigned himself to an Egyptian bride and sent us a photo in which they were both so careful not to smile (and, horrors, show their teeth – a good photo didn't have teeth showing no matter how beautiful they might be) that they looked dead scared; and Rakhiya, finally a divorcée with a choice, married our good friend Salem.

Then Mohammad got work with the Waitaki Freezing Works in Oamaru killing lambs for the *halal* market in Iran. He worked with four or five others who were all Muslims, though only one was Arab. The whole slaughterhouse was orientated so these *halal* slaughter-men faced Mecca, but it was up to them to make sure they were clean and pure before they started, and to say

'*Bis-millah, Allah-u-akbar*' each time they slit a throat – up to two or three thousand times a day each, until either the lambs ran out (the sheep were killed by regular slaughter-men because they weren't exported to Iran), or the union called a strike. The striking drove Mohammad crazy – he was bored at home anyway and wanted to make money, and when they went on strike they didn't get Saturday overtime. When he cut his finger and it took weeks to heal he handed in his notice and we went back to Nelson.

I was bored too. Despite picnics and play groups, bush walking and family, the days in between were hard to fill. I didn't like having to ring friends to see if it was all right to visit. I wanted to just call in, and I wanted them to call in the next day. We started to recognise the things we enjoyed about Jordan and got ready to go back.

I took my vinyl LPs into town and sold them for fifty dollars (the one thing I regularly regret), and, although I remember them whenever I remember my records, I have no regrets about burning six years of teenage diaries in the incinerator down by the chook pen.

We flew back to Jordan ready to settle in.

1981: A New Floor and an Old Lamp

We came back from New Zealand on a hot, hot day in the middle of 1981. I was going to be a Bedouin woman from now on so I put on my *mudraga* and long-sleeves and tied a scarf over my hair before we got back to Petra. I wanted to slip back in where I had left off, and I knew nowadays that image was important.

At Abdallah's tent up by the Palace Tomb, I sat in the shade and met old friends and new babies. Umm Mahmoud had a boy, Maryam had a boy, Shtaya had a girl (she seemed like an ancient grandmother to me and admitted she had even surprised herself).

That night Abdallah made a *mensef* to thank God for our return and we were invited to *mensefs* in our honour at tents around the valley for the next few days.

We took down the wall we had built across our cave door and shook the mothballs I had been relieved to find for sale in Wadi Musa out of the quilts. We didn't find any scorpions. We moved the kitchen (table, utensils, oven and water drum) out to my private room, and we scrounged wire and sticks to make a fence so Salwa couldn't run off the edge of the ledge.

Mohammad had seen another world. He had always come up with clever ideas for improvement anyway – a couple of years ago he had designed a metal table with a lid for his souvenirs so he wouldn't have to pack them up every day – and now, thinking of the comfortable homes he had seen with patios, decks and verandas, he was inspired to renovate.

When he bought sacks of cement to make a floor under the sewn-together-sack awning he had put up to shade the ledge, Abdallah became concerned. He gestured to Umm Sayhoon, where clearing of the construction site for our settlement raised a distant but substantial dust, and he implored, '*Ya waladi*, don't bother yourself with concrete floors, you can't take them with you to *al-Wahidat*.' But Mohammad wanted to be comfortable now, even though it meant investing in something he would have to leave when 'the Units' were completed, and we were moved to them.

Traditionally the Bedouin were nomads; their possessions were mobile and extravagances were generally portable – unlike concrete floors. Women sported gold teeth or tattoos, but the men had a saying: 'When a Bedouin gets rich, he buys a horse, a rifle or another wife.' And while they watched each other jealously to see who got what, their wives encouraged them to buy horses and rifles.

He got Rewe'e, who was always looking for casual work, to help him with his floor. They extended the yard at the same time, adding a few more metres of fresh dirt to the pile below. On the donkey they carted sand from the *wadi* in a split-open sack, and water from the cistern below the High Place. For the next few days they mixed great pats of cement up in the yard and made the *ma-rush* floor and a wide path from the cave to the kitchen door.

The resulting fifteen square metres of floor cost us only as much as a month of food for our donkey but lasted much longer. The move to the settlement didn't happen as soon as some people expected and we enjoyed that floor in the shade for years to come. It was so much easier to keep everything clean.

With the floor our *ma-rush* became our summer room. We sat and ate there. I did our laundry there – spreading my piles of clothes around the big tin tub, the *ligan* – and at night we made our bed there. When winter approached we took the sacking down, so it wouldn't disintegrate in the wind and rain, and so we could still enjoy the floor on sunny days.

We were sitting out there late one afternoon when we saw Mohammad's father wending his way up the hill. It wasn't unusual for him to visit but he wasn't stopping to scratch the sandy surface for possible antique coins, which suggested he was on a mission. I could see he was wearing his usual collection of garments, camouflaging his shape and his slight frame but not his walk. He always appeared to walk sideways, reminding me of a crab, but if I looked closely to see why I got that impression I couldn't tell what it was. He had on the purple sweater I had knitted him over a warm shirt. His old sports jacket provided pockets for tobacco, a trowel and often other treasures. His *mendeel* was red; his black shoes plastic. The woollen army-surplus trousers and greatcoat hung loosely.

Soon he joined us on the mats and, leaning forward, questioned Mohammad. 'What is the meaning of the word howd? Aud? Owd?'

'Old!' Mohammad and I recognised and chorused. '*Gideem,*' we told him it meant.

Understanding spread along the deep smile creases of his face.

'No wonder,' he mused as he extracted a cloth bundle from an inside pocket. He nodded to himself as he unwrapped it in the palm of his hand – it was an earth-pink oil lamp, a little blackened round the wick-hole, but otherwise as perfect as the day it had been fired.

'I just met a tourist down on the Roman Road and showed this to him. He seemed interested. In fact, he looked quite keen, but he became a bit wary when I told him the price. It's only an *inhaidi* [the most common Nabataean style] so I didn't ask for much and that's when he asked me if it was *old*. He looked suspicious so I thought *old* must mean *copy* or *fake* and swore to him, "No, not old!"' Abdallah chuckled and added, with his goateed chin in his coat, 'I should have asked for more, then he would have *known* it was old.'

Despite being illegal, the Bedouin sold the pottery they dug for and the coins the wind and rain uncovered for them. When I realised how many pieces there were in boxes in the basements of museums (which only the people cataloguing them would ever get to see) I wished there was a way the digging and trade could be regulated. A way in which the unique pieces and the historical secrets they revealed could be protected, but the common bits like Abdullah's lamp could go out into the world, interesting other people in Petra, the Nabataeans, the Bedouin and Jordan.

Digging could be productive, but it could also be dangerous. The sandy earth was firm enough to keep the shape of the hole dug into it. If more than one guy worked together they could dig down some metres and follow a seam of pottery under the ground, possibly along a wall, much like miners follow a seam of ore. Sometimes when they divided their spoils they had to take their *mendeels* off to carry all their pieces home in. The Byzantines left lamps and cups that looked immature, as if made by children; the Romans left solid pots, fine tear jars and pornographic oil lamps; and the Nabataeans left pocket-sized statues of goddesses and horses, and plates and jugs – beautifully thin and cleverly painted.

One afternoon I was at home. It was either spring or autumn. The sun was warm and the air had that clear, clear clearness that made me feel my lungs should burst. Umm al-Biyara loomed higher in the afternoons as the shadows subdued the details of its face. There was a raising of voices down at the Keenya, and soon after the Department of Antiquities Land-Rover raced crazily along the track below my ledge . . . and a couple of minutes later raced back. After it had disappeared up the Siq I saw Mufleh on the track and called out to see what was going on. He came up for tea.

It was Basma's husband being taken to hospital. He had been digging in the lucrative area near the Crusader castle, not far from where they lived, when his hole fell in on him. The child digging with him realised he had no hope of moving the earth and screamed for Basma, who had raced straight for the nearest help – the Department of Antiquities office, where there were usually people hanging out, and a vehicle.

They had dug him out. Mufleh told me: 'I don't know how we did it – you should have seen the size of the hole! I suppose it helped that the dirt had fallen behind him so he was trapped but not completely buried. His breathing didn't sound too good though, so they've taken him to the hospital.'

He survived thanks to the unselfish actions of all involved and the incident was smoothed over like the dirt over the hole.

A Car, a Loan

During our trip to New Zealand Mohammad had also learned to drive. He had passed his licence test on a wet, wet day in Oamaru and looked forward to being able to buy a car.

Soon after we got back to Petra, he went off with Ali and came home, creeping along the path, in a smoky metallic-blue Mazda 929 sedan. It had Saudi licence plates. One of the Abu Taya Howeitat – the Bedouin who rode with Lawrence of Arabia and still lived out in the southern desert straddling the border between Jordan and Saudi Arabia – had brought it in and the Jordanian customs duties still had to be paid. We couldn't use it till they were, so we flattened the dirt in the cave below our home and parked the leather-seated extravagance in it till we could borrow the money.

When we went down to the Keenya to ask Gublan (the 'Toktor') for a loan, he produced Miranda and Pepsi from his *thilaaja,* popped the lids off and told us to come over in the evening.

Mohammad reminisced as we climbed up to Gublan's cave on a-<u>Th</u>ineb. 'We used to make cars of wire and milk cans and drive them all over the place. That was when my mother was alive and we lived up here and Ali was an orphan and he lived with us. We scrounged around and made the fanciest cars. We could drive them standing up.'

I had seen children make them even today – just a small squiggle of wire and cans which they managed to manoeuvre with a steering wheel on a metre-long rod.

'We cleared a road all the way down to the shop near the Keenya so we could drive them if Ummi sent us.'

Gublan's family was living in a smoky winter cave; the lamplight didn't reach to the dark walls but lit up the eyes of the children clustered round the fire, and the pages of the notebook spread on the ground beside it into which a little boy, hunched on his hands and knees, was copying his lessons. We sat in our coats and boots on a *jannabiya* by the fire and flicked our cigarettes straight into it. They poured us tea and offered to make dinner (it almost goes without saying), but it was late enough to convince them we had already eaten.

Bekhita went out into the night and came back in with an eight-ounce Nido tin. She knocked the earth out of its rim and Gublan passed over his *shabriya* for her to prise it open with. Pop. She extracted a plastic-covered roll and untied the string. The dinar notes it contained were divided by colour – green twenties, blue tens and two red fives. They had memorised how many notes there were but were unable to multiply them into dinars. Bekhita passed the notes one by one to Gublan and we all counted together. The boy with the notebook paid particular attention. Gublan then counted Mohammad twenty green notes. 'Four hundred dinars,' Mohammad stated and we both invoked, '*Allah y kathr khair-ak,*' for God to increase their providence, and promised to pay it back as soon as we could.

We wandered home. We were lucky – in Mohammad's pocket was a wad of cash (worth about eight hundred pounds) and we would be able to use our car, but it had been in a buried tin can and I couldn't help thinking about the barefoot children doing their homework in the firelight and wondering about priorities.

In the Car to the Khateeb

Once the duties were paid we became busy. Our car was one of only four vehicles in the valley but because it had four doors it soon became the preferred ride for families needing to get to the doctor in Wadi Musa, the hospital in Ma'an, or to *khateebs* with special gifts in sand-blown villages from al-Guweira to al-Gatrana.

Each *khateeb* came to fame briefly and disappeared again into local history once everyone who wished for a cure had tried his and been either healed or disillusioned.

The latest was a man from the Aiwanaat, a tiny cluster of concrete buildings on the side of the Desert Highway. Cure seekers converged on it from as far away as the Syrian border and Saudi Arabia. Everyone was welcome, even if they didn't arrive with a goat or sheep tied in the tray of their pick-up to contribute to the evening meal. The family members prepared *mensef* in a breeze-block shed and served it by the light of kerosene lamps to the women in one room and the men in another.

The women swapped stories and discovered there were others worse off than themselves. There were women who miscarried, children with cerebral palsy and Down's syndrome (unexplained afflictions which could only have been caused by magic spells), and girls who ran away from their husbands, but they came for persistent coughs or colds as well. After dinner the *khateeb* – an ordinary man in army-surplus trousers and a well-worn herringbone-tweed overcoat – came in and the sick people took turns to lie down on the floor so he could step over them, spit at them and cure them, *inshallah*. Men who were impotent or infertile or sired only girl babies underwent similar treatment in the *shig*. This was seldom the first place they had tried. And they rarely restricted themselves to traditional medicine.

They tried cures concurrently so it was impossible to know if the antibiotic injections I was administering or the spit of the man in the herringbone-tweed coat had done the trick.

There were other *khateebs*, too, for lesser dilemmas and for dilemmas other than human health, as I found out when my mother-in-law produced bitter *samin*.

Everyone complained it was bitter when she poured it on our *fatteh*. Even I could detect an unusual taste, a faint earthiness, but wouldn't have known to comment. It was her first lot of new-season *samin*. She had noticed the odd taste when she churned the butter but hoped it would go when she clarified it. She melted the butter to boiling and added flour to collect the impurities and herbs to give it the traditional bright yellow colour. The taste was still there when she licked her fingers after scraping the frying pan. She had poured it back and added more herbs but it hadn't helped. She decided it must be a spell put on by someone's empty, jealous eyes. She imagined she knew whose.

The *si'ins* (skins) she had collected the milk in were new. She had made them last summer when she had prevailed on the *nishaama* slaughtering the goats for a wedding not to slit the skins but to peel them back from the carcasses, so there were holes only where the tails and trotters had been, and the heads. And she had taken herself off to Bir a-Dubaaghaat (the well of the tannin-collectors) on the hills above Bei<u>th</u>a, where she spent a few days with her sister digging down to the roots of the prickly oak trees and scraping the tannin-rich bark, the *dubaagh*, off them. She came home when she had a full sack of it and after curing her skins she had sold the rest (by al-Ghazal vegetable-oil-tin measures) to the other women in the valley. She had scraped the hair off the skins in preparation for curing, then for weeks they had lain in the *ligan*, with the *dubaagh* staining the water and a couple of stones keeping them immersed. Eventually she had closed the holes by wrapping the folded ends over pebbles and tying them with slices of an old skin, leaving only the necks open for pouring the yogurt in.

I wondered if the taste might not be that of the *dubaagh*, if the new *si'ins* hadn't been properly rinsed, but Umm Laafi said, 'No. It's from the empty eyes. I should have denied having produced buttermilk so early. I should have cut a piece off Flana's *mudraga* when I saw her admiring our fat sheep without remembering

God. Then I could have burned it and her envy would have been powerless.'

But the *fatteh* was our only dinner, so we told each other it wasn't too bad and ate a few mouthfuls, and the next day, curious, I went with her and Mohammad to Hmed, a local, low-profile *khateeb* who lived in Wadi Musa.

We pulled up by a doorway in a wall shaded by a huge fig tree. Hmed came out at the sound of the car and invited us in. Two rooms and a kitchen with a blackened window hole and sack across the door opened onto the packed dirt yard; Hmed called to his wife to make tea as he opened the guestroom. We took our shoes off and stepped over a row of cut-glass ashtrays to take our seats on mattresses that lined the walls. Hmed didn't waste any time. He got out some lumps of alum, described circles over Umm Laafi's head with them and disappeared into the kitchen across the yard. The tea still wasn't ready and he was back with his answer. In the fire the lumps of alum had puffed and bubbled, and when Hmed decided they had bubbled enough he took them out and interpreted the shapes.

'*Al-mishkela min al-ar<u>th</u>, mish a-naas,*' he declared: the trouble is from the earth, not the people. Having thus ruled out Umm Laafi's theory, he went on to prescribe a plan of action. 'Burn incense over the *si'ins*, and move them to a different corner of the cave – the enchantment might be ancient.' He wrote some verses from the Holy Koran in tiny squiggles on a scrap of paper and folded it into a piece of tin the size of a large coin. He folded the edges of the *hejab* over with a pair of pliers and tapped them smooth out on the concrete step. Umm Laafi paid him with some balls of yoghurt and when she got home she sewed a tiny cloth pocket around the *hejab* and hung it around her neck.

Eventually her *samin* and *laban* were delicious. She thought the spell had been broken, or the spirits in the earth appeased. I thought the *si'ins* had had enough buttermilk through them to be rinsed of all traces of *dubaagh*. What mattered was that we had *samin* and delicious *fatteh* to dip in it.

In the Middle of the Night to Ma'an

My turn to drive came when a baby was due. The knock on the door in the middle of the night, or insistent calling from the gate, continued until we woke. (We had rigged up gates where the paths led off the ledge to keep Salwa – and the plants Mohammad was growing in steps at the back of the *ma-rush* – safe.) I put a *mudraga* over my nightie, tied a scarf over my hair and backed the car out of the cave below. I picked the huddled group up from their cave or nearest track and, taking the car slowly over the stony surface, wound out of the Siq. The head-lights slicing back and forth highlighted god-blocks between cliff curves, white fig trunks clutching rock cracks and the rem-nant of paving I had sat on to feed Salwa on one walk through the canyon. (God-blocks are cute rectangular shapes carved in Nabataean times as representations of their gods.) The smoky goat-hair smells of mother-in-law and husband competed with the freshly bathed perfume of the woman in labour. She bathed herself once she was sure she was in labour because it was safest not to go near water, the cause of all ill, for a couple of weeks after the delivery. Sometimes we only went as far as Wadi Musa to a midwife, but as the years went by, and incubators and cae-sarean sections became appreciated, we went more often to Ma'an.

In Ma'an we waited in the corridor. When Sister Naifa came out and asked for baby's clothes, we knew the baby was fine.

We asked, 'Is the mother fine too?' but never, 'Is it a boy or a girl?' although that is what we wanted her to tell us. She kept us in anticipation.

Often there weren't any baby's clothes and she would wait, hands on hips and mimed disbelief on face, as the new grandmother took off her floral headscarf or chaff-specked cardigan and handed it over with an ineffectual shake. I saw the drama often enough to know that Naifa melted at this moment, maybe she remembered her own well-meaning grandmother, but her tut-tutting as she went off to wrap up the new bundle of joy fooled others into preparing baby clothes next time.

The next day, or later the same day if our trip had been in the early hours of the morning, we went back to bring them home. Salwa, awake now, cried, '*Widi aroo'h ma'aki Yom*' – I want to go with you, Mum – and my passengers insisted there was room and sat her on their knees. We never had car seats for children nor did anyone use the seatbelts provided for the adults.

The doctor did a morning round and discharged new mothers then if everything was normal, and the accountant had a copy of the Royal Decree for free medical care, so most mothers were on their way home within hours of the delivery.

Grandmothers carried the infants out of the hospital under their *abas* and new mothers shuffled onto the blanket on the back seat. There were husbands who insisted we all go to Abdo's restaurant and breakfast on grilled chicken-halves or fried lamb's liver on plates of humus, husbands who bought the side of lamb that was hanging outside the butcher's shop, and husbands who had the poultry man slaughter and clean enough chickens to take home for *mensef*. There were grandmothers who insisted we stop at the Amrani's shop to buy fenugreek, an infusion of which would help the uterus back into shape, and watercress seeds, a couple of which, administered on the tip of a nipple, would relieve an infant's constipation. Mothers asked their husbands to buy us all cold *manga* (cans of mixed fruit nectar) thick and sweet for the drive home.

Back at home with the car in the cave below and the invitation for dinner accepted, I would have liked to have lain back in the *ma-rush* and felt the mountains, but Salwa had slept in the car and needed watching now, and there were usually dishes to do, or water to get, and often an injection or dressing to attend to, too.

Accidents Do Happen (i)

Oh no, I wondered, seeing Ataima at the gate with her granddaughter on her hip. What have they done to her now? It was obviously not a social visit; she was wearing a plain black everyday *asaba* around her head and an unembroidered fire-pocked *mudraga*, and the two-year-old wore a ragged scrap of dress. I got up from my washing and as I opened the gate wee Basma recognised me and screamed, throwing up her arms in defence, so I could see her right arm was covered in tomato purée. There was the answer to my question: another burn.

Ataima put Basma down on the concrete floor and over the noise defended herself before trying to calm the child.

'I was busy frying cauliflower for the kids' lunch. Basma ran in and tipped the whole lot over: primus, frying pan, oil, food. You know how her mother is and *she* doesn't sit still. Luckily the other kids weren't nearby – look, it splashed on my sleeve too!' She sat down on the mat rubbing her arm, exasperated.

I put a pot of tea on the gas, got the bandage box out of the cave and crouched in front of them, pouring saline solution into the kidney dish. The cries increased. Basma's little mouse-face was a mess of dusty tears and Ataima gave it a wipe with the end of her *asaba*.

'You of all people should know to be more careful,' I scolded her. 'I mean, look at her leg.' The bright red scar from her ankle to her thigh was only a few weeks old – that time she had been scalded by a glass of hot tea. 'And I've told you a hundred times not to put tomato purée on, now it's going to hurt her even more trying to clean it all off. No wonder she's afraid of me. Hold her arm up now.'

Ataima held her on her knee.

Why don't they learn? I thought as I washed the mess off. Luckily it hadn't set. On her leg they had put toothpaste and that had set like plaster of Paris!

Poor Basma. A swatch of skin peeled off.

'*Smallah, smallah*,' Ataima soothed, and slowly Basma's cries ran out as I applied the greasy paraffin gauze and bandaged it up.

I hated having to cover the burn but they lived in an open goat-hair tent with a sandy floor and there was no way Basma was going to stay clean. I had to do my best to protect her from infection, although changing the bandages was probably going to be as painful as cleaning off the purée.

I instructed Grandma again, as we shared the pot of tea, and hoped some of the instructions would sink in. 'Bring her back in two days. Try to keep her out of the sand but if the bandage comes off bring her back straight away – and unless you decide not to bring her back at all, don't let anyone put anything else on it.'

Why Donate What You Can Sell?

One night Mohammad took another Fatima to have a baby in Ma'an and the doctors performed a caesarean section. She

needed blood. Mohammad came back to Petra and took brothers, cousins and other volunteers (all males) who were keen to
donate, but none of them matched her type so he went with a
cousin to find some in Amman. The blood bank didn't have any
either. People with negative Rh factors didn't donate blood –
they hung out at the downtown coffee houses and sold it. Cash
was the currency and luckily the cousin had plenty, because
besides paying the two guys who had the matching type, he had
to pay the doctor in Jerash (60 kilometres north of Amman)
who extracted a unit from each of them, and he also had to buy
a cooler to preserve it during the drive back to Ma'an.

Back at the hospital they checked the type and poured it all in,
or maybe they did have some in store, tested and cleared, and
what Mohammad brought was tested and cleared to replace it.
Either way it must have been good because Fatima and her husband went on to have more children, despite the doctor's
advice – till they reached a grand total of thirteen.

1982: Relations and Home Improvements

For a long time none of my family visited. My brothers Ted and
John were both studying then working, and my sister Anna was
still at school. Mum and Dad had no plans to leave their country of choice. When John and his wife Cathie went overland to
Europe it coincided with our trip to New Zealand. Ted also
eventually left New Zealand and went through the USSR to
Holland, where he arrived in a winter so severe that even the
Dutchmen skating the Eleven Cities Tour found it cold. He flew
straight home.

The closest he got to us was at Yokohama harbour, waiting

for the ferry across to catch the Trans-Siberian Express. The meandering chatter of the gathered travellers eventually took them to the Middle East and Jordan and one of the girls said, 'The most spectacular place is Petra. You mustn't miss it.'

'That's where I'm headed. My sister lives there . . . she married one of the Bedouin.'

'That's so amazing! I stayed with them. They live in a cave, right? Mohammad and Marguerite!'

Finally John and Cathie were coming and Mohammad decided to make a shower. Until now when we wanted to bathe we heated the water in a metal bucket, shut the cave door, stuffed something into the windows for privacy, and then, crouching in the big round flat-bottomed tin bathtub, scooped water over ourselves, or each other. A good scrub with a loofah followed and a few more scoops of warm water washed off all the soap. The hardest part was manoeuvring the *ligan* out of the door to tip the water out in the yard.

I thought our visitors could manage. If they needed a proper shower they wouldn't come I figured, but Mohammad was adamant.

As if he had been a shower maker all his life, he got to work. He got pipe cut and threaded to his measurements, and bought a shower rose and stopcock in Wadi Musa. He put a 40-gallon drum on the rock above the kitchen and connected the pipes down the rock-face and through the roof. Behind the kitchen door he made a shower basin of cement and outside the kitchen he dug a hole for the drain to run into. He put boards over that and buried it again. And he hung up a shower curtain, as much to keep the water in the basin as for privacy. We emptied a couple of jerry-cans in for a test run and found the plumbing to be perfect, though it took a long day in the hot sun for the water temperature to be as good.

When we got the telegram, barely understandable, and almost

unbelievable, in the middle of John and Cathie's visit, I was finally glad of the shower. None of us imagined Mum and Dad would ever leave New Zealand but it said they would be arriving the following week. *Ligan* bathing was not something *they* needed to experience. It was a bit of work to keep the drum full, but Dad enjoyed the trek down to the spring and was often given the job.

Mum and Dad stayed ten days. Until now the Bedouin had found it hard to believe I had a family. 'Don't they want to visit? Are they too old?' they had asked. They had no understanding of the distance or cost. Now, as I showed them Petra, I showed them off. The women came up and shook their hands. They held on while they made sure. '*Haatha abu-ki?*' Or, '*Haathi ummki?*' This is your father? This is your mother?

And then they kissed them. Mum's short hair confused them or she would have got kisses on both cheeks. They invited us for tea, and food. They scrutinised us to find resemblances.

It seemed everyone wanted to make a meal for my parents. It was Ramadan so we were invited for *Fotra* (or *Iftar* as the modern Arabs call it), which is the evening meal to break the fast. We went to Umm Olaidiya where Ali now lived with the smiling wife of the unsmiling photo; to the Palace Tomb where Abdallah's tent caught the afternoon breeze; to a-Thineb where, these days, Maryam had to share her cave complex and her husband Salaama with his new Egyptian wife; and to Dakhil-allah's at the Monastery, where we reclined on plump *farrshas* with the monument dominating like a painted backdrop in a photographic studio. The Monastery was my favourite monument, so big and calm and out-of-the-way.

Dad was adopted by Salaama and Ali who came over to play *shish-bish* with him or John, and by Abdallah when he realised Dad had figured out how to play *sieja*. *Sieja* is a draughts-like game that can be played anywhere a board can be drawn in the sand. They needed about twenty-four 'men' each and collected whatever was in greatest abundance on the spot – stones or Pepsi-bottle tops or hard, dry camel or goat droppings were the most common. Dad won the game occasionally but his major triumph, before even starting, was *not* getting the droppings.

Mum had been an interested birdwatcher in Holland and a holiday botanist in the native bush in New Zealand. Now she carried a notebook and listed plants and birds she recognised and those she wanted to look up, like the large black birds that sat in the rocks above the Theatre and swooped down to scavenge after the group of schoolchildren had eaten their lunches there. Crows, she wrote, or were they ravens or rooks? (But when she got home to her book she was no better off; crows and ravens and rooks, she discovered, all lived in the hills of Jordan.)

A Sinai Blue lizard made an appearance on the steps near the High Place, plenty of ordinary clattery lizards were seen on other paths, and snake-like salamanders, green and orange, slithered into the oleanders as we made our way down by the spring. We found at least one scorpion when we lifted our bedding up from the yard in the morning, but no snakes.

We had made the toilet more private – but you still had to crouch – by building a small wall and covering a deep hole with planks to make a 'long drop'. I kept the toilet paper handy because even I didn't like using a stone – the natural equivalent. It worked well and the shower did too. Over the years I contested many of Mohammad's home improvements and business ventures, but the time usually came when I had to admit how right he was.

The car was great too, although we couldn't all fit in it. Mohammad took my family to Aqaba one day, for grilled fish at the Samaka restaurant and a ride in a glass-bottomed boat, and had great trouble convincing the policeman at the checkpoint that these really were his in-laws and that he was not illegally using his privately licensed vehicle for monetary gain. I was stopped too (when their visit was over and I drove them back to the airport along the King's Highway), but we all showed our passports and were 'welcomed to Jordan' with bows and open arms.

New Zealand Backpackers

One afternoon Mohammad came home from work grinning like the Cheshire cat and as he told the story I pictured the scene.

He no longer worked at the Treasury. The rivalry between the vendors there and his awareness, since our trip to New Zealand, of another way of doing business made him keen to try a spot on his own, so he had moved opposite the Theatre and set up his table outside an open red cave. Over the coming years he developed it into a coffee shop, but that day he just had the table, and I could imagine him lying in the shade of it watching the dusty road between the table legs.

Horsemen passing occasionally called, '*Gow-ak*' (slang for 'your strength'). They knew he was there although they couldn't see him.

'*Allah y-gow-eek, tifuthul,*' he always replied. God strengthen you, come in.

He saw four tourists coming down the road and got up lazily. He leaned over the back of his metal table and appraised them as they got closer. Sun-bleached hair, frayed shorts, Indian-cotton shirts and leather sandals: *im-gatayeen*, he decided – good for a chat, not usually so good for business, although he was learning to be open-minded about that.

Im-gatayeen comes, I think, from *im-gatay turug*, which is a highwayman, so it became a word for hitch-hiker or someone with no (obvious) fixed abode.

The brown-legged girls dawdled by the table. They wore

plaited thread bracelets and one of them carried an army-surplus shoulder bag, like I had when I arrived. The guys headed for the arch and disappeared into the Theatre.

'Where are you from?' Mohammad opened the conversation, having already decided they were Kiwis or Aussies.

They glanced at each other, bored with the question, but allowed him, 'New Zealand,' as they tried on the silver bracelets.

'Whereabouts in New Zealand?'

I could see him cock his head and he probably didn't miss the resigned rolling of their eyes (or the meaning of it: 'He wouldn't even know what a map of the world looks like, let alone where New Zealand is'), but one of them answered politely as she checked herself out in the embroidery-framed mirror, 'Nelson.'

The answer couldn't have been better if Mohammad was writing the joke himself (and I always loved him for his quickness). His eyes must have lit up but he probably managed to straighten his face enough to enquire, tongue in cheek, 'Nelson . . . or Motueka?'

He poured them tea and they reminisced about the Chez Eelco and apple-picking.

A Desert Stage

Dad had likened our ledge to a stage because it had gates to 'stage left' and 'stage right' and a backdrop of mountains. And over the years all sorts of characters flitted onto it. My clothes line, which stretched across the yard and I lifted up with a forked willow pole, wasn't really the curtain but in every photo we have there was something flapping on it.

In the early days, although I hardly knew anyone, women

and girls came to look at me. We sat on the mat on the floor of the cave and they looked around. '*Wheen Mohammad?*' they asked – Where's Mohammad? – though they must have known he was at the Treasury. And they asked, '*Haatha wahadki?*' nodding so incredulously at our bedding (one *farrsha*, a sleeping bag, a blanket and a pillow) that I knew it meant, 'Is that your quilt pile?' and that it wasn't anywhere near big enough. Even their poorest bride's family received a *mahr*, which enabled them to supply her with at least two wool-stuffed *farrshas*; two wool-stuffed, satin-covered quilts; four bolsters stuffed hard with cotton, and covered with satin and white embroidered pillow-cases; a long rug of brightly dyed wool; and a low long wooden cabinet with lockable doors to stack them all on.

But that stage passed as I became one of the tribe, and as my pile grew.

Nora came to beg me for a coin. 'I need it for a potion,' she said, but wouldn't tell me what for. 'I have to beg coins from seven Mohammads and seven Fatimas.' And I was chuffed she considered me enough of a Fatima to count.

A respectable-looking Bedouin, in a pinstriped *thaub* and matching suit jacket, came to ask for money. The son of his cousin had killed a man and a tribal court had ordered his tribe to pay the victim's family twenty-five thousand dinars. He was collecting, as were most of his blood relations, to save the murderer from the death penalty and to save themselves from retaliation.

Laafi brought a plump *shon-nar* (chukkar) – a fawny colour but for black and white striped underwings and a ribbon, like a mask for a masquerade ball, of dark feather across its red eyes. He had caught it in one of his bird traps. Mohammad paid him for it and made a cage, from which it was stolen the same day, so we didn't get to enjoy its morning clucking. *Shon-nar* meat was delicious and we should have known somebody wouldn't resist the temptation.

Another guy came with an eagle he had caught on the cliffs of Umm al-Biyara, way above the spring. He crouched with it on his knee and stretched the wings out nearly as wide as his arms could reach. He had a buyer from Jerash who wanted the blood as a cure for *al-khabeeth* – cancer, the 'devious'. Blood is forbidden to Muslims; they slit the throats of the animals they are going to eat so that the blood runs out, and they like their meat well-cooked, but it features in lots of remedies and magic spells.

A man with a washed-thin shirt and ironed-shiny trousers came with a kit-bag full of *shabriyas*. Lots of the Bedouin had plain sturdy *shabriyas* made by metalworking gypsies, but Abu Riyadh Hoshaan was an artist who made masterpieces for tourists. The blades were reasonable but the handles and sheaths were beautiful – some curved round extravagantly, some were short and straight to the point – and all were studded with coloured glass beads and engraved with leaves and flowers. We bought his whole stock and ordered more.

And late one night a couple of men arrived with whispered talk of gold. They were from Sherig (the east) and had heard of these mountains and the inscriptions and carvings they held. ('There's gold in them thar hills,' Arabic style.) They said they had all it takes to extract the elusive riches: incense, a sacrificial rooster and a Moroccan with an authentic book (spades and picks weren't necessary – the rock would open up for a 'real Moroccan' and the gold would flow out). They were ready to share it with Mohammad if he would guide them to the rock wall they had heard about, the one with a carved snake on either side of the central niche.

We had heard such fairy-tale dreams before, and intricately laid plans to launder the results (for all gold in the land belonged to the crown), but, despite the fact that the only gold we knew had been found had been Turkish and uncovered by a road-gang bulldozer, high on the Sh-rah mountains without a

Moroccan in sight, none of my scepticism had rubbed off on my husband. His eyes lit up and off he went. Besides being illegal, gold, and thoughts of it, had been known to make murderers, so I stayed awake till he was safely home, gold-less, again.

Tuf-leh brought gold – a golden earring, soft and yellow. It had a little round plate which a stone might have fallen from, and a dangling droplet holding a small garnet deep and wine red. It had glinted at her from the belly of the *wadi* early one rainy morning as she crossed it to bring us a loaf of *taaboon*.

Two Italian girls in high-heeled boots came and stayed for the night. Ali-f and Mohammad decided to go to Amman the next day so they all went early to catch the *service*. 'The heels broke off their boots and we had to carry them halfway up the Siq,' they teased me when they got back. And I wondered: the heels off both their boots? But I didn't worry for long because Mohammad was here with me.

A uniformed policeman leaned over the gate and demanded, 'Did you see Flan go past?' He was just a young thing, a Bedouin who would have soon been conscripted if he hadn't signed up for the salary and pension of the police force, but I didn't like him and didn't invite him in. I despised the way he came into Petra with a self-important determination to apprehend the boys who had strayed from the army. From where we stood near the gate he could see Flan too – halfway across the ancient market-place, running for the hills. The policeman pulled up his socks, straightened his beret and raced off in pointless pursuit; for Flan was faster and these were his hills.

The scenes on our ledge continued bringing us comedy, tragedy and regular drama till the day we were to take down the gates and the clothes line, and move to the settlement project at Umm Sayhoon.

The Yarmouk Force

Ever since restoration work began on the Gasr al-Bint, Abdallah had had the job of watchman. At night he slept there in a canvas tent surrounded by sacks of cement, trowels, spades and rubber buckets, and at dawn he was up to '*Wahhid Allah*' and count out the tools to the workers who started at seven. During the day, while the workers rigged up scaffolding to reach the highest arch and applied cement to keep it in place for a few more years, and even after they all knocked off and handed the tools back in at two thirty, he sat on the altar in front of the temple and watched the world go by. One sunny winter's afternoon, before we went to New Zealand, he had called us over as we passed and pressed his transistor radio to Mohammad's ear.

'Iraq is at war with Iran,' Mohammad had told me.

It was such a beautiful day and those countries were so far away that I hadn't given it much thought.

'I can't understand why the Muslims would fight each other,' I might have wondered.

'The Iranians are Shi'ites,' Mohammad might have justified, but a year and a half was to pass before that war was to encroach on our lives.

I seldom bothered to listen to the crackly BBC news, reasoning that if something was going to affect me it would. Then Jordan offered Iraq a fighting force of volunteers and the *nishaama* signed up in droves. Mohammad's brothers Salem and Ibraheem were among them. I couldn't understand it – they all hated the conscription into their own Arab Army and several of them had spent years in the mountains avoiding, or deserting it, and time in prison when they were caught. Maybe it was the promise of action, maybe it was the money – anyway, off they went –

Bdoul, Amareen and even some of the Liyathna from Wadi Musa.

The money lost its attraction when they got to the front and the bombs started falling. Awath and a younger guy, Khaled, signed off and came home on the first troop-carrying flight. From Baghdad they brought generous gifts for everyone: red and blue synthetic dresses for the girls that lasted for ages; battery-run toy racing cars for the boys that didn't; and for the families, glass jugs and matching glasses with modern yellow spots that never washed off.

Mohammad lost track of his brothers. Now and then someone came on leave but there was no sign of Salem or Ibraheem. The BBC reported that the Iraqi troops were getting pushed back out of Khorumshar, so Mohammad set out for Baghdad to look for them.

He took Ahmed, a friend from Wadi Musa, and they were gone about a week. They came back thinner and quietly stunned by the reality. There was no food in Iraq. In the truckers' cafes along the thousand kilometres of desert road to Baghdad, they had been served thin tomato soup with rice. From the capital they were directed out to the Jordanian force. I don't know if they went north or south (it was probably east); I didn't have a map. They asked directions and were told '*gobíl, gobíl*' (further, further). They found the camp, and Ahmed's brother – they even took photos. But you can't tell from the photos that it's forty-five degrees or that Mohammad and Ahmed didn't get *mensef* and pots of tea. The desert behind the little pyramid of soldiers posing in their tin hats is featureless. Warm water and the news that Mohammad's brothers and al-Jimedy were in another division – on the front – was all that they could offer. They gave up and came home.

Word finally got through to Ibraheem and he called to say he and Salem were alive. Before the Iranians got the land back, all the Bedouin I knew had signed off and come home.

Bedouin Bracelets

Mohammad bought two silver bracelets from a craftsman on the streets of Baghdad. They were modern pieces, quite different from the heavy plaited or nielloed styles traditionally worn by the Bedouin in Jordan. Both bracelets had camels and palm trees and tiny boats with square sails engraved on them, stick-like and appealing – but while one was simple, the other was intricate. I knew Mohammad loved the filigree design, with its inlaid engraved onyx and delicately hinged clasp, but for Petra it was frilly and impractical. I slipped the other one, the plain band, beaten thin but with the smoothest of edges, sideways onto my wrist and there it stayed. Mohammad gave the intricate one to Mum and they were both delighted.

Al-Jimedy – A Neighbour

Mohammad al-Jimedy was our neighbour for most of the time we lived in the cave. At first he lived up behind the Ras in a pair of caves that reminded me of Laura Ingalls Wilder's family's sod house on the banks of Plum Creek: hidden completely under the hill until you came round from the front and saw the doors and window in the rock wall. Al-Jimedy was taller than most of the Bdoul, very elegant, but seldom seen in a *thaub*. His cheekbones were strong but his eyebrow bones were stronger, making his deep-set eyes appear fierce until he smiled. He drove the truck for the Department of Antiquities between bouts of alcohol over-indulgence, and he brought wives from Egypt with great panache.

Before he ever went to Egypt he had married two Bdoul women and divorced one of them. He married the first Egyptian wife when Elizabeth and I were first in Petra. That wife didn't stay long, which left only Fatima-n and their two small children in his household.

When Fatima-n popped in to visit we drank tea together while the children ran around wreaking havoc. '*Majnoona*,' she said. Crazy. Thus she excused her daughter's behaviour, and her own lack of discipline. Fatima-n only came up to my shoulder. Her wide open face was emphasised and aged by the frame of the *asaba* she wore. She was pregnant for the third time and crunched with poise on chips of limestone to alleviate the heartburn it was causing her.

Then al-Jimedy went back to Egypt and came home with his next wife, Hanem. Hanem had Egyptian height and held her head haughtily but was accepted by the women as soon as they heard her ululation, which was so loud and long that she became an asset to every celebration.

He moved them all into a cave down the hill from us, on the promontory just above the Nymphaeum. Beside the entrance to the cave he built stone walls for a kitchen, but the old bits of tin he had scrounged to make a roof for it never got put up and the women wrestled with them daily. The tin squawked and twanged as they tried to cover the barley sacks, the firewood, the donkey blankets and the occasional goat or sheep.

I went down there on long summer afternoons. Until their tent was repossessed we sat in its shade out on the cliff edge with the latest crawling child tied loosely to a pole by a scarf round his ankle, and the older children throwing stones at the goats bleating down below. After that, we sat in the cave. The children ran in and out and climbed onto Fatima-n's bedding pile as soon as they were told not to. It tumbled down, to their great joy.

They seemed to know not to try the same out on Hanem, who had a half moon of the almost circular cave, with a curtain rigged up in front of her things. The material of the curtain was heavily machine-embroidered light blue satin, so very, very Egyptian, but so un-curtain-like that I suspected she had made it from her wedding dress, once she had realised she would never wear it here. The cave was smaller than ours and I couldn't help wondering about private time with a shared husband, but they joked – usually bawdily, occasionally tensely – about whose turn it was, and as they were both regularly pregnant I guess everyone just played his part – the family went to sleep, or pretended to, and the couple was considerately hushed, or tried to be.

The fire-pit was a dirt spot in the middle of the rough concrete floor. We sat around it on *jannabiyas* in flowery covers. Blind Fathiya (Umm Laafi's aunt, Fatima-n's grandmother) sat tightly on her staff so the children wouldn't steal it away, and usually held the crying baby. The smells merged: the baby's swaddling clothes, last night's dinner, Fatima-n's *heeshy* (she smoked it when she had papers or chewed it when she didn't), the log in the fire-pit. The log rarely burned well because there was no window or chimney, but they stoked it up and made tea when I got there. The children scrambled round, Fatima-n punctured a can of evaporated milk, holding the point of the *shabriya* in the rim and bashing it against the floor, and we shared it out. The little boy poured tea back into the can and sucked every last drop of milk out before racing to throw it as far as he could off the cliff.

Al-Jimedy blackened his moustache one afternoon (I found him sitting cross-legged leaning over the *ligan*, out in front of his cave), and he went back to Cairo to introduce some other Bdoul to prospective in-laws. Until he opened the 'road' there had been a shortage of women in Petra. Most girls were snapped up and promised before they got to their teens and if a divorcée or widow became available she was barely left for the traditional three months (in case she was pregnant) before she was married again. Now men whose wives didn't produce children, or only produced girls, and men who had extra money and didn't want a concrete floor, had other possibilities. There was a whole suburb of Cairo ripe for the marrying, ripe, young, plump and pretty, and they didn't mind being _thurras_ or second wives. Several of our unmarried friends went off and got wives (though not all of them lasted), and several of our married friends did too. The Egyptian women brought an accent I couldn't understand, a standard of ululation I could never attain and pretty soon were producing a generation with fresh genes at a rate I had no desire to match.

Accidents Do Happen (ii)

And then one afternoon Mohammad sold the car for a wad of cash. I looked out from the ledge when I heard the car pull up and saw him get out with the ammunition box he kept his tools in. The buyer then drove off before I knew he was a buyer.

'It's good, Marg, we will buy another,' Mohammad assured me. 'A better one,' he said, alluding to when it had broken down on the Desert Highway and in Amman, and we had stood around uselessly until a wiser driver had stopped and sandpapered the points apart for us. The garages weren't much good. One time, when the engine was misfiring, an enthusiastic apprentice had used the high pressure air to blow the fuel lines clean, and then when the engine refused to even start, it had taken him several hours to figure out that he had ruined the fuel pump in the process. We had had to stay overnight.

I was happy to pay Gublan the rest of his money back, but even with punctures and breakdowns we had become used to our own car and we missed it for some months before we found one that went well and we could afford, without a loan and with Jordanian licence plates.

Until then we were once again at the mercy of others. When I went to Ma'an to find a dentist to fix my broken tooth, I left Salwa with her grandmother and walked up to Wadi Musa. I found a driver willing to take me and agreed on the fare. On the way we picked up an old couple and closer to Ma'an a soldier heading back to his barracks, and I had to bite my tongue when they offered the driver the money for their fares and he took it – I wanted to be able to cover them too, but they were thankful enough that I had put the car on the empty road, and he had been counting on other fares to complement my own. We had spent our own share of hours, in the days before we got a car, sitting on the side of a desert road praying for any kind of a vehicle, and had always been happy to pay who-ever stopped to pick us up, (and invariably put his children on the back of the pick-up so Mohammad and I could ride in the cab).

'Hiy ummki jet, ya Salwa.' Her aunties raced her up the hill to meet me as I came back into the Wadi Mataha that day. They were living in a cave at the base of the jumbled cliffs.

'What a day!' Umm Laafi was excited to tell me once I was sitting with Salwa on my lap and a tea in my hand. 'They got themselves all wet, her and Hussein, when I washed some clothes and they wanted to help. Then they went off to play, and when lunch was ready we couldn't find them anywhere. We called and called and I was beginning to get worried when I heard them answering. They were waving at me from that wogba up there at the end of the turnaga.' She pointed so far up the cliff that it was obvious why she hadn't seen them till they waved. 'And,' she continued, 'when I yelled at them to get back, for God's sake, they started jumping up and down. Luckily Laafi and Neda got them down. I couldn't have gone up there.'

I just wished she hadn't filled me in.

Accidents did happen in Petra. Apart from the occasional fatal scorpion sting or snake bite, the Nabataean cisterns drowned people and the precipitous rocks claimed unwary victims.

Like the little girl who, knowing that when Mum saddled the donkey they were leaving their cave, toddled off ahead down the wee slope and before Mum could catch her and hold her hand she went over the cliff, instead of along the narrow path that edged around it. The drop was only seven metres, but the rock reached out in bumps and knobs and her baby bones didn't stand a chance – her life was battered out of her before she reached the bottom.

I had been pregnant with Salwa then and suddenly, although I hadn't seen her yet, she became precious. I understood how Asmahaan's mother lost the will to live. I realised why the light went out of her eyes. And I saw how lucky she was to have a loving husband who believed his daughter's death was fated – she happened to fall off the rock, otherwise she would have died of a fever, a burn, or from a donkey's kick – and that having shared such a tragedy together they could do anything. He signed up for the Bahraini army and took her away from the cliffs and the memories.

Destiny and fate were all well and good, I mused as I walked home with Salwa's little hand in mine, but I was no longer in blissful ignorance. I had left Salwa with her grandmother quite happily that morning and I hadn't worried about her while I was away, but now I realised I would never have that luxury again.

Wogbas and Turnagas

Wogbas and *turnagas* can hardly be described in English. They are Bedouin words even the Wadi Musa people don't understand. To me, now, they sound like the shapes in the rocks, which they describe.

A *turnaga* is worn by the wind: a sweeping pathway that takes you around the side of a mountain where you don't dare to look down. Some of them have been embellished by the Nabataeans, who carved laden camels into a rock-face at the end of one and god-blocks into the smooth red side of another, and by the Bedouin, who carved their names or the initials of their wildest dreams, while their goats clattered forward to the blossoming *rattam* bushes in the gully at the end.

A *wogba* doesn't go anywhere. If you find one you can sit in, it feels like a hanging cane chair with wraparound sides, and if you pull your feet up, as our kids loved to do in the one halfway up to the Monastery, you could hide, as they did, until we drew level and then pop out. 'Boo!'

The Elephant and the Bad Baby

It was now the winter of 1982. I was pregnant again. This time it was going to be a boy. The Italian Hospital didn't have an ultrasound machine yet, but I knew anyway – as I had known Salwa would be a girl. We had chosen his name already – Raami, Rami – and as well as the knitting-needle dream of the old lady in Ras-a-Nagb, Mohammad had had a dream of his own: a brand new pistol – another masculine noun!

When we chose the name for Raami, we knew of only one other person with it, but I think it was the name of the year because now there are thousands of Ramis and hundreds of Abu Ramis too. I also chose to spell it with two 'a's in English so people wouldn't pronounce it with a short 'a' sound. I didn't realise the name would become so common that he would have more trouble explaining his spelling than he would have had telling people how to pronounce it.

It was a winter of providence; it had already rained several times since September – quick wet storms after a couple of days of black clouds, with days in between sunny and clear.

We now had a gas light (a mantle on a tall pipe connected to a gas bottle which lasted a month or two) so we didn't have to battle with the temperamental Tilley-lamp any more, and a kerosene heater, which was great, though we still liked to make a fire at night and occasionally argued about the smoke in the kitchen. There wasn't much *rattam* left on our hillside but the wall behind the cave door was lined with a stack of hardwood logs that Abu Awwad's son had brought from Bei<u>th</u>a. The new road went straight there from the settlement and he had made the most of it and filled his pick-up full of wild pistachio and prickly oak, for which we had paid him well. Late in the evenings we used the coals to make crunchy loaves of unleavened bread, which we dipped in fresh *laban* or yellow *samin*.

Soon after dinner I made our bed ready against the back wall of the cave and cuddled up to read with Salwa from the treasures Mum sent. I didn't always speak to her in English, and she spoke mostly Arabic, but through the stories she learned the language.

'And the elephant went . . .' I read.

'Rumpeta, rumpeta, rumpeta,' she recited.

'All down the road with the . . .'

'Ice-cream man . . .'

The Elephant and the Bad Baby had arrived in the most recent parcel and she already had half of it off by heart. She got me to read it over and over again, but now and then I had to read *The Very Hungry Caterpillar* or *Mr Magnolia* to keep me sane.

Ali-f and Salaama still came to play cards most evenings as soon as the sun went down, and once Salwa was asleep I was free to play too. We usually played *Handreemi* (a variation of rummy) or *Banakel*, which we played in pairs. Mohammad was my partner unless we weren't doing well or he was trying to get me to cheat, and then I partnered Salaama because he kept his derogatory remarks to himself when I made mistakes or ignored his hints. Sometimes Ali came and I had to wait for a turn; other nights they tried to talk me out of reading to Salwa so there would be enough of us to start playing straight away.

My bones were loosening and my back got painful pretty quickly so it was always a relief when we took a break. I could stretch my legs and make the dash through the weather to the kitchen, to make tea or sweet hot drinks with powdered milk and instant coffee.

It was on one such dash that I heard a voice calling for help in the darkness near our gate. An Antipodean voice, what's more. I assumed a countryman had been directed to our home and yelled out over the wind, 'Are you looking for me?' I shone the torch in the face of a young guy with a huge backpack.

'I'm looking for anyone who can help but I wasn't expecting a Kiwi!'

I wasn't expecting anyone either but I invited him to stay – people fall off cliffs wandering around in the dark. I didn't want to think about what could have happened if I hadn't gone out just then – and the unbelieving looks on the gathered faces when I came in with a pot of tea *and* an Australian was reward enough.

In 1978 there had barely been an entrance to Petra; just an office where you could rent a horse or guide but nothing else.

After we moved to the settlement an entry fee was introduced for the first time, but some time before that signs were put up forbidding tourists to sleep overnight in the site. Everyone was angry about the signs. Everyone always invited people to stay and the whole of Petra benefited; some tourists gave their hosts money, some bought mats or *mudragas* from them, some sent friends bearing gifts, and all of them went out and told of the hospitality of the Bedouin and the welcome they had been given, encouraging more visitors. That's how I met Mohammad, for goodness's sake. The signs were a reminder, a way of making us uncomfortable, making us look forward to the settlement and homes of our own.

In all the years the Bedouin lived in Petra there was not one foreign casualty in the area (apart from the flood victims). But in the years after we moved, several people lost their lives, simply because no one was around to tell them which was the correct path, or to hear them calling when night fell and they lost their way, or even to notice which way they went – so that when they were missed and a search was initiated, no one knew in which direction to look and they found them too late.

When it rained we went out and lined up bowls and buckets to catch the water from the tin roof to use for washing. We played cards for hours or until Salaama had lost more than he could bear for one night.

Raami Arrives, Feet First

One such night, a week past my due date, Mohammad suggested we get someone to take us to Aqaba the next day to see what was up. On my last visit to Amman, four months before, the doctor had remarked, 'Everything seems to be fine – so far. There is still a chance the baby might turn.' I had put the doctor's remarks to the back of my mind but they were now creeping forward.

I went into labour later that night and woke Mohammad at the first light. He went down to his father's night-watchman tent for help. Abdallah was taking a night off but Laafi and Neda were filling in for him. Laafi went up the Argoob Jmea-aan to get Ali-f, who now had a little Datsun sedan, and Neda sprinted home barefoot to get her mother to come with us. Not long after Mohammad got back, Ali-f pulled up below the ledge and Neda arrived on it pulling her mother along excitedly. 'I'll look after Salwa and tidy up till you get back.'

I had Salwa up and ready. I hadn't planned to leave her and didn't change my mind; as long as she was with us I wouldn't worry about her. I was ready too. I had packed a bag of baby clothes weeks ago, but Umm Laafi fussed around. She refused to move until I produced a razor blade and some string for emergency cord-tying, then she grabbed a blanket to put under me and ordered everyone to the car.

I was breathing and relaxing quietly but the contractions were getting closer together and stronger and I could feel a hard lump below my ribs. Was it a head? 'Maybe we should go back to Wadi Musa,' I said, worried, as we climbed the winding road up the Sh-rah.

'No good,' the others agreed. 'The doctor probably wouldn't be there . . . and you'll be all right till Ma'an, won't you?'

I was feeling less sure about that as Ali-f raced along the road in the lee of the Sh-rah, through the village of Uth-ruh and out onto the Ma'an plateau. A tyre burst like a shot ringing out and he pulled over with a nervous chuckle, 'I don't have a spare.'

'I couldn't wait for you to change it if you did,' I gasped as we all got out on the cold and lonely road. We were in a crisp, clear dome of blue – the land wore a faint green blur. For a few moments as we stood there, the sun warmed us side-on.

Mohammad flagged down the two cars that we had just raced past and both of them stopped. The first was a pick-up and the driver pulled over, but by then the second car had stopped too – a spacious, old, leather-seated Mercedes with a man and two women and room for some of us. We left Mohammad and Ali-f with the pick-up driver to deal with the flat tyre and sped off. The plump, black-clad matron jiggled herself round in her seat to talk to us. They were from Wadi Musa – this was her son who worked for the Civil Defence, and his wife. Assessing my breathing she urged him on.

There was hardly a break between contractions and I was tempted to tell them to stop. The road was empty, the air was cold, but clear and still and dry. I had the blanket, Umm Laafi had a razor blade and the other women were sure to know a thing or two. I would never live it down if my baby came in a stranger's car.

But what if something went wrong? The lump was hard below my ribs. I wavered till we had passed into the outskirts of Ma'an and then there was no going back. The driver turned on a siren (the unbelievable advantage of being in the Civil Defence!) and raced through the early morning to pull up a couple of minutes later at the hospital doors.

Kind faces tried to help me out but I ignored them, breathing, breathing till the contraction passed. Then I ran along the corridor and up the stairs to the maternity-ward office and an easy chair before the next contraction began, leaving my deliverers and Umm Laafi with Salwa to gather their wits behind me.

The Sister wasted no time in getting me to the delivery room and examined. I was glad it was Naifa because I knew she was competent, but I could see on her face that all was not well. Sure enough she ordered, 'Don't push till I get back with the doctor.'

'Oh no. What's wrong?'

'It'll be OK, but the baby is coming feet first and I can't manage on my own. So don't push, I won't be long.' She went out and shut the door. I was all alone.

'I knew I could feel a baby's head,' I told myself silently.

And then she was back with the doctor and in a few short minutes he said, 'It's a boy!'

But I couldn't hear it. I could see his tiny slippery feet in the doctor's grasp as he swung him round and round, head down, to unwrap the cord from his neck. Three times round, then all was well. Raami cried, the cord was tied, and later, as he made me comfortable, the doctor chatted in English.

'I understand you live in Petra.'

I don't need this now, I thought. 'That's right.' I made an attempt to be civil . . . didn't have much choice.

'You're married to a Bedouin there, Naifa told me.'

'Yes.'

'I think you have a baby girl born at the al-Basheer hospital, is that right?'

That's an unusual variation on the theme, I was thinking, then he finished, 'Well, I delivered her as well, remember me? I am Dr Basaam!'

What more could I say? 'Small world, Dr Basaam, *salim-edaik!*' May your hands be blessed.

We had a couple of hours' rest before Mohammad and Ali-f got the car fixed and came to take us home. The morning sun shone onto our bed and the desert outside the window stretched eastwards chalky-white and empty except for scattered black rocks. In this dreamy comfort Raami was soon nursing content-edly and I planned how to make the most of the takeover I knew would start as soon as we got back to the cave.

'Introducing' Raami

On day fourteen I got the *muzferr* out of storage (the red suit-case under my quilt table), put Raami in it, took Salwa by the hand and headed for my in-laws.

Most women waited forty days before they took their babies anywhere, but by the time I had spent fourteen days stuck on my ledge when Salwa was born I decided that that was one of the traditions I was not going to bother to keep. I had already been to the clinic then so didn't see the point.

The destination, or host, of that first visit was very important, I had discovered. In the following months everyone asked, '*A meen dakhelti bintki?*' To whom did you 'introduce' your daughter? But it seemed more a matter of personal choice than tribal tradition.

For those mothers who 'introduced' their babies to the prophet at the shrine on the top of Jabal Haroon it was proba-bly just as well they waited forty days – to get a bit of strength back – but others 'introduced' their babies to neighbours, and Salwa's grandparents had been thrilled when I had appeared at their tent with her. So my own tradition of 'introducing' my children to my in-laws was started.

Now Salwa skipped ahead, also glad to be out. Yesterday it had rained and today the sky was a piercing blue. Water, caught seeping down the rock-faces, glittered in the sun. The ground was sandy, never muddy, and green was glistening everywhere; the smells were almost lush. In front of the Palace Tomb, on our wedding race track, so much grain had sprung up from the spilled feed and droppings of goats, donkeys and horses that it was possible to imagine Bdoul crops were still planted there.

Abdallah and Umm Laafi were still wintering down in Wadi

Mataha, but in a different cave again. The deep shade of the mountainside sat in this one, damp and cold with no promise of sun till late afternoon, but Neda and Maryam scrambled out with a couple of *jannabiyas* and put them for us way out in front in the sun.

'*Ahlan, ahlan ahleeeen.*' They copied their mother welcoming us and kissing Raami, who stretched when I put him down but squinted against the glare. Salwa raced off with her aunties to bring things to make tea.

Ibraheem roused himself and welcomed his new nephew, getting down on his knees to rub his unshaven bristles across Raami's soft cheeks – and chuckling as Raami wriggled a response. Ibraheem had the matches and started the fire.

The sandy gully up in front of me was green in every shade. Among the oleander and *rattam* bushes clumps of barley and wheat grass thrived, as did *khubaiza* (a mallow plant with mauve flowers and edible leaves) and nettles, which the kids came back stung by – licking their fingers and rubbing the spots – after collecting a whole pile of the *khubaiza* in Neda's scarf.

Umm Laafi cooked the *khubaiza* up for lunch like spinach or silver-beet. Ibraheem said how much nicer it would be with a squeeze of lemon but there was none to be had and I enjoyed it as it was – a tangy contrast to the *taaboon* bread we ate it with.

After lunch I lay back in the sun beside Raami, and the girls played with the neighbouring girls by the remnants of a stone wall. They moved stones to make rooms and squealed for Laafi to kill the hibernating scorpion they had rudely awakened. The gully provided a wealth of rusty bottle tops, once-yellow sardine cans and barely red tomato purée tins which they lined up on a rock shelf. They pulled up a *zaknana* bush and used it to sweep their 'home' clear of stones and twigs. They found oblong stones which they wrapped in scraps of rags for dolls which they sang to, put to sleep, woke up and pretended to breastfeed under their scarves. The stone dolls were wonderful because they couldn't lose an arm or leg or break and were easily replaceable, but they were a worry if arguments broke out – then it was best to run.

Laafi was dispatched to his father in the watchman's tent by the Keenya and I wasn't allowed to leave till he got back with some money for Raami. The ten dinars he sent was a quarter of a month's wage, but refusing it was impossible. Saying I would introduce my next baby somewhere else didn't work – they knew I wouldn't offend them that badly, and were thrilled anyway at the prospect of more babies. So I took it and was able to tell the women I met on the way back to my cave how generous my in-laws had been.

1983: Umm Salwa

For a couple of years now I had been called Umm Salwa. It was the latest in a line of names but it was not to be my last.

Mohammad sometimes called me 'Marg' but usually it was 'Fatima' and that's what our early friends still called me.

'*Marrat Mohammad*' – Mohammad's wife or woman – is what I was called by people when they were talking *about* me – even when I could hear them. That was a bit like 'Mrs Mohammad Abdallah' – especially when it was Mohammad's family doing the naming, or proud claiming.

When I became a government employee, I joined a different order. The quick pharmacist in Wadi Musa, when he found out my name was Marguerite, called me 'Margaret Tatcher', whose era we were in, but many of the Bedouin who met me through the clinic called me '*as-Sitt* Fatima'.

When Salwa was born I joined the club of *Umms*. I became Umm Salwa (Salwa's mother), and Mohammad became Abu Salwa. That she was a girl was not a worry.

'Whoever can bear a girl, can bear a boy,' I was constantly reminded. And so I should have been prepared for her name to be swept aside as soon as Raami arrived.

I fought it for as long as I could.

'*Issm al-mowlood?*' The name of the child? The shopkeeper in Amman asked me politely in order to address me appropriately. And, 'We take the name of the boy,' he took the time to explain when I answered 'Umm Salwa' and he could see Raami quite obviously a boy in my arms.

But I couldn't keep it up and quite soon I was Umm Raami, and Umm Salwa disappeared like Marguerite before her.

Salwa's Swing

Mohammad had wanted Salwa to have a swing ever since seeing all the 'rest area' swings scattered across New Zealand's South Island, and if he wanted something he usually managed to get it, somehow, sooner or later.

Salwa was her daddy's girl, *bint abu-ha*, and he spoiled her. Mohammad's father had spoiled him too, with meat – getting up early and waiting with a shotgun for *shon-nars* or quails to come and drink at the *gutaar*, or going hunting with a rifle for gazelles and ibexes. Nowadays we could get freshly killed chickens from Wadi Musa or, on our way back from Amman, a few kilos of lamb from a carcass hanging under a plastic bag on the Desert Highway, so Mohammad spoiled Salwa in other ways. Like letting her drink as much Pepsi as she wanted when she went to the shop with him, or breaking open pomegranates and never telling her not to dribble because it would stain her clothes but letting her suck and squirt the juicy seeds to her heart's content. And for her third birthday he surprised her with a swing.

We were on our way back from the clinic and it was hot. The doctor hadn't arrived and we had had to wait the whole morning. It had been shady and there were plenty of children to play with but now we were getting hungry and the path home was uphill. We climbed the Grand Staircase and were trudging across the ancient marketplaces (we still thought they were marketplaces then) when Salwa broke into an indescribable babble. Just the top of the cave and the fence across the ledge were visible from here, but now the top of the swing frame was too. I hadn't imagined she would know what it was, but she did. 'A-zingea-ha,' she managed. I could see her heart and soul fly ahead and even her body for a couple of jerky steps looked as if it was going to take off. And then it did. She ran the rest of the way home.

Summer Stories

Time went by. If it hadn't been for the doctor once a week I would have lost track of the days altogether. Mohammad went off to open his souvenir table and I was kept busy with Salwa and Raami – mostly washing the red sand they played in from their clothes (it was like dye), but also watching them: Salwa not to fall off the rocks or catch scorpions, and Raami not to eat any of the sand, or cigarette butts which he sieved out of it with his busy little fingers.

I often drove to Ma'an, usually for babies to be delivered but once for the placenta delivery only. Umm Khaled's long-awaited girl had arrived but the placenta didn't follow although her friends in attendance tried all their tricks. They tied and cut the cord then and while one woman stayed home with the baby the others escorted Umm Khaled down to the valley where I could meet them with the car. There was no hurry, they assured me, they had secured the placenta (by tying the umbilical cord round a stone anchor which she carried under her *mudraga*) so there was no way it could slip back inside her body (to float around wreaking havoc). The doctor had seen it all before. An injection and quick massage helped finish the process in no time.

Late every summer, as figs and grapes came ripe in the gardens around Wadi Musa and down by the spring, and bowls of them were set down wherever we visited, everyone got conjunctivitis. Bathing the eyes with an infusion of aniseed helped and we gave out all the eye drops we had in the clinic.

On summer evenings we sat around on the ledge. We made pots of tea with mint, and sliced watermelons on the *siddr* with the crack of a knife. It was easier to stay home, especially as the children got bigger, and we never lacked visitors.

We made our bed in the *ma-rush* – four sponge *farrshas* side by side with two sewn-together sheets tucked round them, blankets for later in the night, and our mosquito-cum-scorpion net like a gossamer room hanging from the poles. Salwa and Raami went to sleep to the sound of Bedouin stories.

Musa told us about his trip down to Wadi Araba. He was from the Amareen tribe, a real tent Bedouin, all skinny bones and buck teeth and a big guffaw for a laugh. He had bought himself an old pick-up and taught himself to drive, but like most of the other drivers in the desert he hadn't bothered to get a licence. It was his cunning alone that got him out of Wadi Araba that day without a heavy fine.

'A couple of weeks ago I went down to Grey-gre,' he said, 'to get a load of tomatoes.' The rocky dirt road down through the mountains usually took a couple of hours, then there was a fifteen-minute stretch along the potash-truck-bearing main highway before turning off to the market gardening settlement.

'I was glad to get to the asphalt and was cruising along without rattles when a policeman stopped me at a checkpoint. As I pulled in I realised it was Ali, a guy from the Amareen I don't think I have seen since the second grade when he dropped out of school. He recognised me too, and pulled his shoulders back to show off his uniform as he asked me for my licence.

'I got out my wallet and handed over my identity card. Ali took it and checked it out. He turned it over and scrutinised the other side too. As he passed it back to me he remarked, "I see you've learned to drive."

'I couldn't get it back in my wallet quickly enough, and then as I tucked that into my jacket pocket the punchline came into my head. Letting out the clutch as smoothly as the old Datsun would allow I replied, "And I see you've learned to read!"'

I don't know if we all believed him but we all laughed.

And al-Jimedy often told us about the tigers his father or grand-father, or maybe a more distant ancestor, had killed.

Tigers? In this area? I was sceptical until I saw a scruffy, stuffed thing in a musty rug-dealer's shop in Aqaba, which Mohammad admired. I certainly wouldn't have recognised it as a tiger without his enthusiasm. The dark brown and ochre stripes were only discernible on close inspection and it was only as big as I imagined a tiger cub to be. It was not what I had been conjuring up when al-Jimedy told how his hunting forebear had spied the tiger on a distant rock and, although he was sure he had shot it, it stood there still. He shot again. Everyone knew he was a good shot but there was still a tiger standing on the rock. The story varied between seven and ten shots until he finally downed the thing and went to look. And there they were behind the rock, dead tigers in a brownish pile.

I got embarrassed listening to this story and always felt like telling them how unlikely and ridiculous it was. But then again it might be true, and that hunter might be singularly responsible for the extinction of the species, for extinct they are.

There were other old characters too. They talked about Salaama Samaheen, who they called Heboob a-Reah – Puffs of Wind. He had drowned in the cistern by the Urn tomb but before that he spent years fighting against the British Mandate, and eventually a television serial was made about him. Mohammad loved telling how, when the soldiers came down from the Wadi Musa police post to arrest him, he was able to evade them but still deliver the famous Bedouin hospitality. He perched with his rifle on the cliff above his tent and ordered the soldiers to slaughter a goat from his herd while his wife made the *shraak* for *mensef*. Then he sent them back where they came from.

The young man who had dared to climb onto the flat Wadi Musa house-roofs to steal drying figs was recalled with similar awe. What audacity, but then again what desperate poverty their tribe must have endured for him to dare such foolishness.

When Mohammad came back from the toilet pit trailing the dead snake he had noticed gleaming in the moonlight on the overhanging rock, and killed with a well-aimed stone, the snake stories came pouring out. Everybody had one.

Awath's father had been bitten on the big toe by a snake years ago, in the days before hospitals and anti-venoms, so he hadn't wasted time thinking about them. He had pulled out his *shabriya*, always sharp, cut off his toe, ripped a bandage from the hem of his *thaub* and survived.

How lucky he was to have been bitten in a body part that could be cut off, I thought, but then there was another man who had been bitten in the heel and survived. I never quite knew if they told me this story about Faraaj to test my gullibility or to describe the hardiness of the Bedou. They described a real old-timer who had never worn shoes in his life.

'His feet were as wide as a camel's,' they said, 'and so cracked and calloused that when he arrived for work at the excavation, with a snake stuck by the fangs in the dead skin of his heel, everyone had just laughed.'

He was lucky he had battered the life out of it as he'd dragged it unknowingly across the stony ground because it was one of the poisonous ones – only they were small enough for him not to have noticed its weight. That kind of snake usually slipped quickly away, so that all we saw of them were their tracks in the sand – little smudges across the ridges, like lizard trails, but without the footprints.

He would have noticed the weight of a *haam*, which was what Mohammad killed – the kind we saw more often. The *haam*s were dark, almost black, and more likely to be a metre long. Thicker and heavier, they left more obvious trails, curling back on themselves like slow-moving rivers, where they had enjoyed the overnight warmth of sandy spots. People said they were harmless, that we should say *seeb* and leave them to go, but most of us never took the chance. (*Seeb* is what we say to a child who is touching something we don't want them to touch – 'leave well alone'.)

My father-in-law Abdallah had woken up once to find a *haam* coiled up inside his *thaub*. '*Sittrik ya-Rub*,' he had prayed as his situation sank in.

The whole family was out harvesting and had stopped for a sleep in the heat of the day. Abdallah had leaned his back against a terebinth tree, which provided leafy shade and probably a home for the snake. He became aware of the snake as it settled into the loose pouch of his *thaub* formed by the belt around his middle. He knew it was a *haam* and believed they weren't usually dangerous, but how to get it out without causing it to attack

in fear? He was always particular about fastening his belt properly and as he set about working it loose he continued his prayer,
his heart thudding so hard he was surprised he didn't alert the
snake. Then he jumped up and released his belt and his load.
The snake lay for a moment on the ground, probably stunned –
then slithered away. Abdallah didn't kill it because it didn't cause
him any harm. He said *seeb* and off it went. A year-old goat in
his herd didn't fare so well. He killed it that night to thank God
for answering his prayers and invited everyone within calling
distance to share.

I was glad Mohammad had killed the snake he found. I couldn't
have used our toilet knowing there was one around, and it was
a long way to the next suitable spot. People told us it was likely
another snake, possibly a more dangerous one, would move into
the vacated territory, but despite (more than daily) checking I
never saw one.

There was a murder story too but it was rarely mentioned. The
murderer had done his time and looked normal with a wife
and children and goats, but to kill a man for his rifle and the
clothes on his back was a sin that no one approved of.

A scorpion arrived in our midst one evening as we sat around
the lamplight, and we killed it and *al-humdulillahed* that it
hadn't crawled inside a jacket or trouser-leg as we sat on the
mats, backs to the darkness.

Some years we didn't see any scorpions, others we saw too
many. In the mornings when I lifted things – jerry-cans, mattresses, the donkey blanket – I uncovered them and they sprang
up or played dead. I had sewn second-hand net curtains together
to make our huge net and I was regularly thankful for it. (It
worked well to keep cats off the bed too. The ginger cat
Mohammad and Salwa had rescued from Aqaba had recently
had kittens and she tried to carry them to softer spots. To keep

her out of my quilt pile I had put a sack for her in a box under the kitchen table and the kitchen was filled with the sound of purring.)

The scorpions usually squeezed in and lay flat under our bed, but we watched from inside the net one night as a large black one made the great traverse up and over.

We couldn't put the net up inside the cave though, and when the rustle of an east wind caused us to make our bed inside I usually put a welcome sack across the cave door for them to settle under. Either I forgot, or the scorpion I found one morning in Salwa's little tracksuit sweater didn't get the hint. Thank God the sweater was inside out because otherwise I would have put it straight over her head. As it was, when I slipped my hand in the sleeve to turn it round, my body reacted to the scaly intruder in a spasm and I had flung it against the wall of the cave before I even realised what my hand had touched.

We were collecting our own stories too fast for my liking.

Smoking

I smoked for years – the more pregnant I got, the more I smoked, and once I had the babies I enjoyed a *cikara* whenever I sat down to breastfeed. Most of the guys smoked and few of the women said no if I offered them one. Mohammad and I smoked Gold Star cigarettes produced by the Jordanian Tobacco Company, but sometimes the cave shops ran out of them and then we smoked the poorer quality Reems or Kamaals, or even rolled *heeshy*, which made us cough and stained our teeth and fingers brown but were cigarettes none-the-less. Whenever I found myself scavenging in the windswept corners of my yard for leftover butts and smoking whatever dried-out scraps I found I knew I should stop, but I mightn't have if Mohammad hadn't stopped first.

One morning I found his packet after he went to work and thought he had forgotten it, but when he got home he declared he had given up. For the next few days I tried not to smoke in front of him, and wondered how he managed, then one morning he left me to look after his shop for a few hours. I had had tea and cigarettes for breakfast and nearly finished my packet as I waited. My mouth felt dry and disgusting – the Bedouin description, 'like the donkey's blanket', seemed apt. I thought: It's now or never. I stuffed the rest of the packet down the back of the wooden chest and hoped that no one would notice. I didn't want them betting on how long I would last.

I got through the first few days by saying, 'I just put one out,' whenever I was offered (and by eating a whole kilo of candy-coated almonds to keep my fingers busy).

I thought I had made it – a non-smoker for ever more – but one night Mohammad didn't come home and I nearly cracked. Early in the evening he had offered three Aussie girls, with tank-tops and sparkling smiles, a lift up to a tent near the Rest House so they could easily catch the dawn bus. Jealousy crept in as night fell and he didn't come back. It filled me up as the waning moon slipped behind the Crusader castle.

I searched the cupboards for a hidden cigarette swearing, 'If he hasn't spent the night in hospital or prison I'll leave in the morning!'

I searched the yard but had swept it clean. I sat by the fence in the starlight praying for a smoker on the path but there wasn't one. And so my night of weakness passed.

I didn't leave Mohammad. He had spent the night in prison for arguing with the pompous policeman who thought only *he* spoke English and who had tried to use his uniform to prevent the (ignorant) Bedouin from 'harassing' the foreign women.

Mohammad had had no trouble getting himself a cigarette to ease the stress!

On a few occasions over the years I had moments of jealousy like this. I had to remind myself it was Mohammad's generosity and freedom of spirit that I loved, but I did resent our children on such occasions because they were his excuses not to take me on whatever adventure he was going off on.

A Part of It All

We were at another wedding on another summer's night. Or it might have been a circumcision party – the celebrations were similar. Instead of a bridal procession the *Shalabi* went from tent to tent with a little leather suitcase and an excited crowd. (I was to convince Mohammad to have our boys circumcised in the hospital but later realised what a quick and clever artist the *Shalabi* was. I was brought a few babies who needed attention after the operation but it was usually because the mothers were careful not to let them get near water and the little bandages had stuck.) Once circumcised and dressed in a miniature *thaub*, the boy was practically ignored for the rest of the celebration as his family was so busy playing host. Most of the boys were only a year or two old at the time, so hopefully too young to remember.

Anyway, circumcision or wedding, three families had gotten together so everyone could celebrate at once and share the costs. They had set up their tents side by side along the Argoob Jmea-aan looking out across Petra.

The decorative *hubble-m-wad-aa* hanging along the front of the tent was mine. Now that I worked from home and had figured out how to sew under-dresses, everyone brought me material to make up and the *makeena* never got folded away. If the leftover scraps weren't big enough for a child's dress, or a pair of sleeves, I added them to my 'rope of celebration'. It became a bit like my story – some swatches, like some people, were brighter or starred more often, while others only appeared subtly once or twice, and the rope was like me connecting them to each other, and showing them off.

I lent my *hubble-m-wad-aa* to whoever came to borrow it for whatever celebration was happening. They returned it, tangled and smelling of juniper-smoke, but with a box of Nashed Sweets to show their thanks.

The singing and celebrating went on, as usual, till late. In front of the tents the row of dancers swayed sensuously. A couple of budding *nishaama* shyly joined at each end of the line but most of the smaller kids were asleep in the darkness of the tents. The poetic verses of the traditional *samer* resounded round the otherwise silent valley.

I sat with Mohammad among the men for a bit, chatting with three young American anthropologists who were staying with Abu Sha-her while they studied the Bdoul of Petra. As I watched them observe, I recognised myself at my own wedding – seeing the Bedouin in that same collective light. Now, I realised proudly, I knew them personally. I got that sensation (the heart-swelling one, till it felt it would burst) as I watched the row of dancers, firelight flickering on their faces. Awa<u>th</u>, Salem, Ali, Ismayeen, Ali-f, Sliman and Mufleh – our crowd was all there. And the feeling continued as I took in the old men crouched by the fire, Eid and Huwaymil sharing *heeshy* out of a cloth pouch, and the women, Jidaya and Umm Mahmoud, building up the fire to make tea and more light to flicker on their faces. These ordinary people, good and bad, happy and moody, ignorant and clever, were the only 'People of Petra' in the world – and they were my friends.

I often sat with the men. In the beginning when we were invited for meals I always sat with Mohammad and ate with the men and it was only as I got to know the women and a bit of the language that I started sitting with them. However, during weddings or longer celebrations, there were often moments when Mohammad extracted me and took me to sit with him; he knew I loved the coffee and to lean back on the pillows. And if he wasn't around I made a point of wandering in so it wouldn't become unusual. In the future it was my confident behaviour in any situation that earned me the compliment '*tigool rajul*', she's like a man.

Later in the celebration the younger guys with their kohl, *thaubs* and fringed *mendeels* changed the mood and danced the *dub-ka* round and round. Twirling his *mendeel*, Abu Saksooka sang in the lead, '*Reda ha, reda HA!*' and they all stamped the ground. The dust flew, the drum beat, arm in arm around they swept. A burst of gunfire sparked at the sky demanding attention. Pistols came out of shoulder holsters and were unwrapped from cleverly beaded handkerchiefs. Sisters and wives were sent to bring rifles from bedding piles in the backs of dark tents. The pistols were held high, *puk puk*, but their shots were drowned by the *t-r-r-a* of Umm Gurin, the Kalashnikov, named Mother of the Horn for its curved magazine, and the echoes went round and round the valley before fading, making even the singing sound quiet.

In the women's tent the young girls were vying for attention just as fiercely. Khatma and Khatma-h were singing together, their nasal voices, strangely beautiful and strong, were aimed at their hearts' desires who, even I knew, were dancing just outside in the *dub-ka*. This was as close as they could be – unseen but not unheard. '*Yaabu jacket a ra ma di*' – you with the grey jacket – more girls crowded round in new *mudragas* and headscarves and sang after them, '*La ti-ta-masha bil wadi, al ain lag-eeni, al ain stan-eeni*' – don't walk in the valley, meet me at the spring, wait for me at the spring – back and forth, back and forth. When the original song lyrics ran out they carried on – making up their own. '*Bokra b-yinzil a sarookh, ya yomaa!*' – Tomorrow the rocket will fall, oh mother! – they sang, referring to the Skylab they had worried about before it had broken up on re-entry and dropped into the Indian Ocean.

Jidaya, Umm Awwad and a couple of others from their generation sang the more staid *hejeeni*, stretching the words out and twisting them round to fill up the lines. Usually they just sang over each other but the girls stopped for a bit so that the older women could record themselves on a cassette without too much conflicting noise. Basma had bought new batteries for her tape-recorder and managed to scrounge a partly empty cassette from one of the *nishaama* and we were to hear her recordings broadcast on the open air from her cave below the Crusader castle every afternoon as long as her batteries lasted.

We hadn't brought our blankets so we wandered home. The path was clear in the moonlight, the *samer* and occasional gun-fire echoes chased around the cliffs, little blobs of light pin-pointed Bedouin homes. Salwa was fast asleep on her father's shoulder, Raami was on my back in his *muzferr*, and I felt surrounded by the blissful feeling of being a part of it all.

Bekhita's Tent

In the summer of 1983 the Gublan family set up their tent on the hill across from us in the afternoon-shadow of the Crusader castle, and now Bekhita set up her loom along the back of the tent and prepared to weave a new goat-hair strip for it. I decided it was now or never if I was to learn to spin and weave, and made an effort to go every day.

As soon as Mohammad left for the Theatre, I swung Raami in the *muzferr* across my back and, with Salwa skipping ahead, I made my way past the tents of Ali-f's sister and Rakhiya's sister and past the Pharaoh's column (which they all called Zibb Faroon but told me not to because it means Pharaoh's dick) to Bekhita's tent.

At the end of the winter the Gublan boys had dragged their tent out of the back of the cave and rolled it out in the sun in a black rectangle on the bare rock of a-<u>Th</u>ineb. Other families up there had done the same. (Salaama al-Mokhtar no longer had a black-hair tent but he made a summer *ma-rush* on the top of his cave out of planks and sacking and scraps of old canvas.) The women had helped each other, mending holes and rearranging strips and making sure the pieces of carved wood which cupped the tips of the tent poles (so they wouldn't poke through the fabric) were all in place. They wrapped their fingers in rags, for thimbles, to push needles like 10-centimetre nails through the heavy fabric. Their tents were all of similar size, though some younger families around the valley had smaller tents, shorter and narrower too, with fewer strips.

Bekhita's tent was made up of eight strips each about 16 metres long and 60 centimetres wide. When it was set up on its twelve poles there were about 60 square metres of living space. Usually she hung a dividing wall to separate one third of it into the *shig*, but then she would have had to weave her strip outside and rig up some kind of a shade. The *r-waag* was a separate piece of three strips, with white cotton woven in bands along its length and with a *mukhul* at the top. The *mukhul* was a strip only about 20 centimetres wide so when it wore out, from having whittled sticks poked through it to join the back to the roof, it was more economically replaceable.

Early every summer the *nishaama* worked their way around the valley, clipping goats for a different family each night. It

was a festive time with *fatteh* and tea and flirting and fun.
Spinning was the summer pastime for women in motion. Girls
going out with the goats had tresses wrapped softly around their
arms and bulging their bags, and by evening they had converted
them all into fat balls of spun yarn wrapped round the handles
of their simple wooden spindles. Women arrived at the clinic and
sat separately so they wouldn't expose others to the hair they
inevitably spread around. When the doctor pulled up they
stuffed their spindles into the woven-plastic grain sacks they
had adapted as shoulder bags (but carried over their foreheads)
and wedged them into the clumpy forks of the oleander bush.

It took the hair of about fifty goats to make a strip and when
Bekhita had it all spun into balls and two-plyed into loose
skeins, she got out her loom of sticks and stones and set it up
with the help of Nora, a crowd of children, and cries of '*haak
ya ayil*' – here you are, child, '*emsik ya walad*' – hold this, son,
and '*shwy, shwy*' – slow down, to harness and control the
enthusiasm.

Bekhita measured the yarn out in heads, one, two, three . . .
forty times she held it round her head and played it out for one
strand of the warp. It took some running back and forth to lay
enough strands side by side for the width of the strip. The loom
was set up close to the start and a couple of times a day, as the
weaving got close to it, we took it down and set it up again a few
hand's lengths ahead.

Although I learned how to spin and weave in the ten days
it took to complete the strip, it took quite some determination.
Every day before letting me sit beside her – so I could pull each
thread tight with a hooked gazelle-horn *nutty*, then push the
threads down and poke the weft yarn through with a stick –
Bekhita tried to treat me like a visitor, putting down a
jannabiya and offering tea and breakfast to me and the children.
One or two other women came most days to 'sit' on the strip
and they were more experienced and helpful than me so I

learned carding and plying while I waited for a turn. But most discouraging was Fraija, who arrived to help and found me plying two wet strands of yarn together (the wet hair expanded and would dry tightly) and who was vehement. 'You don't want to know!' she insisted, holding up her own gnarled and cracked examples. 'It will ruin your hands!'

Although I learned to spin I never really took it up. I didn't *need* a tent. It had been handy to be able to borrow one recently when we celebrated Raami's circumcision in conjunction with Ibraheem's and Salem's weddings, but I could imagine that in the future that would be all they would be used for. The cloud that was the settlement was spreading slowly over the hillside of Umm Sayhoon – in wide ovals with absolutely no allowance made for the lie of the land or the path of the winter flood, let alone the direction of the sun, the wind or the view – and it was already affecting our future.

Dakhil-allah – A Sick Man

A pick-up pulled up below our ledge late one evening. Rakhiya's husband Salem paid the driver and as he helped his brother up our path I realised they were coming to stay. Dakhil-allah was bent double and there was no way he would make it back up to the Monastery, or even to Salem and Rakhiya's cave, which was closer but almost inaccessible on the steep side of the Monastery valley. I put *farrshas* down in the *ma-rush* as they came through the gate, and Dakhil-allah, with barely a '*salaam*', kicked off his *ship-ships* and lowered himself sideways onto one. He wrapped his *mendeel* around his head and curled up in a ball under the quilt.

Dakhil-allah was as tall as Mohammad but seemed smaller because he had narrower features. He looked serious, and he was when he needed to be, but he had an impish wit and a twinkling smile. He lived at the Monastery with his wife, who was also named Rakhiya, but had been called Umm Khaled since the first of their nine sons was born. (They had previously lived on a-Thineb and Mohammad had pointed out the cemented-up hole in the rock – the cistern opening into which their second son had fallen and drowned before he could walk.) Up at the Monastery they were closer to firewood and goat grazing and they served tea to tourists who made the forty-minute climb. Dakhil-allah went down to work daily as a stone-cutter and builder for the Department of Antiquities and he was so good at it that he could always get extra work with visiting archaeologists on their excavations. His shop, which he opened after work, was in a cave below the museum and we wandered down there on summer afternoons, drawn by the shade of the mountain it was carved into, and the pot of tea and chat that could be had. He sold the usual packets of tea, cans of sardines and plastic shoes and was sometimes helped out by one or other of his good-looking sons. Those boys ran faster than their goats in the mountains and broke the record for 'the run up to the Monastery and back' just about every time they were sent on an errand.

I poured tea for Salem, who reached for the glass with a shaking hand. 'We've come from the *mustashfa*,' he said, the health centre in Wadi Musa. 'I went down to get cigarettes and found him sitting in his shop biting his *mendeel* to stifle the pain. Luckily Abu Zela'a had been delivering barley and I was able to stop him on his way back past. He took us straight up to the doctor who gave him an injection – but he doesn't feel much better yet.'

'*Khuthoo rahetkoo*,' we invited him to make himself and his sleeping brother comfortable. And, '*Twakil ala-Allah*,' we advised him before going to bed.

In the middle of the night when I heard voices out in the *ma-rush* and recognised that of Musa-a, the red-hot-nail specialist, I shrank back under my blanket.

I had first met Musa-a a few days into my marriage and after that sensational introduction I never had any trouble recognising him, or his voice. Mohammad had developed a sharp pain in his side that brought his head to his knees, and a trip to the doctor had resulted in an injection and an order to drink as much as he could. Kidney stones were suspected. The injection had worn off before all the tea he drank could work its way through, and the pain had returned. Abdallah, who had raced over when he heard we had been to the doctor, sent for Musa-a. The pair of them had pumped up the primus and heated the head of a 10-centimetre nail to red. They hadn't hidden it from me, but neither had I imagined the barbaric treatment they were preparing – and I barely believed it even when I heard the 'pssst' and smelled the wisps of burning skin.

'*La! La!*' I cried, and I know they understood but they ignored me, so I grabbed Musa-a's jacket and tried to pull him away.

Mohammad told me to go outside until they had finished. I couldn't believe he was letting them burn him intentionally. He had three pink spots like fingerprints on the pale skin of his hip. He looked as if he was in too much pain to know what was good for him but he waited for me to go out and then his father held him down while Musa-a did the same to his back.

By morning the pain was gone.

'*Shoofi, a-nar quayas,*' Abdallah had claimed – see, the fire's good. But I reckon the stones had been flushed out as Mohammad had made several trips during the night to pass urine, which he admitted had been painful.

I figured Dakhil-allah must have sent for Musa-a – the doctor's injection would have worn off and as I had nothing else to offer

242 Marguerite van Geldermalsen

I was better off staying in bed with my head covered where I could neither hear nor smell.

Dakhil-allah was already sitting up when I got up to make breakfast, but although he drank tea he barely touched the fresh bread. He said that he didn't remember anything but pain before Musa-a's ministrations, but while he was applying the 'nail' it was as if something had snapped and relief had come as the pressure had been released.

I could get away with being nosy because of my job, and asked to see the cure.

Despite having seen Mohammad's *kowe* spots and lots of others since, I was not prepared for so many on one body. Dakhil-allah's right side, from his collarbone down to the draw-string of his trousers, was like a polka-dot singlet – there were at least twenty burns, and on his back there were also as many. As if the internal pain had not been enough, I thought. Or was that the aim, to divert his attention?

I applied antiseptic cream.

It didn't take long for people to hear that Dakhil-allah wasn't well and they came to sit with him in our *ma-rush* and to speculate on the cause of, and a cure for, his condition. He held forth on the saga from the first stab in his side through the visit to the health centre and back to Musa-a's therapeutic hands in the night. No two visitors came up with the same diagnosis or herbal remedy.

'Do you have *sheh*, *baytheraan* or maybe *hunedia*?' they suggested.

What I didn't have didn't take long to get. Hassan sent over a scruffy child courier with sage leaves twisted in a scrap of bright material, and others were sent home to caves and tents to delve into precious supplies of herbs. Mohammad had gone to work, the visitors kept Salwa and Raami entertained and helped to make food, and I boiled up concoctions. Dakhil-allah was game to try anything but he only managed a mouthful or so of each, and although he chatted and dozed and drank a little soup, he deflated as the day wore on.

The next night passed, pain-free. Soon after dawn Umm Khaled arrived. She had loaded the little children onto the donkey and come for the long stay. Although she had been told her husband was fine she needed to see him for herself, and I didn't blame her – around here people would put off the inevitable and tell you he was fine even if he was dead. She didn't feel any better on seeing him. He was pale this morning, said he had not slept comfortably, and his worry was showing through.

I was worried too and convinced Mohammad and Salem to take him back to the doctor. They decided to go to Aqaba, which was only half as far as Amman but had a military hospital – better doctors and better facilities than Wadi Musa or Ma'an. Salem lifted his brother and carried him down to the car, which was enough to set Umm Khaled and several of the other women wailing.

The day dragged. Visitors came and when they didn't find Dakhil-allah they waited with us. It was a hot day, and would be unbearable in Aqaba, which was always a good five degrees hotter. Fraija suggested *geasoom* was very good for stomach pain. Umm Khaled knew the plant and went off determined to gather some. She was gone ages, and returned shaking and empty-handed. While scrambling nervously among the perpendicular rocks below the High Place she had lost her footing and nearly fallen. She was worried about losing Dakhil-allah, and now she was worried about losing control.

'Dakhil-allah will be fine,' we reassured her. 'You think about the children – there are plenty of people to help.'

And help they did. Someone brought more firewood. Maryam made a wheel of bread. Heyaiya-f brought *laban* and made soup. There was *fatteh* for lunch, pots of tea and chatter. Many of the women hadn't seen each other for ages and they caught up on everything – goats, horses and crops; illnesses, children and vaccinations; newlyweds, husbands and scandals.

We were all relieved to see the patient get out of the car that afternoon. He had been X-rayed and diagnosed with a kidney infection or kidney stones, I didn't understand exactly, but he had had an injection and brought packets of pills with instructions on them which I could deal with. I made sure he took his medicine, and his medicine only.

He didn't look any better the next day but I persevered, and it was while I was insisting he eat some of the custard I had boiled up, smooth and bland, that he confided, 'Nothing has come out since I came here, Fatima. I feel full to my neck and cannot manage even a spoonful.'

So as soon as Mohammad came home, he and Salem bundled Dakhil-allah into the car again and headed for Amman in the night. They took him straight to the Italian Hospital where he was operated on almost immediately.

When Dakhil-allah came round, the doctor demonstrated just how lucky he had been. He held up a glass jar containing the appendix they had removed. It had been inflamed (causing the pain), then burst (releasing the pressure), and become gangrenous (causing the blockage).

When Dakhil-allah came home his family moved down to a cave in the cliff opposite the clinic and set up their tent on the ledge in front so they could better accommodate all the guests who came to wish him *al-humdulillah-a-salaama*. Everyone speculated on the operation scar too – how long it was, whether it went from up to down or across, and how many stitches it had. But it was all speculation, I noticed. Dakhil-allah was not exhibiting the scar like he had the nail-head burns. When I went to change the dressing Umm Khaled hung blankets round to form a screen so no one could lay unclean eyes on the wound.

Dakhil-allah appreciated the modern medicine he had

benefited from, but he had his own views on how to keep things running smoothly. From then on whenever he came to stay he asked at breakfast for a glass of deep green olive oil which he drank in one smooth swig before reaching for the bread or lighting up his cigarette – and he is still going strong.

1984: Queen Elizabeth – A Royal Visit

One day in early 1984 Nyazi arrived with a small contingent of 'beautiful people' on our terrace where I sat cross-legged surrounded by my piles of dirty clothes and the *ligan* of washing water. Nyazi was a Wadi Musa man, the local Director of Tourism, so I scrambled up and put mattresses on the low wall in the winter sunshine, wondering what was going on.

He introduced the young men and women with him. 'In a few weeks the Queen of England is to visit Jordan and these are her public relations officers,' he said.

One of the young linen-suited visitors continued. 'Her Majesty will be the first British monarch ever to visit Jordan and we are trying to organise a diverse programme for her. We heard from Nyazi about you and your Bedouin husband, and how you live here in this cave. It sounds so unusual we are sure Her Majesty would be interested to meet your family . . . especially as you are her only subject in the area.'

I went into the kitchen to put on a pot of tea and to keep me from throwing him off the ledge. I was not sure how I felt.

I tried to think back. Had I hoped that by marrying into this Bedouin tribe in the remote ruins of Petra, in the middle of the Jordanian desert past the end of the tar-sealed road, that I could disappear and nothing would be expected of me again?

For a moment I tried to look through their Ray-Banned eyes – our daily life was strewn about the packed-earth yard: the water jar, jerry-cans and wooden donkey saddle; the pot of steaming water and twists of wrung-out clothes; Salwa swishing something around in the soapy water. What was so ordinary that I didn't usually notice, suddenly looked primitive, but I had to look beyond – to the whorled face of our cave standing over the yard, to the blue sky you could touch, and to the attention-seeking cliffs pocked with antiquities. Petra noises seeped into my wide-open picture window.

Raami toddled over and I picked him up. I felt proud and embarrassed, shy and amazed.

I poured tea remembering how in 1963 the royal yacht *Britannia* had moored at sea off the Boulder Bank, which forms the natural harbour of Nelson. We went down to the docks, as did everyone else in the district, to wave and cheer and hope for a glimpse of the young Queen – or at least of her gloved hand – as she came ashore. For weeks we had imagined being invited for tea at Buckingham Palace, kinking our little fingers and prac-tising curtsies.

And now I had a chance. Who was I to deny her her only sub-ject in the area? Of course I would meet Her Majesty.

Mohammad didn't bat a beautiful eyelid. He lived in a country with a reachable king. 'My father met King Hussein when he came by helicopter and landed near the Palace Tomb,' he said. '*Aady.*' A common occurrence.

I was more fazed. I wasn't sure what the occasion would entail and now there was no one to ask. I chose an outfit for each of us and put them away so there wouldn't be last-minute burns or olive-oil stains to contend with. I was really happy with the sky-blue *mudraga* I had recently finished embroidering for Salwa, using remembered cross stitch and crimson thread. I went searching in the Amman cloth *souq* and found matching material to make a blouse for underneath.

Mohammad thought the Queen would expect flowers – a posy from Salwa – and so she might, but Interflora didn't work in these parts so we had to think of something else. I wanted it to be something particularly from Petra and that's when Mohammad decided to make a bottle of coloured sand. I had seen some of these in Aqaba, where they filled miniature whisky bottles with artificially coloured sand creating designs of camels and flowers, but I was sceptical of Mohammad's ability to make one, let alone one 'fit for a Queen'. He said it wasn't difficult, that when he was younger he had made them, crushing the naturally coloured rocks to make sand.

And he did it. I argued as he used my good sewing scissors (which I couldn't replace this side of the Souq-al-Bukharia) to cut up an old cooking-oil can, which he soldered to make a funnel – he had a soldering iron in his suitcase. I ranted as he sieved crushed rocks through my flour sieve to obtain fine enough sand, and I cried in disbelief when he finally produced his masterpiece – in a Tabasco sauce bottle!

I had to admit it did look good. Tabasco sauce aside, the bold, wavy lines of rust, ochre, white and grey looked much more beautiful than I had anticipated. It was the ultimate souvenir of Petra. In the future we taught ourselves to make patterns and pictures and filled many thousands of bottles with sand, and Mohammad eventually demonstrated the art as Jordan's representative all over Europe, but for now we didn't need camels or flowers, the lines looked just like the rocks. We had Salwa's bouquet.

On the 30th of March the Badia spread out decoratively across the hills. The Badia was the desert police force made up mostly of Bedouin *nishaama*. Their khaki *thaubs*, dramatically belted with bullet-filled bandoliers of red leather and complemented by red and white *mendeels* flung into crowns, made even the fatties amongst them appear tall and elegant. We were to meet the Queen at the tent that had been put up down at the Keenya, and from where the rhythmic sound of coffee being pounded in a wooden *jorin* now echoed on the air. Rug-laden donkeys were being led there from all directions and a crowd was gathering noisily. Vehicles revved and bounced up and down the paved road.

As we neared the Gasr al-Bint a crowd descended on us. They were reporters and they were firing questions like a cliché. I blustered a bit but when one of them called out, holding his hands up to imply the temple and the blue sky, 'Tell me – what is your reason for living here in this ancient city of beautiful mountains?' I knew the answer.

I glanced at Mohammad walking beside me, looking gorgeous, and said without hesitation, 'He is.'

The tent was huge. The poles were so tall no one would have to stoop. They said it belonged to the king himself but the Bdoul were furnishing it. The sponge-rubber *farrshas*, piled three deep to make soft benches, were draped with tapestries I recognised from Salaama's cave, and woven carpets from Hassan's and Abu Sha-her's; the entire floor area was covered in the hand-woven rugs of other families – long and thin, the linear patterns emphasising the length of the tent.

The Badia and Bdoul were working together; they had set up a fireplace in front of the tent to prepare tea and coffee. The smell of burning prickly-oak wood perfumed the air, mingled with coffee and cardamom. The coffee pots lined up in the embers of the fire were Abu Mahmoud's family heirlooms. There were different sizes for boiling water, brewing coffee, adding cardamom and serving, but they were all made of lovingly pol-ished brass with round bottoms, narrow waists, hinged lids like pointed minarets and spouts like the beaks of flamboyant birds.

We drank tea and sat about. No tourists had been allowed in today so it was a rare day off. Lots of the men were hanging around in order to get a glimpse of their king, and mothers and children sat beside the road with the same intentions. The day stretched on and no one seemed sure what time anything would happen. When Raami finally fell asleep in my lap, the cavalcade came into view.

There were two white cars followed by a horde of Land-Rovers approaching along the Colonnaded Street, through the Triumphal Arch and across the Temenos. The cars pulled up: Sheer Rovers – white, open and luxurious. We all stepped back as King Hussein and Queen Elizabeth alighted from the first car, but as he escorted her into the tent my attention was stolen by Queen Noor, a stunning figure in pink and white, who along with Prince Philip arrived in the second. She started at the end of the line, shaking hands with each and every Badia soldier and greeting him with a smiling '*Masa-al-khair*', good afternoon, before entering the tent.

The rest of the entourage spilled out of the canvas flaps and soldier-held doors of the other vehicles and filled the tent. They settled back on the cushions and were offered Bedouin tea, boiled up on the fire in a big blue enamel pot and served in tiny gold-rimmed, waisted glasses.

An English archaeologist, Crystal Bennet, went forward to have tea with the Queen. We hadn't been given directions by anyone but it didn't look like we were invited for tea after all. We stood in the crowd outside the tent, among the soldiers, the press and the Bedouin who had gathered.

'Soon it will be your turn,' someone whispered. 'Put the baby down over here.' Raami was fast asleep on my shoulder. I tried to wake him but he was well trained to sleep when he was tired, no matter what was going on, and there was no way I was going to put him down – there were TV cameras around and Mum and Dad hadn't seen their grandson yet.

'Go on in,' people on either side of us urged.

My mind raced. I had imagined someone would present us

but we were obviously expected to go it alone. Where to go? We made a beeline for King Hussein. He was standing directly ahead, but the message in his gesture was clear: welcome, but approach the guest of honour first. We veered left and the Queen of England was in front of us. In her blue dress she was as soft as in photos. I couldn't curtsey – Raami would have fallen off my shoulder.

There was a blur. Salwa was trying to offer the bottle of sand, reciting, 'My dad made this specially for you,' too softly to attract the attention of the Queen, who was talking to me. I couldn't hear her; I was overwhelmed, holding back tears. Mohammad was chatting, cool as a cucumber, with the Duke of Edinburgh. By the time I recovered my composure enough to explain the sand bottle, it had disappeared. Did they suspect a security breach? I'll never know.

As the Queen enquired about our life I got the feeling she had been briefed too well and already knew the answers, so it was a bit of light relief when Queen Noor came over and quipped, 'You sound like an Australian,' and Queen Elizabeth filled her in. (Queen Noor was an *ajnebiya* herself, King Hussein's American-born fourth wife.)

They ruffled Raami's hair and admired his ability to sleep – then our time was up. We shook hands all round, including at last His Majesty King Hussein's, and with that honour, left the tent.

As the cars lined up and the guests prepared to leave, we stood around the fireplace and the Badia boys poured us coffee. I felt much more comfortable with them.

The press gathered. 'What did she say? She talked for a long time . . .' But the balloon had deflated; we left them and wandered home.

There was an article about me in the New Zealand *Woman's Weekly*. I didn't mind the story. The reporter hadn't picked up that my name was Fatima (or Umm Salwa, or Umm Raami) and for some reason it pleased me. It almost felt as if she was writing about someone else – which was just as well when a friend sent the article from a South African newspaper with the title 'The Kiwi and the Caveman'.

We made the TV news all around the world. Friends in Australia and England who had last heard of me as I headed back to Jordan, to Mohammad, could see that I had settled in. For Mum and Dad it was a bit more traumatic. They did get a glimpse of their sleeping grandson but when the announcer concluded: 'And then they parted – the head of the Commonwealth for a palace, and her subject (a most unusual one) for a cave,' Mum cried.

Fasting

After that Mohammad was occasionally recognised by British tourists, and I was occasionally asked after. I found I enjoyed the interest people had in us and in our lives, and sometimes took Salwa and Raami to sit with Mohammad at the shop. Otherwise, apart from the extra work of rock-crushing and bottle-washing for our sand-bottle souvenirs, our lives continued much as before – bread-making, water-carrying, clothes-washing, clinic work and hospital trips all interspersed with plenty of visiting and tea-drinking in shady black tents.

The units at the Umm Sayhoon settlement were finished now but the decision to move hadn't been made yet. Rumours flourished: one day we heard we were going to refuse the units unless they were enlarged; another day we heard the number of family members needed to get two units would be seven instead of ten, and fathers made the trip to Ma'an to register previously unimportant children. Some fathers used the extra time to arrange marriages for unmarried sons, knowing all married men would get homes.

There were impromptu gatherings down by the Keenya and the raising of voices. The families collected money for Salaama's *service* and taxi fares, and accommodation in case he had to stay overnight, and sent him back to Amman to negotiate some more.

Ramadan came round, and I realised I should be able to fast. I had always despaired when people who hadn't had a cigarette all day reached for their pouches or packets as soon as the sun went down – I used to think enviously that if I could go without a cigarette from dawn till dusk I would not only fast, I would give up smoking. Now that I had given up smoking, I imagined going without food and water would be easy.

Mohammad and Ali had fasted back in 1979, I remembered: from dawn at four thirty to dusk at seven forty-five. They got a ride up to Wadi Musa after work and bought food. As the afternoon passed they put dates in bowls, filled the water jug with reconstituted Tang, and cut a watermelon open and set it, pink and green, to cool on the *siddr*. They made salads: cucumber, tomato, lemon juice and tahina; tomato with olive oil and onions. They boiled chicken and deep-fried the pieces, spitting vegetable ghee all over Mohammad's jeans. They opened a can of humus and mixed it to a smooth cream. I made *shraak* and a pot of tea. There were no batteries in our cassette player so we carted the food up to the smooth rock on top of the cave and Umm Mahmoud, who had a radio, gave us a signal when she heard the *athaan*.

They said, 'Oh God, for You we have fasted and now, with this food You have provided, we will break our fast, in Your name, oh God,' and ate and drank and smoked . . . and ate and drank and smoked until they couldn't move. They had lasted two days.

I didn't tell anyone I intended to fast. By the time Mohammad got home though, it was obvious. I had a splitting headache and no energy. I had put half a jerry-can of water in the *ligan* to keep Salwa and Raami occupied. Sunset wasn't for ages. Mohammad set to and made his favourite one-pot stew with corned beef and asked Umm Mahmoud to make us some bread.

Was it worth it? I wondered, as I put the kids to bed. Could I handle another day like that?

But Umm Mahmoud looked so pleased (as did everyone else who came in, and Mohammad told) that I couldn't give up, and with all their encouragement it got easier as the days went by. Fasting was now another thing I did the same as them, and it gave me another connection to the tribe. Now when they were describing me proudly to strangers (wedding guests and tourists alike), they added, 'She fasts in Ramadan,' to my usual list of credits, which went something like: 'She speaks Arabic, she makes bread and she became a Muslim.' The wedding guests always nodded approvingly, but the tourists usually looked as embarrassed as I was.

I had become a Muslim slowly. I didn't have a certificate to say so yet – that came years later when I went up to the court and swore with my hand on the Koran: 'There is no god but Allah and Mohammad is his prophet' – but as my Arabic had improved I discovered that Mohammad (peace be upon him) was the latest in a long line of prophets preaching about 'one god', and that the other prophets were the ones I had learned about in Sunday School. I had also discovered Allah in just about every sentence and found He fitted.

For the rest of the month I got up for a meal in the early hours of the morning. I sat on the ledge with a pot of tea and some bread and cheese segments to see me through the following day. The spots of light at tents on the Argoob Jmea-aan and a-Thineb were barely visible because the light of the night was so bright. And it was still – the dogs and donkeys had quietened down and the roosters hadn't started up yet. I enjoyed going back to bed, too, for another couple of hours' sleep.

Mohammad didn't fast. He tried the next day but by eight in the morning his tongue was dry, a swollen lump in his mouth, and not long after we raced him to the hospital in Ma'an in a diabetic coma. The insulin injections they gave him made him feel better than he had for a long time, but the diabetes, that silent killer, changed the flow of our lives. Mohammad started a routine of injections (we could now buy disposable syringes at a pharmacy in Ma'an), specified food (too much of ours was animal fat), and no sweet tea (which meant that once Ramadan finished I made two separate pots to drink on our ledge in the mornings because I had acquired a taste for the sweet stuff). It was a routine quite different from our Bedouin lifestyle and quite difficult to adhere to.

A Girl and Two Boys

Ibraheem and his wife Hunda lived in a cave hanging way up on the side of the Monastery valley. When Hunda went into labour Ibraheem called their neighbour, Rya, to help. Besides delivering the long-limbed boy, tying the cord and crumbling sneeze-provoking *heeshy* under Hunda's nose to encourage the afterbirth, she had her boys bring water and stayed around to help. She was still there when I went across the next day – I don't think she would have told me otherwise.

I was intrigued when she looked up at me across the fire-pit and said, 'I had a dream about you.'

I could feel her trying to guess my reaction. She was not sure what it would be, but I loved hearing their future-telling dreams and seeing which prophecies came true, so I said, 'Did you?' giving her the go-ahead. 'Was it good or bad?'

'I came to visit you because you had given birth', she said. 'And you were sitting in the corner of your cave nursing a baby boy. When I congratulated you, you answered, "*Al-humdulillah – bint ou walad-ein b-kaffi.*"' A girl and two boys are enough.

I felt as if she had dreamed herself into my head.

I didn't discuss the planning of our family much, though I often encouraged my friends to plan theirs. The women who considered themselves lucky had a baby (boy) every two years and breastfed him till they fell pregnant again; they never had a menstruation. But that kind of natural contraception didn't work for everyone, as one young mother in particular discovered, when she gave birth to her second child within a year of her first and was so worn out by then that she had no milk and soon fell pregnant with the third. I tried to encourage her to use contraception. 'You're taking advantage of iron and vitamin injections, of antibiotics and powdered milk, you should be compelled to take advantage of contraception too.'

But pregnancies, she said (as they all said), were 'up to God'.

Rya's dream was my dream too and the following year, apart from the fact that I was sitting in the corner of our brick unit on Umm Sayhoon, it did come true.

In-Laws Again

I think I need some time out.

My in-laws moved in below us a few weeks ago for winter, and I'm already wishing for spring so they can move away and set up their tent. I had thought this would never happen – that none of the caves nearby were habitable – but Abdallah is deter-mined and has dug a ramp down into a snug low-lying one that neither I nor Umm Laafi can stand up straight in. He's made a wall round the entrance and a channel to divert the rainwater away down the hill.

Neda, Maryam and Hussein come up early in the morning to play with Salwa and Raami, putting paid to any hopes I have of routine. Before long Salwa runs off down the hill with them, and depending on my need to control her or my need for some peace and quiet I bring her back or leave her there. The children's play is a choppy ocean of peace and war: in peacetime they 'salaam' and kiss and pretend to serve tea, but it can deteriorate in seconds into fighting – with spitting, cursing and the throwing of stones.

Abdallah has a herd of eight sheep and Inzela is sent off daily to the windswept Hrai-miya to graze them. She comes home at dusk, a slight figure buffeted by the woolly creatures as they bounce their fat tails down past our cave. Her hands are chapped and her face disappears into the shadow of her scarf. It's a poor winter with little rain and there isn't much in the way of forage so they have to buy barley to feed them as well. I am relieved for Inzela when the first sheep dies and they decide to cut their losses and sell the rest.

Often Umm Laafi makes unleavened taaboon. She has set up her oven just below our ledge and made a rough stone wall to protect it from the west wind. The pottery dome sits over a bed of pebbles and has a loaf-sized hole in the top which she closes with an old pot lid. The whole thing is covered with a slow-burning dung fire, like a quilt of ash, which she feeds twice a day after baking the bread with a few handfuls of dry goat-dung marbles. The wintry-smelling smoke wafts up over our ledge. She asks me to make lentil soup with laban so we can have fatteh for dinner altogether.

'What's the point in lighting two fires when your cave is warm and big enough for everyone?' she says, and her suggestion is so practical I cannot disagree. Before sunset our home is full, and when Umm Laafi and Abdallah leave we help them carry the sleeping children down the path.

There is no way I can shut the door and pretend we aren't home. There is no way I can tell them I want to be alone or to ask them to leave. I learned that early on.

That was when we were first married and I was going to work daily to the health centre in Wadi Musa. A couple of times I found unwashed glasses or tea leaves in the pot when I got home, and as I had hardly any dishes to wash I knew I hadn't left them that way. And the batteries in the cassette player were running out much faster than usual.

I came home early one day to find my cave door open and Salem inside with a couple of friends, a pot of tea and the cassette player on so loud they didn't notice me till I blocked out the light at the doorway.

'*Iglib whoojak*,' I had learned by that time – and loved the sound of. Literally it meant 'turn your face', which seemed quaint, but to them it meant, 'Get out!' And they weren't happy.

Mohammad wasn't impressed either; neither with my behaviour, nor my language. 'Salem's my brother,' he said. 'He's used to coming here with his friends. What's a little tea and sugar to us, Marg?'

Not only was asking someone to leave unacceptable, it was incomprehensible. 'As long as people call on you, you will prosper,' the Bedouin firmly believe, so every person who comes to you deserves a welcome and respect. I should have seen that Salem was saving me the trouble of pumping the primus and sat and enjoyed the tea and company.

A little tea and sugar was nothing I agreed, but where I grew up even my mother knocked on my bedroom door, and didn't enter if I wasn't in. I don't know whether Mohammad understood or agreed, or just wanted to keep me happy, but he went to Wadi Musa and bought a bigger padlock that wouldn't open with a sharp tug.

Now Salem comes in the evenings too. He and his wife Jmea and their new daughter live in the cave with my in-laws. Inzela or Tuf-leh carries the baby up and a little later Jmea arrives leading an old man supporting himself on a short stick. He has his *thaub* up round his knees, and his grotty *mendeel* inside out with bits poking up like goat's ears where he's tucked it into his *mirreer*. He crouches arthritically on one knee and warms his sooty hands over the fire. We all know it's Salem but the children crowd round to listen to him stutter and snort and they never fail to laugh hilariously at his satirically idiotic behaviour, a rerun of their favourite comedy.

It's fun but it's every day and every night and it could go on for months. Now and then we give up and close the door and go off to play cards with Salaama. He has already moved into one of the units at Umm Sayhoon. Besides being the mayor and involved in the logistics of the resettlement, he really thinks living in a house is better, and makes him better. He looks forward to and talks incessantly about his whole tribe living in real houses like civilised people.

A high-pressure waterpipe from a subterranean well near Ma'an supplies the site. At the centre of the settlement is a watering trough for animals and a tap to get water from, so we fill our jerry-cans and pack them into the boot for the drive home before squashing into Salaama's place to play cards. The sitting room where we sit with him and his bigger boys is less than 12 square metres, but it is the biggest room of the unit and the only one that doesn't share a wall with the neighbouring unit. Maryam, and Senna, her Egyptian co-wife, sit with their children in the smaller room and come in to bring tea or hot-milk Nescafé. Every time someone opens the door, a gust of cold air replaces the warm, and when there is rain on the wind, wet spots reach halfway across the floor. 'Shut the door,' Salaama reminds constantly. (In New Zealand we used to say, 'Why don't you shut the door? Were you born in a tent?' Here half the people were. It is obviously a hard habit to break.)

The units are all the same. They are made of red brick, unrendered and even on the inside only very roughly pointed. There are *haraamis* like prison bars across the windows – the Jordanian equivalent to contents insurance. All the rooms have concrete floors and flat concrete slabs for roofs. The floors are smooth but the ceilings are roughly patterned by the boards they have been poured on. The doors are solid metal and I am not surprised that they claim several fingers in the first few months of settlement as they blow shut with 20-kilogram bangs.

'Electric City', as Mohammad called it when I met him, is still three years away but there are wires already; in metal pipes running up the walls and across the ceilings, connecting the switches to the bare bulbs. To run his television Salaama has a generator just outside the yard, shattering the silence. He likes the TV on, even though the boys spend a lot of time on the roof adjusting the antenna, and the channel with the best reception is Israeli and in Hebrew.

I have to stop thinking of the unit as a house; it is more basic than any New Zealand holiday bach I ever stayed in. At right angles to the living rooms, a lower concrete roof sits tightly on the kitchen, storeroom and toilet. The unrendered brick décor continues. The kitchen is bare but for an enamelled-concrete tub and a tap connected to a waterpipe that enters through the roof. There is a small storeroom but no bathroom; Mohammad's shower-making skills are going to be put to use again I can see. The toilet is a cold-water tap beside a concrete squat bowl in a windowless space so small you have to flatten yourself against the rough brick wall in order to shut the door – absolutely no comparison with the isolated privacy or the sweeping views at my toilet pit.

When it rains, the hillside outside Salaama's house turns to mud, and Salwa and Raami squeal with excitement as the car, helpfully weighed down by the full jerry-cans, slithers until we reach the middle of the settlement and the gravel road. Thoughts of the future are displaced by reality as we navigate the stream in the Siq – getting out here and there to test for holes or to move boulders washed by hurrying water. Skinny foxes escaping the headlights push future thoughts aside too as 'The Fox Went Out on a Chilly Night' comes bubbling up from my memory and we sing, 'And he prayed for the moon to give him light . . . for he'd many miles to go that night before he reached the town-o, town-o, town-o', at the tops of our voices as we wind back home along the mountain. When we pull up below our ledge the smouldering log smell that emanates from Abdallah's cave reminds me of my neighbours. They don't seem so close after all. In the settlement we might share a wall.

I pray for the red tape to be tangled and the move delayed.

And I sympathise with the Italian girl who confides in me when I escape with my children to sit at the shop. She is here in Petra with her dark and handsome Jordanian husband, and her parents who have come to Jordan to visit her. She met her man in Milan where he studied engineering, and when he finished his degree she came home with him to his parents' house in a village in the north. They have a room in the house; another son and his wife have another room. They all spend their days together, they all eat their meals together and her mother-in-law teaches her how to cook things her husband likes. Her trip to Petra is the first time she has been out of the family fold and she doesn't think she can go back.

I can sympathise with her, but I don't have any advice. I am the one who benefits, as I do from other tourists on other occasions over the years. I call these people who carry my worries away my itinerant therapists.

I can see now how lucky I am. I met Mohammad and got to

know him in his own world, in his own home, alone. We adapted
to the changes in our lives together as they happened. His family
lived in Beitha for some time most summers, on the opposite hill
in Petra for the rest of them, and until now they have spent their
winters over in the Wadi Mataha too. I have the practical advan-
tages of Bedouin in-laws – a woollen quilt, *taaboon* bread and
young helpers who fight frantically over which of them will get
to bring us a load of water – without too much emotional
involvement and without restrictions. (I wonder if it would have
been different if Mohammad's mother had still been alive but I'm
not going to dwell on it.) I decide not to worry about the future
but to make the most of their company for the rest of the winter.

Statues

On those winter evenings Mohammad carved statues from the
soft white limestone of fallen-down pillars – or, more precisely,
from their capitals and bases because the drums in between were
usually local sandstone. It took time to find good chunks of the
rare imported rock because the sand, the wind and the rain had
worked together and rendered the rubble that covered the hillsides a similar, bland hue that belied the colours and textures
inside. He brought suitable pieces home and sliced them into
oblong bits with a new saw from the Hajj Raja's shop up in
Wadi Musa. The made-in-China saw was intended for wood so
he wore it out quickly and had to buy a new one for each piece
of antiquity he remodelled.

Surrounded by family and friends, sitting on a sack by the
mangle of coals, Mohammad would prise and scrape the stone
with a plastic-headed screwdriver that he had hammered to a

sharp flat edge. He had square hands with thick veins that stood out under the brown skin. His thin wrists exaggerated that squareness, as did his fingernails, which he kept short, pared with his *shabriya* so that they were wider than they were long. The white scar on his forearm reminded him of childhood goat-herding with Heyaiya up on Jabal Khubtha. He had been whittling a stick to make a *shon-nar* trap, when he had cut himself badly, and she had helped him staunch the blood. (Heyaiya had moved with her family to Amman shortly after Rakhiya's wedding, and had died there three years ago).

He produced several of the little rectangular statues each evening. He called them Nabataeans and carved their sitting legs and clasped hands identically, although he sometimes carved a cat for one to hold, or gave it a Cleopatra hairstyle, or a twisted-snake headband, or what looked like a Statue-of-Liberty crown. From his seat on the sack, now surrounded by limestone chips and dust and cigarette butts, he buried them straight into the fire. They came out blacker (older with each passing minute) and he sold them to the tourists at his shop for whatever price they offered.

1985: The Gold Tooth

Early in the spring of 1985 I got a gold tooth. It was a sunny afternoon, goats were spreading out over the hillside nibbling at the thistles and my mother-in-law was making tea for the girls who looked after them. I went down to have a glass. They were chattering about the Tooth-gypsy who had come to Petra and how Abdallah had treated both Salem's and Ibraheem's wives to gold teeth. The girls sounded envious.

Quite a few of the Bedouin, both men and women, had gold teeth. I had wondered how they could afford them but now I knew they were just thin caps, either as a piece of jewellery, when it was on the right eye-tooth, or to hold a false tooth in place, and then it usually wasn't.

Just then Abdallah arrived with a guest.

'That's him – the gypsy.' The girls giggled and scattered, picking up their bundles of twigs and urging their goats, '*Hup ineegh!*'

Umm Laafi went in to get a mat and I tried to see how they could tell he was a gypsy – he looked just like the Bedouin to me: his dusty *thaub*, not old but already with a few holes across the knees from falling *heeshy* embers, his black and white *mendeel* and his plastic sandals were uniform with half the Bdoul. The only difference I could see was the cardboard suitcase under his arm, tied round with a strap.

Abdallah announced that he had brought the man home to fit gold teeth for us too. I tried to get out of it. I wasn't much into gold and had so far managed to refuse every bit Mohammad had offered to buy from the gold *souq*. But my father-in-law insisted: we were all equally important, he had sold the sheep and had money in his pocket, both his new daughters-in-law had already produced babies – life was good, and he wanted to show it.

'Couldn't I get a different treat?'

'No, that wouldn't do. Imagine the talk – "He got all of his women a gold tooth except Fatima" – that wouldn't do at all!'

Within minutes he had me and Umm Laafi squatting side by side in the sun against the outside wall of their low cave. The gypsy crouched close in front of us – he had a black moustache streaked with grey. He lifted my lips and had a look at my teeth, then did the same to Umm Laafi. I felt like a horse. I giggled to ease my discomfort at crouching so close to a strange man. Umm Laafi seemed quite unbothered. It intrigued me how easily these people took new situations in their stride. I had often observed how uninhibited they were when they came to get injections. Usually they just bared the obvious buttock by making a window between their *thaub* or *mudraga* and their trousers, but occasionally someone came with no trousers on underneath and still managed to stand just as modestly for the occasion.

The gypsy opened the suitcase on the ground beside him, poked around in the jumble of tools, rags, tubes and stuff, and produced a glass jar of teeth. Now I could see they were only gold caps, barely making a rustle against the glass as he tipped them into the lid. There must have been ten or fifteen, which he sorted with long tweezers – big, small, long, short. They reminded me of the silver caps we made from cigarette-packet tinfoil when we were children. He picked one and tried it on Umm Laafi, on her right eye-tooth. It was a bit long; he trimmed it with his scissors, careful to drop the parings back in the jar. Then one for me; it wouldn't fit over; another, good; he put it aside. Abdallah hung over the proceedings to make sure the price was what they had agreed on. Yes, we had regular teeth, no big surprises.

Our dentist wiped the dust off a smooth flat stone and got out his tubes of glue. Fifty-fifty, he squeezed a tiny bit from each and mixed it up with the matchstick he had used to light his cigarette.

'*Uf-ta-hi.*' Open wide.

He scooped glue into the cap and held it onto my tooth for a few moments, then checked that I could close my mouth without gnashing my teeth. He left me to hold the tooth till the glue set while he stuck the other one in my mother-in-law's mouth.

Abdallah chuckled. '*Jemeela.*' Beautiful.

I didn't have the heart to wiggle it off again.

When I got to the mirror I could see it was actually a different shape from my own pointy eye-tooth. It felt huge for a couple of days but although I got used to it I wasn't allowed to forget it. Everyone noticed my gold tooth and congratulated me on it – and on my generous father-in-law. It was another unintentional step on the road to belonging – and, unlike our floor, when we moved from our cave I was able to take it with me.

Moving

The settlement had become the major topic of conversation and cause of fiery argument at tents and caves around the valley. Even waiting under the oleanders outside the clinic I couldn't escape the politics and petty jealousies. I missed the days when I couldn't understand Arabic and had been excited by the passion with which the language had raged around me. Now I wished I couldn't understand the pointless talk. Now I wished we could move so I wouldn't hear any more about it; we were unsettled here, but unable to settle there.

We had been allocated a unit, despite a sparsely signed and thumbprinted petition being presented to the Wadi Musa District Governor arguing that, as Abdallah Othman and his sons were al-Manajah, not Bdoul, they shouldn't be able to claim houses. The governor had thrown it out. The Umm Sayhoon housing was for the inhabitants of Petra, he pointed out in response, and as Abdallah and his three married sons lived in Petra they would get one unit each. We already had the keys. Now I wanted the red tape to unravel so we could move and get on with our lives.

In April we celebrated Salwa's fifth birthday. Although Mohammad didn't know when his own birthday was, he loved the tradition, and our children's birthdays were fast becoming popular social events. My in-laws and our neighbours came for dinner. Mohammad hung decorations (bought in the Souq-al-Bukharia) across the cave from the rock loop in the back wall to the window in the front. The children called them 'krishations' and they delighted them more than the *maglouba* (the upside-down Bedouin risotto of chicken, vegetables and rice) that I cooked; more than the oranges Mohammad handed out (one each, even for the babies); more even than the cream-smothered sponge birthday cake with candles that Ali brought from the restaurant (built on Abu Argoob's cave) which he now managed – but not more than us singing 'Happy Birthday' *that* delighted adults and children alike. It was our last birthday in Petra; before the end of April we had all moved to Umm Sayhoon.

I was at the clinic when I heard the go-ahead for the move had been given. After all those months of arguing and negotiation, no changes in the size of the units or the number of family members you needed to get two units had been made. Changes had been made since the drawing of the plans I had seen back in 1979 though, because now there were no domes on the roofs, nowhere to stable the donkeys, horses and herds of goats or to store the sacks of fodder or cooking pots, and very few views over the neighbouring units to the mountains.

'And,' Rakhiya came to tell me, 'they say that if we don't move within a week we will forfeit our unit.' A week might well have been a rumour, but most of the tribe thought like Salaama their mayor – a 'house', irrespective of size, shape or construction material, was more civilised than a cave or tent – and they didn't want to miss out, so no one stayed long enough to put it to the test.

We dawdled on the way home that day. I took the children the long way round up the hill behind the Gasr al-Bint. I wanted to savour the experience that had become routine but would soon become history. I was pregnant again so Raami walked and I held his hand as we negotiated our way between prickle bushes and the blocks of fallen buildings. Our path turned towards home and we found Ali-d's family – wives, children, married daughters and their children – crowded into the shade of a weathered rock wall with their quilts, sacks and boxes of belongings piled around them.

'Ta'alu ishrubu shay,' they called – come and drink tea – so we stopped for a glass. They chattered excitedly. 'B-nistana al-Jimedy.' We're waiting for al-Jimedy. 'Min a subuh wa ehna b-nerihil.' We've been moving things since morning (from beneath Umm al-Biyara by donkey). 'Meta widku terihuloo?' When are you moving? 'Aiy wahida wahidetku?' Which is your unit?

Al-Jimedy was once again employed driving the Department of Antiquities truck and he was already busy with it and the other employees acting as the removal men.

The time had really arrived.

We had considered not moving – of staying in our comfortable cave, on the ledge with the million-dollar view, but we couldn't. Apart from the tables of the souvenir sellers and the cooling thilaajas of the Pepsi vendors, everything else to do with the community was moving. Two units had been allocated to the school, another to the clinic, and the shopkeepers would cram their stores into one of their rooms until they could build something. Mohammad's family was going, and so were all our friends. 'Jan-na bela naas ma b-tin daas,' Mohammad quoted – Paradise without people isn't worth entering – and I agreed. Much as we enjoyed not having close neighbours, we knew we couldn't live without the community.

And the truck was busy reaching into isolated valleys and up carefully constructed tracks to make it as easy as possible for everyone. It pulled up at the clinic between the oleander bushes and the clump of aloes that flamed flamboyantly orange for a few weeks each spring, and the gang of Bedouin workers pushed and pulled without coordination but with plenty of enthusiasm – 'Shid min endak.' Lift from your end. 'Mish heek!' Not like that! 'Khuleeni a wherijeek.' Let me show you how – till they got everything out of the cave and haphazardly loaded. It was hard to believe I had run a clinic there, in that hole in the rock. I left the door wide open but took the key to remind me.

In seven days all seventy-eight families had been moved from the bowl of Petra. The tribe had grown as I predicted and the families living near Jabal Haroon and the Beitha plains had to wait another year for more units to be completed.

And so the truck had pulled up below our ledge.

If we had had to move to Umm Sayhoon when I first arrived and between us we had had a suitcase and a backpack, it would have been really easy, but now as the *nishaama* carried our belongings out of the cave and down the path I was amazed at how much we had accumulated. Each piece had a story: the two tall cupboards, which we had taken the glass out of and carried on donkeys from behind the Crusader castle when Mufleh sold them quickly and for cash; the chest of five precious drawers I had wedged into the boot of a Mercedes *service* as soon as I found it in Ma'an, for fear of never seeing another; the gas cooker Mohammad had seen in Wadi Musa on the same day that the gift-cheque had arrived from my great-aunt for its exact cost; the sewing machine and pile of under-dresses in progress; the kerosene-fired fridge (we had recently borrowed Musa's pick-up to bring it all the way from a small village on the Syrian border because we needed a fridge for Mohammad's insulin and they now had electricity) and the water drum from Mohammad's first trip to Amman as a married man. I even had quite a pile of blankets, sponge-rubber *farrshas*, cotton-stuffed pillows and satin-covered quilts.

The guys carried everything down with an air of festivity and had great fun helping Mohammad take the door, the wooden window-frame and the sheets of roofing-tin off the kitchen. They dug, with excited swings of the pick, the *ma-rush* and Salwa's swing out of the concrete that held them down in the yard. Despite being one of the smallest families, we had more stuff than most, and it wasn't until I saw it all together on the back of the truck that I dared to think it might just fit into our little brick box. We loaded the clay water-jar and potted hibiscus into the car with our children and ginger cat, and followed the truck along the dusty track. We didn't look back; the cave will be there for centuries to come.

'*Twakilna ala-Allah*,' Mohammad said. We had done what we could; the rest was up to God.

As we wound out through the Siq I wondered if I would regret not shedding a tear, but none came.

It was too exciting. There were none of the goodbyes usually associated with moving because everyone was going and there were all sorts of things to look forward to. The house was ours – what we did to it would be for us (we could make all the concrete, and tile, floors we wanted) and because of the glass windows I would be able to shut the door to keep warm on winter days – and still see. The school, which Salwa would soon attend, was only minutes away and the clinic was in the next unit to ours. Besides all that, we were expecting another baby. He was a boy – I knew even without the predictions (and my doctor still didn't have ultrasound) – and I had decided to call him Maruan after the valley beyond the Monastery.

The future looked bright.

Epilogue

So a way of life disappeared. The Bedouin no longer set up their tents of woven hair on the long, wind-catching ridges of Petra and they no longer dwell in the security of its ancient caves or sleep out in front of them under the sheet of stars. Even the cave entrances and kitchen walls they had made were knocked down so not much remains to show they ever did – though I know there are thousands of tomato purée tins and battered blue enamel teapots waiting to be discovered by future archaeologists.

I have mostly remembered the good times, but that is how I like to look at life. I have not written about the little child who died days after pulling a bucket of boiling water over herself, or the babies who got sick and died so quickly I could only guess at what illness had struck. The stories of the shop that was broken into, and the binoculars that were stolen and sold before the thief could be caught are not here. I have not told of the girl who crept from her husband's bed, stepping from rock to rock to carry her footprints so she couldn't be followed when she went to meet her lover in the mountains, nor of how caring friends convinced her husband to overlook her behaviour and not commit a crime of honour but an act of *sutra* and forgiveness by treating her child as his own.

But life in the settlement wasn't any less exciting than life in the cave had been, in fact with three growing children and our Petra shop which soon became a family business (to which we had to commute) it got more so. Maruan was born, with little of the drama of Salwa and Raami but with just as much joy and postnatal support, and just as big a *mensef* to give thanks. The unusual name I had chosen turned out to be the second most popular Jordanian name of the decade. I gave up running the clinic, partly because we now lived too close to everyone (before they had only walked the distance to our cave if their cut was long and deep enough), but also because I discovered that I loved working with Mohammad in Petra. As soon as the children were big enough I commuted with him daily. As Mohammad became renowned for his sand-bottling – starring on in-flight entertainment for the Royal Jordanian Airline and attending Travel and Tourism Fairs in major European cities – I got good at it too and was able to hold the fort while he was away. Business boomed (and busted during *intafadas* and Gulf Wars) but picked up again reasonably quickly after.

I no longer tried to hide when tourists came past and I was forced into thinking of answers to confronting questions like, 'What about your children's education?'

What I really hoped was that we could give them a wide enough education so they could make their own decisions. I had chosen this life but I wanted them to be able to make their own choices. Mohammad hoped he could buy them what they wanted and they would go on to get university degrees.

Salwa went to New Zealand to Nelson College for Girls as a boarder for one year but then came home to complete high school in Wadi Musa and the important degree from the University of Jordan. Raami went to Nelson for all his secondary education. It was easier to convince Mohammad to let him go because he was alone in his class here by the time he was twelve. His classmates all dropped out and went down to Petra with their donkeys and came home with tourist dollars. Raami went on to do a diploma in electronic technology in Sydney. Mohammad wouldn't let Maruan go though; 'He is my crown prince,' he said, and anyway fewer of Maruan's classmates had dropped out. Maruan was our chauffeur as well; by the time he was twelve he could drive us home on the dirt track from Wadi Araba – across the desert and up the crumbling granite side of the Great Rift Valley – a two-hour drive in the Nissan Pathfinder we had by then.

They were years of travelling adventure too. Whenever Mohammad tried to buy me a piece of gold I said 'Get me a ticket instead.' We visited my grandmother in the Hook of Holland and friends in Germany and Switzerland. We went backpacking to Turkey and Thailand, both so different and so much fun, and we visited my brother John and his family when they lived in Amsterdam, in London and in Sydney. Now and then we made it back to New Zealand. Mum and Dad visited again and again and one year we all went with our car over on the ferry to the Sinai Peninsula. We climbed Mount Sinai and for days after we lay around on the beach at Dahab soothing our aching muscles.

All the time Mohammad carried his insulin in a tub of ice and monitored his blood-sugar levels – which went up and down. So much for a diabetic leading a normal life . . . the changes were slow but insidious. We went to the doctor who did tests, prescribed him tablets for high blood pressure and said, 'Be careful what you eat', the same thing, every few months. How careful could you get?

In the late 1990s the vendors in Petra were forced, by the new Petra Regional Council, into cooperatives – a bad idea considering how much the Bedouin lifestyle is one of individual cunning and hard work (and how different the enterprises in Petra were one from another), and especially bad for us considering how much our lives had revolved around our shop. But we had started together with little more than our enthusiasm, a language barrier and what we had decided was love, and we didn't stop then. Mohammad was soon buying new ventures and I was soon running them.

Mohammad's brothers and sisters married and had babies. Our birthday parties got bigger and bigger. If I were to turn fifty in Petra there would be sixty-four relations to invite (*ma'sha'allah*), before considering the families of our friends.

Now everyone lives near the local school and buses run regularly to the high schools in Wadi Musa and to higher education facilities in Ma'an. Several homes have computers, and the *nishaama all* have email addresses.

Most families have added so much to their homes that they are barely recognisable as the original units. However, more rooms meant a lot more housework and I'd often think of my cave – only one room to clean and no cracks for the dust to get in through – but then winter would come again and I could enjoy watching the black clouds spilling over the western mountains from my warm, light-filled rooms, and I'd be thankful.

More rooms also meant my determination not to gather clutter waned. Mohammad never had any such determination – he collected things spontaneously: dolls and roller skates from Europe; video cameras, water bottles and army knives from the US marines; huge *siddrs* and gas rings for special occasions which called for *mensef*; and from Thailand, fifty more kilograms of luggage than we had gone with.

Mohammad went into pulmonary oedema in May 2001. We were in Amman waiting to pick Mum and Dad up from the airport. Luckily, because I doubt he would have made the hospital if we had been at home. All the roads out of Wadi Musa were undergoing major reconstruction at the same time. As it was, the hospital was just around the corner from the hotel yet he could barely breathe when we got there. His kidneys had shut down, we were told, probably battered by years of uncontrollable blood-sugar levels, and he would need dialysis twice a week to stay alive.

The Bedouin rallied round. They drove him, or went as part of his 'support crew', to Aqaba for the dialysis and to Amman for various tests. They found out their blood groups and offered their kidneys, until his young brother Hussein's was found to be compatible and was successfully transplanted at the Queen Alia Hospital in Amman. But as it turned out that was only a temporary reprieve.

The day Mohammad died, in February 2002, the Shergiya was blowing its cold dusty wind across the valley; he went home from Petra before me and passed away there, on a *farrsha* in our comfortable sitting room, during his afternoon snooze. By the time I was brought home our house was full. His friends came and washed him and wrapped him in a plain white shroud, his *caffin*. Someone handed me his wedding ring and I slipped it perfectly onto my middle finger. It was the one he had bought for himself on that trip to Amman, when I had been sceptical about his ability to know my finger size – and he had them both right.

There were so many hands to help that Mohammad's grave was ready before the night fell and he was buried on the day he died which is a blessing for a Muslim.

For the traditional three days of mourning the people he had touched came to pay condolences. The tents the *nishaama* quickly put up (for the men), and our considerably built-onto house (for the women), were full. Mohammad's sisters came and stayed, friends came daily and everyone else made an appearance. I was kept busy. Emails poured in and I printed them out and stuck them up till my kitchen wall was covered. Bdoul families slaughtered goats and sheep to make *mensef* which they boiled up and delivered, steaming on big round *siddrs*, for our lunch and dinner.

For a few months I continued going through the motions of my life. My visitors didn't stop coming, and I didn't stop prospering, but my reason for being there had gone.

Since then we have been living in Sydney. My brother and sister live there and it's not quite as far from Petra as New Zealand.

But we haven't really settled. I think of the question the Jordanians always used to put to me in those early days, trying to comprehend my leaving a western country to live in theirs (not crediting the power of love): '*Yet ahsen al-Ordon ow New Zelanda?*' Which is better?

I knew then it wasn't like that, and it still isn't. Some things are better in Jordan – some things are better in Australia, and there will be somewhere else where other things are better. It's best to look at the good things of where you are at the time, and to do what feels right in the circumstances. I can't really speak for Salwa, Raami and Maruan but they are old enough and I hope they have had enough experience to choose their own futures. I love the way they all still call me *Yom*, the colloquial, almost extinct, Bedouin version of Mum, because it takes me back to Petra.

I might go back and see if I can find a Petra I can live in without Mohammad. I know that it is still an exciting place to be. The Bedouin have settled in to Umm Sayhoon, but by day they inhabit the ruins of Petra. They bring them back to life – using donkeys to take tourists to the High Place and Monastery, camels to get them to Wadi Sabra and Jabal Haroon, and almost any means at all to get them into the shade for a glass of mint tea. And, if there's one happening, they invite them with typical enthusiastic hospitality back to up to their village for a Bedouin Wedding.

But I wasn't in Petra for the mountains or the history – nor even for the culture. Without Mohammad to hold me I am no longer married to a Bedouin and, despite all the things we have accumulated, I have become a nomad once again.

Glossary

A note on my Arabic: I have written most of the words as they *sounded* to me when I learned them, consequently many of the names that should have 'h's on the end, don't. I have chosen to underline 'th' when it's said like in '<u>th</u>en', otherwise it's said like in 'thing'. And the 'r' is always pronounced.

Aba, square cloth cloak

Ahlan-wa-sahlan, welcome

Ajnebiya, foreigner (female)

Al-humdulillah/al-humdulillah-a-salaama, thanks or praises to God/praise God for your deliverance unto safety

At<u>h</u>aan, call to prayer

Al-Wahidat, the Units, referring to the settlement

Dub-ka, line dance

Eid, special days: **Eid Ramadan,** the celebration at the end of Ramadan; **Eid a-<u>Th</u>e-hiya,** the commemoration of the sacrifice/ also used for birthdays, independence etc

Farrsha, thick, cloth-covered mattress made of sponge-rubber or stuffed with wool

Fatteh, staple meal of bread mushed up in yoghurt or soup

Gismih o naseeb, fate and destiny

Gtaar, wedding procession

Gutaar, a place where water drips out of the rock and gathers in pools

Hajj/Hajja, the pilgrimage to Mecca or one who has undertaken it/a female pilgrim

Halawa, brittle, melt-in-your-mouth sesame-seed sweet

Heeshy, home-grown Bedouin tobacco

Jannabiya, thin, cloth mat

Jorin, pestle and mortar, also called a *mihbash*

Keenya, gum/eucalyptus trees

Khateeb, one who heals, usually using amulets, spells, or traditional herbs

Laban, goat or sheep's yoghurt/also mother's milk

Ligan, shallow, circular, flat-bottomed, galvanised tin washing basin

Mabruk, congratulations

Mahr, Bride Price or kind of male dowry

Majaneen/majnoon/majnoona, various forms of crazy

Mangle, brazier

Ma-rush, awning or shade made of bamboo, sacking or cultivated grape-vines

Mendeel and **Mirreer,** the Bedouin words for the man's head-dress; cloth and cord ring

Mensef, typical Bedouin feast of meat, rice and bread with yoghurt sauce

Misfah and **Asaba,** together make a woman's head-dress

Mudraga, woman's over-dress

Muzferr, sling to carry a baby in

Nishaama, the Bedouin word for youths

Quayas, good

Ramadan, the Muslim month of fasting (it moves forward about 10 days each year)

Rattam, white broom (*retama, raetam*)

Rishoof, *laban* and lentil soup

R-waag, the woven back wall of the goat-hair tent

Saj, dome of tin used to make flat bread/*shraak* on

Salaam, greeting/peace

Samer, traditional chanting dance

Samin, clarified goat's butter

Service (pronounced serveece), shared taxi

Shabriya, double-edged Bedouin knife

Shay, tea

Sheikh, representative (religious, tribal, parliamentary)

Shergiya, east wind

Shig, men's quarters

Shish-bish, backgammon

Shon-nar, a plump game bird a little bigger than a quail called a chukkar in English

Shraak, typical, flat, unleavened bread

Siddr, circular, flat, serving platter with a small rim, usually 70–80cm in diameter

Si'in, cured skin used to hold milk, yoghurt, butter or clarified butter

Sitt/as-Sitt, a respectful title for a woman

Taaboon bread, leavened bread made in a traditional dung-fired oven (a *taaboon*)

Tanaka, a 20 litre tin can with a round pop-out lid, used for olive oil, *samin* and cheese

Thaub, man's robe

Thilaaja, a container that water can evaporate from, used to cool drinks/also a refrigerator

Wadi, river or creek-bed, often dry except when it rains/also valley (**Wadi Musa**)

Wahhid Allah, to state the oneness of Allah